Colorado Nature
Almanac

COLORADO NATURE ALMANAC

A MONTH-BY-MONTH GUIDE TO WILDLIFE & WILD PLACES

STEPHEN R. JONES AND RUTH CAROL CUSHMAN

Illustrations by Dorothy Emerling

PRUETT PUBLISHING COMPANY
BOULDER, COLORADO

Printed in the United States
10 9 8 7 6 5 4 3 2 1

Library of Congress Cataloging-in-Publication data

Jones, Stephen., 1947-
Colorado nature almanac : a month-by-month guide to wildlife and wildplaces / Stephen R. Jones and
Ruth Carol Cushman ; illustrations by Dorothy Emerling.
  p. cm.
Includes bibliographical references (p.273) and index.
ISBN 0-87108-883-5 (pbk.)
1. Natural history–Colorado. I. Cushman, Ruth Carol, 1937-
II. Title.
QH105.C6J65 1998   98-24096
508.788–dc21   CIP

Cover and book design by Julie Long
Book composition by Lyn Chaffee
Illustrations by Dorothy Emerling
Maps by Julie Noyes Long; base art by Kathleen McAffrey, Starr Design
Cover photograph by Eric Wunrow, "Moonrise over Anthracite Range and autumn colors,
from near Kebler Pass"
Interior photographs by Stephen R. Jones and Ruth Carol Cushman except where noted otherwise

To Morgan Jones, who loved ideas, delighted in mysteries,
reveled in beauty, and questioned everything.
—Steve

And, as always, to Glenn, who shares my joy in nature
and my sorrow when wild things disappear.
—Ruth Carol

Contents

Preface

Certain events—the booming of prairie chickens in April, the blooming of gentians in August, the bugling of elk in September—define the seasons in Colorado. This book is for those people who want to know when and where the first wildflowers of the year bloom, which butterflies flit across the tundra in summer, why leaves turn red and gold in autumn, and what wondrous events happen in winter. It's sort of an observation guide for people who follow the flow of seasons.

However, the seasons do not always flow evenly. Sometimes Easter daisies bloom at Christmas, sometimes it snows in July, and sometimes bluebirds or warblers surprise us in the depth of winter. Encountering the unexpected is one of the joys of nature and of living in Colorado.

We also rejoice in the diversity of nature in Colorado. There are hundreds of bird and mammal species, thousands of plant species, and some fifty thousand insect species. How can we see and understand everything from hawks overhead to fungi underfoot? Obviously, we can't. So, this book focuses on the seasonal events that most fascinate nature-watchers.

Each month features a description of an ecosystem that is especially colorful or interesting during that season. The monthly chapters also include profiles of plants, mammals, birds, and insects you are likely to encounter. Most months showcase an owl species because almost everyone, including us, is partial to these seldom seen birds. The "Where to Go Directory" (p. 247) gives directions for reaching places mentioned in the text.

This book is not a field guide. We urge anyone interested in nature to refer to the detailed field guides listed in "Selected Readings." Remember, you can't identify the players without a program!

SOURCES

We once thought scientific plant names were immutable. Not so. A plant may accumulate over a dozen common names and almost as many scientific names. For instance, in *Guide to Colorado Wildflowers,* G. K. Guennel lists seven scientific names and four common names for mountain parsley and five scientific names and eleven common names for bog wintergreen. If it is proven that a species was described at an earler date under a different name, the older name has priority. We have used William Weber's *Colorado Flora: Eastern Slope* and *Colorado Flora: Western Slope,* revised editions, as our authorities for plant nomenclature.

The poems that begin each chapter are from *The Path on the Rainbow,* edited by George Cronyn, and from bulletins of the Bureau of American Ethnology, Smithsonian Institution. A selective list of books on natural history concludes this almanac.

Stephen R. Jones
Ruth Carol Cushman
April 1998

Acknowledgments

Through the years many people have helped us understand and appreciate Colorado's natural world. We have singled out the people listed here because they had a direct impact on this book, and we wish to thank them.

The following scientists from the Colorado Division of Wildlife were especially helpful: Tom Beck, Howard Funk, Janet George, John Gottl, Ron Kulfeld, and Bill Weiler. Nolan Doeskin and Jim Harrington from the Colorado Climate Center supplied all the weather data.

Other people who provided information included Sherry Chapman, David Chiszar, Kristine Crandall, Ed Engle, Martha Evans, Mike Figgs, Fern Ford, Steve Frye, Kathy Granillo, Dave Hallock, Paula Hansley, Bill Jennings, Mary Lu Jacobs, Hugh Kingery, Boris Kondratieff, Nancy Lederer, Peter Lipman, Dan Murphy, Christina Nealson, John Pape, Pam Piombino, Michael Sanders, Ken Spies, Janeal W. Thompson, and Glenn Wallace. Earl Mosburg helped with computer conversions.

We also acknowledge the contributions of Jim Knopf to the *Boulder County Nature Almanac,* coauthored by Cushman, Jones, and Knopf, on which this book is modeled.

The resources at the University of Colorado Libraries were invaluable, as was the assistance of Daria Carle and Pat McClure.

We particularly appreciate the help of Randy Gietzen, Tim Hogan, Clint Miller, and Mike Weissmann, who provided us with essential information and critiqued large sections of the book.

We thank all these people for generously sharing their knowledge with us. Any mistakes are ours, not theirs.

We're also grateful for Marykay Scott's skillful editing; for Jim Pruett's enthusiasm in publishing the book; and for the talents of Cheryl Morris, Trevor Munoz, Dorothy Emerling, Libby Barstow, Merrill Gilfillan, Julie Noyes Long, and Lyn Chaffee.

Above all, we thank our spouses, Nancy Dawson and Glenn Cushman, for their help, their wit, and their support.

S.R.J.
R.C.C.

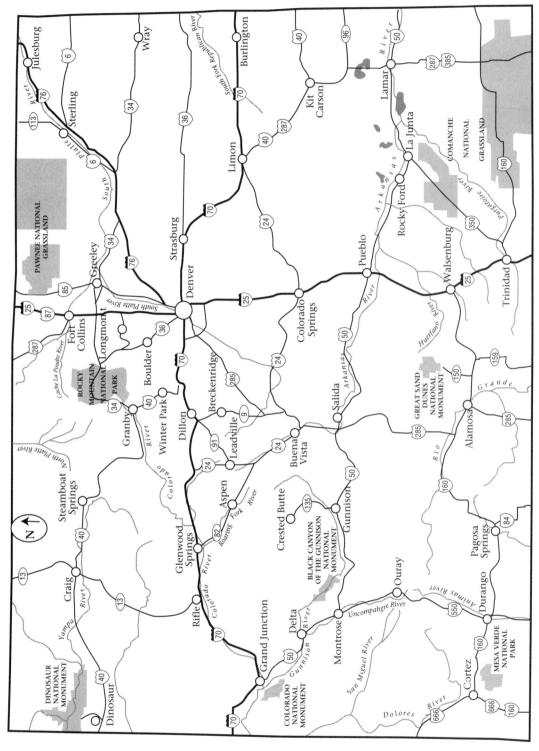

Colorado's main roads and landmarks.

Prairie, Peak, and Plateau:
An Introduction to Colorado Life Zones and Ecosystems

Sitting in the heart of North America and rising almost 3 miles above sea level, the central Rockies receive and modify weather blowing in from all directions. The same Pacific storms that dump snow on the Western Slope bring warm, drying winds to the eastern foothills. Arctic cold fronts chill Front Range cities while the mountains bask in sunshine. Humid southerly winds bring 100-degree temperatures to the Arkansas Valley, drenching rains to the San Juan Mountains, and tornadoes to the northeastern plains.

COLORADO CLIMATE SUMMARY

Annual Means and Extremes	Grand Junction (4,824 ft.)	Steamboat Springs (6,760 ft.)	Alamosa (7,536 ft.)	Berthoud Pass (11,310 ft.)	Denver (5,282 ft.)	Lamar (3,620 ft.)
Ave. high (°F)	66	54	59	40	64	69
Ave. low (°F)	40	22	23	18	36	38
Max. high (°F)	105	98	96	76	104	111
Min. low (°F)	−23	−50	−50	−34	−30	−29
Ave. prec. (in.)	8.64	23.38	7.57	38.03	15.40	14.62
Max. prec. (in.)	15.69	35.89	11.55	58.47	23.31	24.51
Ave. snow (in.)	25.4	168.7	37.4	399.8	59.8	27.4
Max. snow (in.)	55.7	251.0	69.1	591.1	112.0	63.3

State record high: 114°F at Las Animas (1933) and Sedgwick (1954).
State record low: −61°F at Maybell (1985).

Averages are for 1961 through 1990 for all stations except Berthoud Pass (1950–1985). Extremes are for the following periods: Grand Junction, 1891–1995; Steamboat Springs, 1931–1995; Alamosa, 1946–1995; Berthoud Pass, 1950–1985; Denver, 1934–1995; Lamar, 1931–1995.

Sources: Colorado Climate Center (Fort Collins), Colorado Climate Summaries (monthly); National Oceanic and Atmospheric Administration, *Comparative Climatic Data* (1996).

When viewed over time, Colorado's climate is more predictable than it appears at first glance. The mountains are consistently colder and wetter than the eastern plains and western valleys. As a general rule, mean temperatures decrease 3 to 5 degrees (Fahrenheit) with every 1,000 feet of elevation gain; the summit of Pikes Peak averages about 40 degrees colder than the floor of the Arkansas Valley. In terms of climate and vegetation change, the drive from the plains to the Pikes Peak summit is analogous to a 2,700-mile journey from Denver to Point Barrow, Alaska.

The spruce-fir forests that grow between 9,000 and 11,500 feet in elevation in the central Rockies contain many of the same plants and animals that thrive at 1,000 feet in northern Canada. The low tundra vegetation that grows above tree line in the central Rockies is structurally similar to the vegetation you would encounter on the shores of the Arctic Sea. Nineteenth-century biologist Charles Merriam introduced the term *life zone* to describe this distinct grouping of plant

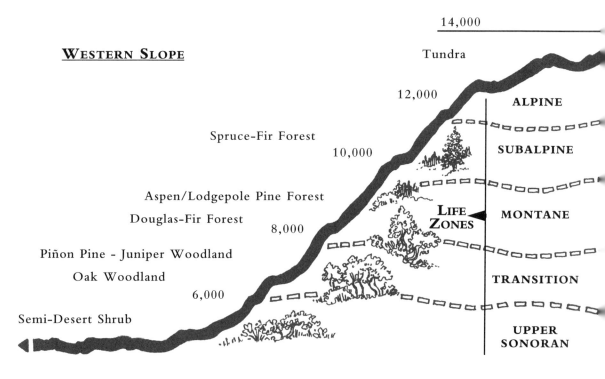

COLORADO LIFE ZONES AND ECOSYSTEMS

communities in response to climatic differences at various elevations and latitudes. Each life zone in Merriam's system supports a characteristic assemblage of ecosystems. For example, the subalpine life zone, in the high Rockies, contains these ecosystems: Engelmann spruce–subalpine fir forest, limber pine forest, bristlecone pine forest, mountain meadows, and mountain willow carrs (thickets). Each of these ecosystems is a distinct community of plants and animals that functions as an interconnected unit. Grassland, ponderosa pine forest, aspen forest, and tundra are other examples of Colorado ecosystems.

The life zone concept was first applied to Colorado by University of Colorado plant ecologist John Marr during the 1960s. Marr described five life zones in the Front Range region. Marr's classification scheme, with minor modifications, works well for all of Colorado (see illustration below).

The **upper Sonoran** life zone encompasses most of the eastern plains and

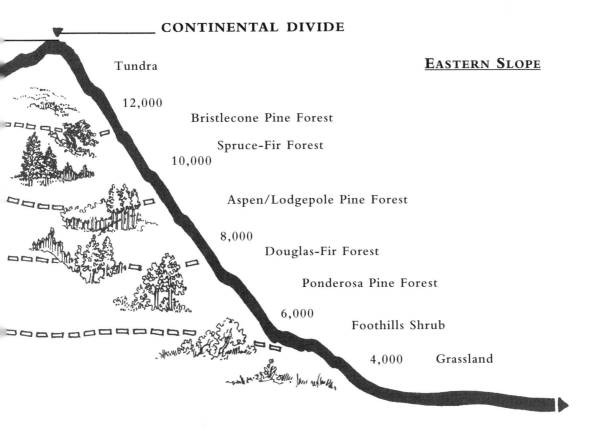

CONTINENTAL DIVIDE

Tundra

EASTERN SLOPE

12,000

Bristlecone Pine Forest

Spruce-Fir Forest

10,000

Aspen/Lodgepole Pine Forest

8,000

Douglas-Fir Forest

Ponderosa Pine Forest

6,000

Foothills Shrub

4,000   Grassland

western valleys. This zone extends northward into Colorado from the high elevation steppes and deserts of northern New Mexico and northern Arizona. Grasslands dominate in eastern Colorado, semidesert shrublands in the west. Cottonwood-willow woodlands grow along streams and rivers. Annual precipitation averages 8-18 inches. The cities of Grand Junction, Cortez, Denver, and Fort Morgan lie within this zone.

The **transition** zone begins at the base of the western mesas and eastern foothills where grasslands and shrublands slowly give way to coniferous forests. This zone extends into the lower mountains. Ponderosa pine woodlands dominate in the east, piñon pine–juniper woodlands in the west. These woodlands consist of scattered trees interspersed with grasses and shrubs. Annual precipitation ranges from 12 to 25 inches. Steamboat Springs, Durango, Evergreen, and Estes Park all lie within this zone.

The **montane,** or Canadian, zone includes mid-elevation aspen, lodgepole pine, Douglas-fir, and ponderosa pine forests, along with mountain grasslands and shrublands. Riparian woodlands of willows, aspens, maples, and river birches grow along mountain streams. Annual precipitation averages 20 to 35 inches. Telluride, Dillon, and Grand Lake lie within this zone.

The **subalpine,** or Hudsonian, zone is dominated by Engelmann spruce–subalpine fir forest. This is a majestic forest with tall, robust trees and verdant undergrowth. Scattered groves of limber pine and bristlecone pine cling to rocky, exposed ridges. Annual precipitation, mostly snow, ranges from 30 to 45 inches. Most of Colorado's major ski areas lie within this zone.

The **alpine** zone begins at tree line and extends to the summits of the highest peaks. Krummholz, a stunted forest of windblown spruces and firs, grows at the lower elevation limit. Higher up, the krummholz gives way to tundra, a treeless ecosystem of grasses, perennial herbs, low shrubs, mosses, and lichens. Annual precipitation can exceed 40 inches, but fierce winds blow much of the moisture away. Many of our high mountain passes, including Loveland, Cottonwood, and Independence, are in the alpine zone, and Trail Ridge Road in Rocky Mountain National Park traverses this zone.

Throughout this almanac we feature seasonal profiles of selected ecosystems and their inhabitants within all of these life zones. For more detailed ecosystem descriptions, we recommend *The Southern Rockies,* by Audrey Benedict, and *From Grassland to Glacier,* by Cornelia Mutel and John Emerick.

FRAGMENTED ECOSYSTEMS: CAN NATIVE SPECIES SURVIVE?

Everything in nature has its place, but some species occupy more places than others. The American robin, a habitat generalist, nests in four Colorado life zones and

COLORADO THREATENED AND ENDANGERED WILDLIFE[a]

MAMMAL	STATUS
BISON	Captive populations only
GRIZZLY BEAR	Colorado endangered; Federal threatened
BLACK-FOOTED FERRET	Colorado and Federal endangered
GRAY WOLF	Colorado and Federal endangered
RIVER OTTER	Colorado endangered (reintroduced)
CANADA LYNX	Colorado endangered
WOLVERINE	Colorado endangered

BIRD	STATUS
PEREGRINE FALCON	Colorado threatened; Federal endangered
BALD EAGLE	Colorado and Federal threatened
PIPING PLOVER	Colorado and Federal threatened
GREATER SANDHILL CRANE	Colorado nesting population threatened
WHOOPING CRANE	Colorado and Federal endangered
GREATER PRAIRIE CHICKEN	Colorado threatened
LESSER PRAIRIE CHICKEN	Colorado threatened
PLAINS SHARP-TAILED GROUSE	Colorado endangered
WESTERN SNOWY PLOVER	Federal threatened
INTERIOR LEAST TERN	Colorado and Federal endangered
MEXICAN SPOTTED OWL	Colorado and Federal threatened
SOUTHWESTERN WILLOW FLYCATCHER	Federal endangered

AMPHIBIAN	STATUS
WOOD FROG	Colorado threatened
BOREAL TOAD	Colorado endangered

FISH	STATUS
RIO GRANDE SUCKER	Colorado endangered
COLORADO SQUAWFISH	Colorado and Federal endangered
HUMPBACK CHUB	Colorado and Federal endangered
BONYTAIL CHUB	Colorado and Federal endangered
RAZORBACK SUCKER	Colorado endangered
GREENBACK CUTTHROAT TROUT	Colorado and Federal threatened
ARKANSAS DARTER	Colorado threatened

[a]Species in **boldface** probably have been extirpated from the state as wild populations.
Source: Colorado Natural Heritage Program, 1997. "Colorado's Natural Heritage: Rare and Imperiled Animals, Plants, and Natural Communities." 103 Natural Resources, Fort Collins, CO 80523-1401.

most Colorado ecosystems. In contrast, the golden-crowned kinglet, a habitat specialist, nests almost exclusively in old-growth Engelmann spruce–subalpine fir forest.

When natural ecosystems are disturbed or destroyed, habitat generalists often fare better than habitat specialists. Colorado populations of raccoons, mule deer, great horned owls, common ravens, and robins probably have increased since Europeans settled here. Many specialists, including black-footed ferrets, river otters, burrowing owls, and prairie chickens, have not fared nearly so well (see table above).

Some generalists have wreaked havoc after being introduced into new environments by humans. In 1890, members of the American Acclimatization Society, wanting to ensure that all the birds mentioned in Shakespeare were represented in North America, released sixty European starlings in New York's Central Park. Today, about 200 million starlings make life difficult for many North American native species. The starlings take over nests of woodpeckers, bluebirds, and other cavity-nesters, often eating or evicting eggs or young.

Many North American native generalists have proliferated as natural ecosystems have been fragmented or disturbed. Brown-headed cowbirds once lived primarily on the Great Plains, where they fed on insects that swarmed around herds of bison. With the introduction of domestic livestock and the clearing of eastern deciduous forests, brown-headed cowbirds expanded their range into almost all of North America south of the Arctic Circle. Cowbirds lay their eggs in nests of other songbirds, who then feed and care for the cowbird young. Nest parasitism by brown-headed cowbirds has decimated breeding songbird populations in rural and semiurban regions. Because cowbirds inhabit open country, they have thrived in areas where native forests have been broken up by agriculture or urbanization.

Many other adventive species have disrupted native bird and mammal populations. Scrub jays invade shrubby areas on the urban fringe, eating eggs and nestlings of other songbirds. Fox squirrels, who entered eastern Colorado as they followed the lines of deciduous trees that settlers planted along prairie rivers and streams, now compete with native squirrel populations. Raccoons thrive in urban areas, where they aggressively outcompete other mammals.

Exotic weeds such as Russian thistle (*Salsola* spp.) and knapweed (*Acosta* spp.) have invaded much of the state. These weeds, which often gain a foothold along roadways and in overgrazed pastures, can crowd out native plants. Knapweed, a noxious plant harmful to livestock, has already taken over millions of acres of prairie in eastern Montana, placing Montana's cattle industry and some of the state's native prairie plants in jeopardy.

The Colorado Native Plant Society lists more than one hundred plant species as "of special concern." Many of these plants are naturally rare. Many others are threatened by urbanization, mining, overgrazing, groundwater depletion, logging, weed infestation, and plant collecting.

Perhaps more frightening than the loss of individual plants is the loss of entire ecosystems. A recent Forest Service inventory of northern Front Range (Denver to Fort Collins) ponderosa pine forests determined that only 1 percent were "old-growth" (defined as forests that had survived more than two hundred years without being logged off or burned down). Several habitat specialists, including Abert's squirrels and flammulated owls, depend on old-growth ponderosa pine forests for their survival. Every square foot of grassland in eastern Colorado has been altered by farming, ranching, or urbanization. We can only speculate about what the original grasslands really looked like.

The 1996 Federal Endangered Species List classified forty-four Colorado birds and mammals as sensitive, threatened, or endangered. More than half of these species (twenty-four) live primarily in grasslands on the eastern plains. Seven Colorado fish were listed as threatened or endangered. Many are victims of municipal and agricultural water projects that have depleted natural stream flows. Competition with rainbow trout, northern pike, and other introduced sport fish has also made life difficult for some natives.

Despite all the threats to native species, much of Colorado's original fauna remains intact. Since 1850, two nesting birds (harlequin duck and ring-billed gull) and three to six mammals (bison, black-footed ferret, gray wolf, and, possibly, grizzly bear, Canada lynx, and wolverine) have been extirpated from the state. Since the turn of the century, river otters (which are native to Colorado) and moose and mountain goats (which may be native) have been successfully reintroduced. Elk and beaver populations have recovered. Bald eagles, osprey, and peregrine falcons have returned to historic nest sites. Ongoing wolf and black-footed ferret recovery efforts may soon include Colorado. These successes have been achieved with moderate expense (a fraction of the cost of one B-1 bomber) and minimal inconvenience to humans.

Future survival of native plants and animals will depend on our commitment to limiting destruction and fragmentation of natural ecosystems. If we fail, we'll have a lot of starlings, fox squirrels, and knapweed to enjoy.

This old mining cabin in Mayflower Gulch has endured many a Colorado January. (Photo by Glenn Cushman.)

I

January

Whirlwind! Whirlwind!

The snowy earth comes gliding,

the snowy earth comes gliding.

—ARAPAHO

WE CELEBRATE THE new year by gliding out on cross-country skis, exulting in mounds of snow piled on the branches of spruce and fir. Silvery icefalls take away our breath with their crystal flow-stone formations. The wind sweeps loose snow into eddies all around us, and the fine airborne snow scatters the light into glittering jewels. We are surrounded by iridescence—"rainbow" clouds in the sky, prismatic colors glinting from sun-lit snowbanks, and sparkling "snow-dust" in the air.

Many creatures are active in this exhilarating weather. Mountain lions stalk snowshoe hares. Geese and ducks seek out open water. Great horned owls are courting, and on rare occasions, we may be gifted by the visit of a snowy owl. While black bears continue to sleep, their cubs are born, the perfect emblem of a just-born year.

The year's first snowstorms come gliding in and create a blank sheet on which nature will write dramas, romances, comedies, and mysteries during the coming months.

January Weather

	Grand Junction (4,824 ft.)	Steamboat Springs (6,760 ft.)	Alamosa (7,536 ft.)	Berthoud Pass (11,310 ft.)	Denver (5,282 ft.)	Lamar (3,620 ft.)
Ave. high (°F)	36	27	33	21	43	44
Ave. low (°F)	15	0	−4	1	16	13
Max. high (°F)	62	55	62	42	73	80
Min. low (°F)	−23	−50	−50	−33	−25	−29
Ave. prec. (in.)	0.56	2.36	0.26	3.49	0.50	0.42
Max. prec. (in.)	2.46	5.86	0.75	7.37	1.44	1.43
Ave. snow (in.)	7.3	35.1	4.5	49.8	7.9	5.0
Max. snow (in.)	33.7	111.6	13.8	99.0	24.3	13.5

Avalanche Danger

Avalanches killed 404 people in the lower forty-eight states between 1950 and 1995. Almost 40 percent of these deaths (152) occurred in Colorado. Washington was a distant second with 58 deaths, followed by Utah with 42 and California with 38. Experts recommend taking the following precautions:

❀ Avoid slopes of 25 to 60 degrees.

❀ Avoid treeless slopes and obvious avalanche chutes.

❀ Be cautious in loose, powdery, or windblown snow.

❀ Carry avalanche cord and/or an avalanche beeper.

❀ Heed avalanche warnings and obey "out of bounds" signs in ski areas.

Source: Colorado Avalanche Information Center.

Strong Pacific storms bring heavy snows to the Western Slope and fierce winds to the Front Range foothills. A series of snowstorms in January 1996 dumped 196 inches of snow on the Steamboat Springs ski area. A four-day storm buried Wolf Creek Pass under 100 inches between January 11 and 14, 1997. In 1971 winds gusted to 147 miles per hour in Boulder and 165 miles per hour on Marshall Mesa, between Boulder and Denver.

Cold Arctic air "pools" at lower elevations as relatively warm westerly winds sweep across the mountains. On a January 1975 morning in Gunnison, the thermometer read −16°F, while at Mount Crested Butte, 2,000 feet higher and only 20 miles away, skiers enjoyed temperatures in the low 30s above zero.

See "Colorado Climate Summary" (p. 1) for information on averages, extremes, and sources.

january ecosystem

Snow Forest

Snow begins falling in the spruce-fir forest in early September and stays on the ground through early July. It comes in waves, with short, intense storms sandwiched between longer intervals of clear skies and fierce drying winds. In January 1996, 20 feet of snow blanketed some Western Slope spruce-fir forests. A March 1899 storm dumped 141 inches on the small mining community of Ruby in Gunnison County.

These winter and spring storms bring the moisture that enables Engelmann spruces and subalpine firs to survive in their high-altitude environment. The snow blanket insulates many of the forest's inhabitants from the subzero chill. Weasels, voles, and mice sleep and burrow at the base of the snowpack, where the temperature rarely falls far below 32°F. On the coldest nights some birds, including white-tailed ptarmigan, blue grouse, and snow buntings, snuggle into the snow to keep warm.

Engelmann spruces and subalpine firs have evolved to live in an extreme climate. Their slender silhouettes and down-sloping branches limit snow loading and wind exposure. A waxy coating on their needles seals in moisture, and the luxuriant needle growth shields branches and trunks from windblown ice particles. When temperatures warm above freezing in early spring, Engelmann spruces and subalpine firs can begin photosynthesis long before deciduous trees leaf out.

> ### Fir, Spruce, or Pine?
>
> To tell whether a conifer is spruce, fir, or pine, grab a branch. If it sticks you, the tree's a spruce. By comparison, fir feels almost feathery, while pine needles are long and pliant.
>
> Spruce = sharp, square (needles in cross section).
> Fir = flexible, flat (needles in cross section).
> Pine = pliant, pointed, in bundles.

While skiing or snowshoeing in these spruce-fir forests, note the circular depressions in the snow around the larger trunks. The trees absorb warmth from the sun throughout the day, and the heat radiates outward at night, causing the snow to sublimate, or evaporate. Note, also, that most of the larger trees are the red-barked Engelmann spruces, while the majority of the smaller trees are the white-barked subalpine firs. Scientists do not fully understand this discrepancy of age distribution but believe it reflects the Englemann spruces' longer life span and greater tolerance of sunlight.

Dumbbell-shaped tracks of pine martens and long-tailed weasels thread their way through the trees. The weasel tracks sometimes vanish suddenly where these slender predators have plunged into the snow. Long-tailed weasels spend most of the winter under the snowpack. They sleep in a nest of rodent fur in a burrow or a hollow and scurry through dark passages sniffing out voles, mice, chipmunks, pikas, and young cottontails. Being a hyperkinetic, sausage-shaped, lightweight predator has its pitfalls in winter. Long-tailed weasels must constantly stoke their metabolic fires to keep from freezing. In winter they consume up to 40 percent of their weight daily and cannot go more than a few days without eating.

Pine martens slither beneath the snowpack to hunt voles and mice. They also prey on snowshoe hares and scamper up into the forest canopy to nab pine squirrels and an occasional songbird. These 1- to 4-pound members of the weasel family den in tree cavities, logs, and rock piles. They frequent old-growth forests, where large snags and downed logs provide denning sites and easy access to the subnivean (literally, "under snow") environment.

At dusk snowshoe hares sit motionless in the shadows, waiting to make their nocturnal rounds. Under the cover of darkness they bound cautiously across the snow's surface on furry, oversized feet, browsing on conifer needles, conifer bark, aspen bark, and willow shoots. The hares' relatively large size and thick fur enable them to spend the winter on top of the snowpack. During the day they huddle up in a small scrape in the snow, usually in a thicket of young conifers or willows.

Engelmann spruce–subalpine fir forests occur throughout Colorado at elevations of about 9,500 to 11,500 feet. Owing to difficulty of access and low commercial value of their timber, some of these forests have never been logged. Whether seen in

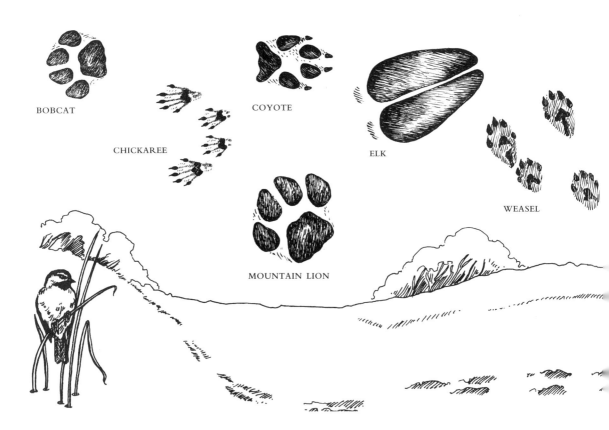

BOBCAT

CHICKAREE

COYOTE

ELK

WEASEL

MOUNTAIN LION

winter, when the soft conifer needles and snow muffle every sound, or in summer, when hermit thrush song filters through the shadows and red-backed voles scamper over moss-covered logs, these ancient forests offer a rare glimpse of Colorado's mountain environment as it might have appeared several thousand years ago.

Where To Go

🐾 Most high mountain passes, especially Wolf Creek, Independence (closed in winter), Monarch, and Cameron.

🐾 Weminuche and South San Juan wilderness areas, near Pagosa Springs.

🐾 Bowen Gulch trail, near Granby.

🐾 Trail Ridge Road (closed in winter), from Rocky Mountain National Park west boundary to Milner Pass.

🐾 Long Lake Nature Trail in Indian Peaks Wilderness, west of Ward.

DEER MOUSE

SNOWSHOE HARE

COLORADO CONIFERS[a]

Species	Location	Identification
WHITE FIR *Abies concolor*	Mountain canyonsides, mostly Colorado Springs southward.	A tall fir with long needles and erect grayish-green cones.
CORKBARK FIR *A. arizonica*	Wolf Creek Pass area, 8,000 to 10,000 feet.	Flat, short, blunt needles; upright purple-black cones; white bark checkered and spongy to touch.
SUBALPINE FIR *A. bifolia*	Areas of permanent winter snow, usually associated with Engelmann spruce; 9,500 to 11,500 feet	Flat, short, blunt needles; upright purple-black cones on upper branches; whitish bark.
ENGELMANN SPRUCE *Picea engelmannii*	Areas of permanent winter snow; 9,000 to 11,500 feet.	Dark green 4-sided needles; tall trees; reddish, scaly bark; cones hang down.
COLORADO BLUE SPRUCE *P. pungens "Glauca"*	Moist habitats, often along foothills streams; 5,500 to 10,000 feet.	Bluish 4-sided, sharp needles; Christmas-tree–like shape; cones hang down.
BRISTLECONE PINE *Pinus aristata*	Dry, windswept slopes and ridges; 10,000 to 11,500 feet.	Short, twisted needles, 5 to a clump, flecked with white pitch; gnarled trunks; bristle-tipped cone scales.
LIMBER PINE *P. flexilis*	Rocky, windswept ridges and exposed slopes, 7,500 to 11,000 feet; also Pawnee Buttes area.	Short needles in bundles of 5; trunks often gnarled; cone scales not bristle-tipped; needles not flecked with pitch.
MEXICAN WHITE PINE *P. strobiformis*	Mid-elevation forests, southwestern Colorado.	Tall, straight trunk; 5 needles with minute teeth near their apex.
PONDEROSA PINE *P. ponderosa*	Relatively dry, often south-facing sites; 5,500 to 9,000 feet.	Long (4- to 7-inch) needles in clusters of 2 or 3; textured, reddish bark on older trees.
LODGEPOLE PINE *P. contorta*	Disturbed sites; 7,000 to 11,000 feet.	Short, twisted needles in clumps of 2; tall, straight trunk; cone-scales bristle-tipped.
PIÑON PINE *P. edulis*	Lower elevations of plateaus and mesas, mostly south and west.	Low, bushy tree; 2 or 3 needles; cone-scales not bristle-tipped.
DOUGLAS-FIR *Pseudotsuga menziesii*	Shaded, often north-facing sites; 6,000 to 10,000 feet.	Short, flat needles; female cones hang down and have 3-pronged bracts protruding from between cone scales.

[a]This list does not include shrublike conifers, such as junipers and ephedras.

SUBALPINE FIR

ENGELMANN SPRUCE

BRISTLECONE PINE

PONDEROSA PINE

LODGEPOLE PINE

LIMBER PINE

DOUGLAS-FIR

WATERFOWL SAUNAS

While many ducks, geese, and swans undertake long migrations, others move south in a leisurely manner, staying just ahead of the line where lakes and rivers freeze. With a thick layer of feathers and abundant fat to insulate them from the cold, most waterfowl can tolerate severe winter conditions. All they really need is

15

a reliable food supply and a predator-proof place, such as open water, to spend the night.

Colorado State University ornithologist Ronald Ryder coined the phrase *waterfowl sauna* to describe Hamilton Reservoir, north of Fort Collins, where warm water released from the Rawhide Power Plant keeps much of the surface ice free throughout the winter. Over the years Ryder and others have observed more than thirty species of ducks, geese, and swans at Hamilton Reservoir, including rarities such as red-necked grebes, snow geese, white-fronted geese, tundra swans, white-winged scoters, and oldsquaws. The Public Service Company's Valmont Reservoir, east of Boulder, also attracts a diversity of rare migrants and wanderers. Notable winter sightings during the 1990s have included double-crested cormorants, tundra swans, white-fronted geese, snow geese, and an oldsquaw.

Waterfowl also gather along ice-free stretches of streams and rivers, often at the base of a large reservoir where constant releases keep water temperatures a degree or two above freezing. Open water in and below Pueblo Reservoir has attracted such winter rarities as red-throated, Pacific, common, and yellow-billed loons; greater white-fronted geese; and white-winged scoters. In the Dolores River

Canada geese bask in a waterfowl sauna.

Canyon, north of McPhee Reservoir, the quacks of fast flying mergansers echo off salmon-colored cliffs, while colorful mallards and green-winged teal bob up and down in the icy rapids.

Where To Go

❧ Horsethief Canyon and Walker State Wildlife Areas. Colorado River west of Grand Junction. Ducks, great blue herons, and bald eagles.

❧ Dolores River Canyon, north of Cortez. Ducks and raptors.

❧ Sweitzer Lake State Park, near Delta.

❧ Pueblo Reservoir. Loons, swans, and rare ducks. Spotting scope or telescope recommended.

❧ South Platte River at 88th Avenue bridge in Thornton. Rare ducks.

❧ Valmont Reservoir, east of Boulder. Uncommon grebes, loons, and rare ducks. Spotting scope or telescope recommended.

❧ Boulder Creek at Walden Ponds Wildlife Habitat. Close views of hooded mergansers, great blue herons, and bald eagles.

❧ Hamilton Reservoir, 18 miles north of Fort Collins. Loons, uncommon grebes, swans, and rare ducks. Spotting scope or telescope recommended.

❧ Bosque del Apache National Wildlife Refuge, near Socorro, New Mexico. Tens of thousands of snow geese and sandhill cranes.

SNOWY OWLS

A rare winter visitor to the eastern plains and foothills of Colorado is the snowy owl, a bird of the far north that breeds on the tundra of Canada, Alaska, Siberia, Russia, Scandinavia, and Greenland. Snowy owls feed chiefly on lemmings, which undergo wild population swings, and also eat other small rodents and hares. In good lemming years, the owl population surges. In years when the lemming populations crash, some owls come south in search of food.

Because of these periodic invasions from the Arctic, which usually occur every three to five years, snowy owls (*Nyctea scandiaca*) are called a "cyclic" or "irruptive" species. However, a 1988 study by P. Kerlinger and M. Ross Lein ("Population Ecology of Snowy Owls During Winter on the Great Plains of North America," *The Condor* 90 [1988]: 866–874) shows that large numbers of them migrate to the

Rainbows 'Round
the Sun and Moon

Some of the most beautiful atmospheric astonishments occur in winter when ice crystals in cirrus clouds refract the sunlight into opalescent colors. Sometimes these sundogs or mock suns are circular, but more often they form a broad sheet of iridescence. They occur near the moon as well as the sun. The brightness is enhanced when the crystals are more numerous and uniform in size.

northern Great Plains every winter, remaining till late February or March. Kerlinger and Lein found no cyclic variation, but they say more research is needed since their result contradicts earlier observations. Their research did not include Colorado, where the snowy owl is considered an irregular winter straggler, with numbers fluctuating over the years.

In *Birds of Colorado,* Alfred Bailey and Robert Niedrach write, "Most unusual conditions must prevail for many [snowy owls] to be forced into Colorado. A considerable flight occurred during the severe winter of 1886–87." An irruption also apparently occurred in 1918 when "seven or eight were sent to local taxidermy shops" in Weld and Washington Counties. Except for a sighting in Rio Blanco County and at Breckenridge, the reports all came from the eastern slope. The most southern record was from Custer County.

Immature males are the ones most likely to be seen this far south. During winter they prey on birds, including ring-necked pheasants, grouse, waterfowl, rock doves, and domestic poultry, as well as rodents.

Perfectly camouflaged to disappear against snow and ice, the soft plumage of snowy owls is white with light gray-brown barring. Some males are almost pure white; females tend to be darker. This ghost of the tundra glares out at the world through slightly mad, bright yellow eyes. It lacks ear tufts and is a bit larger than a great horned owl. It rarely calls except during the breeding season.

As far back as the Stone Age, people seem to have had a reverence for these owls. Petroglyphs of snowy owls and chicks in the Trois Frères Cave in France, dating to a time when glaciers covered much of Europe, may have had religious significance.

Owls are often associated with death and the supernatural. Many American Indian peoples said that if the owl called your name, you would die soon. The ancient Romans and Chinese also believed the hoot of an owl foretold death. The Ojibwa called the bridge over which the dead pass, the "owl bridge," and the Kwakiutl believed the owl represented both the dead person and the soul—a benign guardian spirit. The Micmac Indians translated the snowy's mournful "Koo, koo, koo" as "Oh, I am sorry, Oh, I am sorry" and said the owl was lamenting the golden age when humans and animals lived in harmony, before their quarrel caused the Great Spirit to sail away.

Where To Go

Listen to the Rare Bird Alert (303-424-2144), sponsored by the Denver Field Ornithologists. If there has been a sighting, it will be noted on this recording. If you see a rarity, thank Ullr, god of the north, for the gift and call the number above to alert others.

COUGAR KITTENS

On a sparkling January morning, we followed a fresh set of mountain lion tracks through 18 inches of snow in Gregory Canyon, west of Boulder. The tracks led into a narrow side canyon to a fresh deer carcass partially covered by pine boughs and continued up the hillside to a pine stump shredded with claw marks. We looked around warily, almost certain the lion was sleeping in a ponderosa pine somewhere overhead. After a few minutes, we left the way we had come. Superimposed on our old boot tracks were the round, perfectly formed prints of a mountain lion silently skulking back down the canyon and into the forest.

In winter mountain lions become more than ghostly apparitions. We see their tracks in the snow, stumble upon their kills, or glimpse their shadowy forms darting across a highway at dusk. With fewer of us abroad in the woods and with cold temperatures increasing their need for nourishment, cougars become a little less secretive, a little more inquisitive. We may not see them, but we can sense their eyes watching us.

Deep snows may give mountain lions an advantage over their common prey, mule deer. The snow muffles a lion's stealthy approach, and a deer may become bogged down just long enough to enable the predator to leap onto its back and grasp it around the neck with viselike jaws. Winter scarcity or hardship does not appear to impinge on the lions' breeding cycle. In the Rocky Mountain region they may give birth during any month of the year.

Individual mountain lions defend enormous home ranges of around 15 to 250 square miles. Males and females come together only to mate. After mating, they go their separate ways, and the females take full responsibility for rearing the cubs.

Words for Mountain Lion

*Mountain lion, puma, cougar, and panther are different common names for a single species. **Puma** is a Spanish adaptation of the Quechua (Peru) word for this cat. **Cougar** is a French adaptation of the Tupi (Amazon Basin) sua-suarana, meaning "false deer" (possibly an allusion to the mountain lion's tawny color). **Panther** means "leopard" in Greek.*

Felis concolor was once the widest ranging of all North American mammals—from southern Yukon territory to Tierra del Fuego. It has been extirpated from most of eastern North America and from large areas of South America.

Prior to giving birth, the female scrapes out a nest in a shallow depression under an overhanging conifer bough or in a small cave or hollow. Newborn kittens weigh less than a pound, cannot open their eyes, and mew softly while flopped together in the nest. Fortunately they already sport a thick layer of fur, and their kitten-sized ears and tails receive enough blood flow to resist frostbite in winter.

Before the kittens are a week old, their mother may leave them for twenty-four hours at a time to hunt and feed. Except when nursing kittens, females usually sleep close to their nearest kill, often a mile or more from the den. A single deer can sustain a cougar and her newborn kittens for a week or so, but as the youngsters grow larger, she may need to kill a deer every three to four days. The kittens stay with their mothers for twelve to twenty-two months. Females with dependent cubs generally skip a year before mating again.

Mountain lions roam throughout the foothills, plateaus, and mountains of Colorado and occasionally appear on the eastern plains. Look for their tracks in areas

COUGAR ATTACKS

Dale Johnson was preparing for bed in his mountain home west of Boulder when he heard a thump on the bedroom window. He looked out the window at a full-grown mountain lion in a low crouch, apparently preparing to pounce. A few weeks earlier, in October 1994, a hiker on nearby Green Mountain had fought off a crouched mountain lion with rocks and sticks. Earlier that year a cougar attacked a wildlife officer near Cortez. While struggling with the lion, she somehow managed to stick her fist down its throat. The cat, an old, emaciated female, eventually gave up and ran off.

An apparent outbreak in mountain lion–human confrontations throughout western North America has alerted recreationists to the dangers posed by these predators. The California Division of Wildlife reported six attacks, two of them fatal, between 1992 and 1995. The Colorado Division of Wildlife documented a half dozen attacks during the 1990s. In January 1991, a seventeen-year-old jogger became the first Coloradan killed by a mountain lion when he was ambushed by an adult female near Idaho Springs. On July 17, 1997, an 88-pound female lion killed a ten-year-old boy who was hiking with his family on a popular trail near Grand Lake. Earlier that week, a four-year-old boy sustained minor injuries when a lion attacked in Mesa Verde National Park.

Are cougars losing their fear of humans? Some people argue that removal of bounties and decreased hunting pressure have created a new generation of relatively fearless lions. They point to two fatal attacks in California, which occurred four years after citizens passed a state referendum banning mountain lion hunting. However, almost half of North American mountain lion attacks in this century have occurred in British Columbia, where hunters kill up to two hundred lions a year. In Colorado, hunters annually kill about 20 percent of the state's estimated population of one to two thousand animals.

Some biologists assert that the increase in mountain lion–human confrontations merely corresponds to the recent surge in mountain lion and human populations in the West. Mountain lion populations have benefited from a proliferation of mule deer and a softening of public attitudes toward predators. Humans have expanded their dwellings into prime mountain lion habitat.

Researchers have documented a total of fifteen fatal mountain lion attacks in North America since 1880. Eleven of the fatalities were children under the age of fourteen. Eleven fatal attacks occurred during the past twenty-five years. During that time period, hundreds of North Americans were killed by rattlesnakes or domestic dogs, several thousand were killed by bee stings or lightning strikes, and several hundred thousand were killed by automobiles.

In the rare event of a mountain lion confrontation or attack, experts recommend you take the following steps:

- Stop and then back away slowly.
- Raise your jacket or open your arms to appear larger.
- If the lion becomes aggressive, throw rocks or stones and speak firmly.
- If the lion attacks, fight back.

And remember, statistics indicate you're about as likely to be killed by a vending machine as by a mountain lion.

that support high deer populations, such as ponderosa pine forests, piñon–juniper woodlands, and foothills shrublands. The illustration on p. 12 shows the difference between cougar (mountain lion) tracks and dog or coyote tracks.

Where To Go

Finding mountain lion tracks requires patience and exertion, and actually seeing a lion can be a once in a lifetime experience. The following places support year-round populations:

✂ Dinosaur National Monument, northwest Colorado.
✂ Dolores River Canyon, north of Cortez.
✂ Great Sand Dunes National Monument, northeast of Alamosa.
✂ Golden Gate Canyon State Park, west of Golden.
✂ Boulder Mountain Park.
✂ Buttonrock Reservoir, west of Lyons.

ICEFALLS

Waterfalls freeze in layers, with the water on the sides or in contact with rock surfaces freezing first. Some form giant ice cones with hollow centers. Others congeal into rows of slender icicles hanging down over dark, damp grottoes. Still others coalesce into fluted blue-green veils draped over black cliff faces.

BEAR BABIES

Bear cubs are usually born in January or early February while the female is still sound asleep. Born blind, they find the nipples by sensing heat. As the mother continues to sleep, the cubs remain awake and suckle on her rich milk, growing from about 12 ounces to as much as 15 pounds by the time they emerge from the den in May.

Bears are one of several mammal species that undergo delayed implantation, an ingenious form of birth control. The female is impregnated in early summer when life is rich and easy and food is plentiful. However, the blastocysts float in the fallopian tube until midfall. If food continues to be plentiful and the female has stored fat, the blastocysts will implant in the uterus and start to grow. If food is scarce, implantation does not occur.

For some reason not yet understood by scientists, litter sizes in the eastern United States are larger than in the West, ranging from one to six in the East, one to three in the West. Researcher Tom Beck says that within a region, body size and annual food supply influence litter size, "but even big, fat western bears do not exceed litters of three while small, lean Michigan bears will have three to four cubs."

For more bear stories, see pp. 186 (September) and 222–224 (November).

The appearance of movement in icefalls is not entirely illusory. The weakness of molecular bonds in ice enables it to flow more freely than other solids. Ice in some of the largest glaciers flows several hundred feet each year. Since the degree of ice flow is determined by the size of the ice mass, the ice on the surface of most icefalls probably moves only a few millimeters during the winter season.

Because blue-green light penetrates more deeply than other wavelengths through ice and snow, icefalls often take on a bluish or greenish color. Penetration of blue-green light, which is a near optimum wavelength for chlorophyll absorption by plants, permits some plants growing under the snowpack, and behind icefalls, to continue a low level of photosynthesis throughout the winter.

Icefalls in South St. Vrain Canyon.

Where To Go

🦆 Rifle Falls, north of Rifle. Three massive, blue-green ice floes over mossy sandstones. Popular with ice climbers.

❀ Bridal Veil Falls at Hanging Lake, east of Glenwood Springs. A 1-mile hike on a steep, snowy trail leads to an emerald-green lake framed by veils of ice.

❀ Whitmore Falls, west of Lake City. Henson Creek drops 30 feet into a deep pool surrounded by dark cliffs.

❀ Ice Climbing Park, Ouray. A mile of natural and artificial ice falls south of Ouray attracts climbers from all over the world.

❀ Ouzel Falls, Rocky Mountain National Park. A 3.2-mile ski tour through lodgepole, aspen, and spruce-fir forest leads to a shimmering cascade and a 40-foot-high falls.

For additional waterfalls, see pp. 120–122 (June).

JANUARY EVENTS

MAMMALS

❀ Beavers breed in January or February.

❀ Black bear cubs are born while their mother is dormant.

BIRDS

❀ Rosy finches flock by the hundreds at higher elevations.

❀ Great horned owls court.

❀ Snowy owls may stray into the northeastern part of state; other winter rarities may include redpolls and snow buntings.

❀ Large flocks of Bohemian waxwings feed on juniper and mountain ash berries in urban areas. Because these birds follow the fruit crop, their arrival cannot be predicted, and they are called "erratic."

PLANTS

❀ Some buds, such as pussy willow and Rocky Mountain maple, start to swell.

IN THE SKY

❀ "Moon of Frost in the Lodge" (Cheyenne).

❀ Quadrantid meteor shower peaks around January 3. Look low in the northwest after sunset.

♑ Orion, the "Great Hunter," is high in the southern sky around 9:00 P.M. Orion contains the Great Nebula, observable with binoculars, and the first-magnitude stars Rigel and Betelgeuse. Rigel is 460 light years distant but is fourteen thousand times brighter than our sun. The red giant Betelgeuse has a diameter of 215 million miles, greater than the diameter of earth's orbit around the sun.

Impressive Battlement Arch in Rattlesnake Canyon, near Grand Junction. (Photo by Glenn Cushman.)

February

2

Hare is jumping and singing;

   Hare is jumping and singing,

While the wind is roaring.

   While the wind is roaring.

—PIMA

THE ROARING WIND cannot obscure the signs of spring that appear in February. Our hearts jump and sing along with Hare when we find the first Easter daisies on sun-drenched rock outcroppings, when we see the first bluebirds of the year return from the south, and when we discover the first nests of great horned owls.

On sandstone and granite cliffs golden eagles also begin to nest, and peregrine and prairie falcons establish territories as the cliffs echo the cascading songs of canyon wrens. Hormones also arouse foxes, coyotes, wolves, and raccoons to woo a mate.

During warm spells we even catch glimpses of summer as Milbert's tortoiseshell and mourning cloak butterflies drift past on a gentle wind that can change overnight to a roar.

FEBRUARY WEATHER

	Grand Junction (4,824 ft.)	Steamboat Springs (6,760 ft.)	Alamosa (7,536 ft.)	Berthoud Pass (11,310 ft.)	Denver (5,282 ft.)	Lamar (3,620 ft.)
Ave. high (°F)	45	33	40	24	47	50
Ave. low (°F)	24	3	5	2	20	18
Max. high (°F)	70	59	66	47	76	84
Min. low (°F)	−21	−48	−35	−34	−30	−21
Ave. prec. (in.)	0.48	1.99	0.29	2.90	0.57	0.42
Max. prec. (in.)	1.77	5.13	1.42	5.12	1.66	2.07
Ave. snow (in.)	4.3	29.1	4.6	43.2	7.5	4.4
Max. snow (in.)	18.8	65.8	16.0	76.5	18.3	30.4

Temperatures fluctuate wildly as Arctic air masses and warm southwesterly winds wash back and forth over the state. On February 1, 1985, Maybell recorded a state record low of −61°F. A few hours later, Maybell's temperature had risen to a balmy 15 above zero. Taylor Park reached −60°F on February 1 of the same year. Denver experienced its all time record low of −30°F in February, 1936. The month's state record high of 90°F occurred in Blaine in 1904.

See "Colorado Climate Summary" (page 1) for information on averages, extremes, and sources.

february ecosystem

Cliff Communities

At a place called the Devil's Kitchen in Colorado National Monument, a horseshoe-shaped formation of red sandstones faces southeast, receiving the full force of the morning sun. Summer temperatures in this aptly named spot can exceed 120°F, causing many life forms to wither or scurry for cover. But in late winter the south-facing cliffs of the Devil's Kitchen become islands of life-giving warmth in an otherwise quiescent landscape. Delicate blue-green leaves of pasture sage (*Artemisia ludoviciana*) unfurl and reach for the sun. Rock squirrels bask on the slickrock. A canyon wren's sweet song floats on the still air, while amorous ravens croak and cackle overhead.

Sandstone cliffs throughout Colorado absorb and store enormous amounts of solar radiation, creating microclimates where spring begins early. In the Flatirons, west of Boulder, the bright yellow flowers of Oregon grape (*Mahonia repens*) may

Dramatic cliffs in Knowles Canyon on the Colorado River west of Grand Junction.
(Photo by Glenn Cushman.)

begin blooming in December. In Cottonwood Canyon, south of La Junta, mustards and milk vetches growing at the base of ocher-colored cliffs bloom four to six weeks earlier than their counterparts growing on the surrounding mesas.

Cliffs also collect water, which streams down the cliff face to nourish small oases of greenery or emerges from seeps where ferns, mosses, or wild grapes form hanging gardens. Later in the year, these cool, shady "alcove" habitats support moisture-loving wildflowers such as orchids, columbines, primroses, and monkeyflowers.

Ledges, potholes, and caves on cliff faces provide nesting sites for golden eagles, prairie falcons, peregrine falcons, turkey vultures, great horned owls, and other birds of prey. Great horned owls lay their eggs as early as mid-January. Golden eagles begin incubating by late February or early March. Early nesting enables these raptors to take full advantage of available food resources and gives their relatively slow developing young time to mature and become independent prior to the onset of another winter. Great horned owlets generally hatch in early spring when baby cottontails, prairie dogs, and other prey species are emerging from their burrows. Golden eagle chicks don't leave the nest until late June or July and usually require several months of flying lessons before they can fend for themselves.

White-throated swifts, who winter in Mexico and Central America, arrive at cliff crevice nesting colonies in early spring. These sickle-winged aerialists hurtle across the cliff faces, dodging, diving, and swerving to snatch insects from mid-air. They can sleep on the wing and mate while tumbling earthward in a brief and perilous embrace.

Many cliff community rodents, including most chipmunks and ground squirrels, hibernate or sleep through the winter. Rock squirrels, woodrats, and most mice species remain active. Rodents with nocturnal leanings, such as the bushy-tailed woodrat, deer mouse, and cañon mouse, often increase dirunal activity during the colder months.

Bushy-tailed woodrats, one of many species known as "pack rats," collect sticks, branches, bones, rags, tin cans, and other artifacts and pack them into caves or crevices high on cliff walls. A typical den may contain 20 cubic feet of scavenged material cemented together with feces and urine. Within this debris pile, the woodrat constructs a cup-shaped nest lined with plant fibers.

In *The Desert World,* Colorado ecologist David Costello tells of an Oregon woodrat that stole the booties from the feet of a sleeping baby and of a Colorado woodrat that stored a cache of dynamite in a miner's cookstove. Costello and other scientists have puzzled over why pack rats store so many diverse objects in their dens. The debris may help to insulate young woodrats from cold spring or hot summer temperatures, but no one has ever proved this.

Though unable to explain the method behind the pack rat's madness, humans have benefited from this rodent's collecting mania. Plains Indians raided woodrat middens to find prickly pear fruits and other delicacies, and scientists have used carbon-dated remains from pack rat dens to trace the vegetative and cultural history of North America back thousands of years.

Artifacts found in southwestern Colorado rock shelters indicate that humans occupied the sandstone cliffs of this region more than seven thousand years ago. Like the Anasazi much later, these early peoples preferred steep, south-facing cliffs that soaked up the winter sun and provided protection from wind and snow. Human occupation of rock shelters in the chalk bluffs and sandstone cliffs of eastern Colorado began more than six thousand years ago and continued into the eighteenth century.

Where To Go

⅋ Dinosaur National Monument, north of Rangely.
⅋ Colorado National Monument, near Grand Junction.

☙ Mesa Verde National Park, near Cortez.
☙ Garden of the Gods, Colorado Springs.
☙ Castlewood Canyon State Park, south of Denver.
☙ Pawnee Buttes, Pawnee National Grassland, east of Greeley.
☙ Comanche National Grassland, south of La Junta.

EASTER DAISIES

Easter daisies (*Townsendia hookeri* or *T. excapa*) grow on dry slopes on western mesas and on Front Range foothills. Despite their name, these small composites with yellow disk flowers and up to thirty narrow white ray flowers often appear in

February, six weeks or more before Easter. Before the flowers unfurl, pale pink buds nestle into a soft mound of gray-green leaves. The earliest bloomers grow near shale outcroppings or on gravelly ridges. Although these sites seem exposed, the rock collects both heat and moisture, giving these plants a head start.

At higher elevations and on the eastern plains, look for Easter daisies in April. It seems a paradox that plants usually bloom later on the prairie than in the foothills. A partial answer to this puzzle may be that warm Chinook winds keep winter temperatures relatively moderate in the foothills compared to the prairie.

Easter daisies.

A closely related but showier species, *Townsendia grandiflora*, blooms in late May and June, favoring eroded clay banks. *Townsendia*s were named by botanist Thomas Nuttall for the ornithologist John Kirk Townsend. Both men made many discoveries on an 1834 expedition across the United States to Oregon.

CLIFF-NESTING RAPTORS

As the winter days grow longer, golden eagles renew pair bonds and begin to refurbish their nests. During courtship the male performs a roller-coaster flight, swooping and soaring over the female's head. Pairs sometimes lock talons in mid-air,

WINTER WILDFLOWERS

On foothills shales west of Denver, we have found Easter daisies (*Townsendia* spp.) blooming as early as December 15 and spring beauties (*Claytonia rosea*) blooming by the first of the year. Look for early bloomers on bare or disturbed ground or nestled against rock slabs. Expect to find them first in areas with relatively warm microclimates, such as the Grand Valley, the Front Range foothills, and the Arkansas River Valley.

SPECIES	DESCRIPTION	HABITAT
EASTER DAISY *Townsendia* spp. Sunflower family	Pinkish-white flowers with yellow centers on low mats; stems with long, slender leaves.	Shales, sand hillsides, and rocky slopes at lower elevations; **WS** and **PL.**
SPRAWLING FLEABANE *Erigeron colo-mexicanus* Sunflower family	White flowers with yellow centers, 1 per stem; narrow leaves in a basal cluster.	Dry areas, disturbed areas, and meadows at lower elevations; **WS** and **PL.**
SALT-AND-PEPPER *Lomatium orientale* Parsley family	Dingy white flowers in small umbels; plant low growing with parsleylike leaves radiating from center.	Grassy hillsides and gravelly slopes at lower elevations; **WS** and **PL.**
WILD ALYSSUM[a] *Alyssum* spp. Mustard family	Pale yellow flowers on edge of circular flower head; plants grow in dense masses.	Waste areas, fields, and hillsides at lower elevations; **WS** and **PL,** introduced.
STORKSBILL (FILAREE)[a] *Erodium cicutarium* Geranium family	Pink to lavender 5-petaled flowers on fernlike leaf stalks that radiate out from a rosette.	Disturbed areas, fallow fields, and parking lots at lower elevations; **WS** and **PL.**
SPRING BEAUTY *Claytonia rosea* Purslane family	Small white to pinkish, 5-petaled flowers on erect, slender stems bearing 2 to 4 leaves.	Moist meadows and open forests at low to mid elevations; **WS** and **MT.**
PASQUEFLOWER *Pulsatilla patens* Buttercup family	Translucent flowers with pale lavender sepals and bright yellow centers; hairy, basal leaves and leafless flower stalks.	Grassy hillsides, fields, meadows, sagebrush, and open forests at almost all elevations; **WS, MT, PL.**

MT: Mountains above 7,500 feet; **PL:** Plains and eastern foothills to about 7,500 feet; **WS:** Western Slope valleys and plateaus to about 7,500 feet.
[a]Introduced species.

tumbling eagle over eagle toward the ground. Occasionally, the female will fly several thousand feet up into the sky with a rock or stick in her talons, drop the object, and watch as the male snatches it out of the air.

When a female eagle decides where she wants her nest, she may place a stick on the intended spot, signaling to her mate that it is time to get to work. According to journalist and eagle watcher Dan True (*A Family of Eagles*), the male does the bulk of the work while the female watches with a critical eye. True reported one instance when a female, dissatisfied with her mate's work, shoved the poorly constructed nest off the cliff face, forcing him to start over.

Each year a golden eagle pair may construct an entirely new nest or refurbish an old one. Some cliff faces contain ten or more nests. By not using the same nest every year, golden eagles probably reduce their exposure to nest parasites and increase their nestlings' chances of survival. Favored nests can grow to enormous proportions. A nest on the Lefthand Palisades in Boulder County, first described by naturalist Denis Gale in 1884, has grown to 10 feet across and 6 feet high. Nesting pairs will not tolerate other golden eagles, except their own immature offspring, within a mile or two of the nest.

To determine whether a golden eagle nest is in use, look for bits of greenery such as pine or fir boughs on top of the nest. Then wait and watch. Males and females take turns incubating, with exchanges occurring every forty-five to ninety minutes. After the young have hatched, the female usually stays on the nest or close by, and the male flies in only to deliver food.

Golden eagles breed throughout the state, laying their eggs between late February and early April. Their young fledge between late June and early August. After leaving the nest, the young eagles stay near their parents for a year or more and do not reach sexual maturity until their fourth or fifth year. Eagles may live for thirty years or more. One female in the Boulder Mountain Park nested on the same cliff face for thirteen years.

Prairie falcons, which spend the winter months hunting songbirds on the plains and deserts, return to their nesting cliffs in the mountains, foothills, and lowland canyons in March or early April. They usually lay their eggs right on the rock, on a ledge, or in a small cave or pothole. Sometimes they occupy an abandoned red-tailed hawk or golden eagle nest. Streaks of whitewash (excrement) coat the rock face below the nest site, and the screams of the loquacious and frequently agitated adults echo off adjacent cliff faces.

During the first half of this century, illegal hunting and illegal nest robbing by falconers depleted Colorado nesting populations. Numbers appear to have rebounded during the last several decades, but urbanization is beginning to destroy prairie falcon foraging habitat. In addition, peregrine falcons have begun to displace nesting prairie falcons along the Front Range foothills. In aggressive interactions between these two species, the peregrines often dominate, driving the prairies away from prime nesting sites. Peregrines also may adapt better than prairies to urbanizing environments. While peregrines have nested successfully on skyscrapers in East Coast cities, prairie falcons have abandoned nest sites close to Front Range cities.

Thirty years ago, when accumulation of DDT residues in peregrine reproductive tissues threatened the species' extinction, Colorado supported fewer than five nesting pairs. Since then, the banning of DDT and the initiation of reintroduction programs have contributed to the peregrine's gradual recovery throughout the

CLIFF-NESTING RAPTORS

SPECIES	NESTING HABITAT	ESTIMATED COLORADO POPULATION
TURKEY VULTURE	Remote caves and crevices; mountains and canyons	Unknown
RED-TAILED HAWK	Mostly trees, but also cliffs; statewide to 10,000 feet.	10,000+ pairs
FERRUGINOUS HAWK	Trees and low cliffs; eastern plains and northwestern canyons.	100 to 250 pairs
GOLDEN EAGLE	Remote cliffs, occasionally in trees; statewide to 10,000 feet.	200 to 500 pairs
AMERICAN KESTREL	Tree cavities and cliff faces; statewide to 10,000 feet.	10,000+ pairs
PRAIRIE FALCON	Cliff faces in or near open country; statewide to 10,000 feet.	200 to 500 pairs
PEREGRINE FALCON	Remote cliff faces in mountains and canyons; mountains and west to 10,000 feet.	50 to 100 pairs
COMMON BARN OWL	Cliffs, embankments, barns, and silos; statewide to about 7,500 feet.	Unknown
GREAT HORNED OWL	Trees, buildings, and cliffs; statewide to 11,500 feet.	10,000+ pairs

Sources: Colorado Division of Wildlife; Robert Andrews and Robert Righter, *Colorado Birds*; Hugh Kingery, ed., *Colorado Breeding Bird Atlas*.

Rocky Mountain region. Between fifty and one hundred pairs now nest in Colorado. The much publicized Division of Wildlife effort to establish nesting on Denver skyscrapers has not yet succeeded, but peregrine populations have expanded steadily in the central mountains and western valleys.

The future survival of all cliff-nesting raptors in Colorado depends on our success in protecting nest sites and foraging areas. On the nearly treeless eastern plains, where nest sites are at a premium, several raptor species may occupy the same nesting cliff. Unfortunately, these prominent cliff faces attract hikers, photographers, and rock climbers, who may unwittingly disturb nests. In the Front Range foothills, nesting golden eagles, prairie falcons, and peregrine falcons are rapidly running out of places to hunt, as housing developments and shopping malls replace native grasslands. Several historic nest sites have been abandoned.

Nesting raptors need lots of space. We have found that an approach to within .5 miles or less of an active nest causes some consternation among nesting eagles, falcons, and hawks and may disrupt their nesting routine.

Where To Go

🦢 Colorado National Monument, near Grand Junction. Golden eagles, red-tailed hawks, and peregrine falcons.

🦉 Cedar Mountain, near Craig. Golden eagles.

🦉 Mesa Verde National Park, near Cortez. Golden eagles, red-tailed hawks, turkey vultures, and American kestrels.

🦉 Castle Rock, above the town of Castle Rock. Golden eagles and prairie falcons.

🦉 Boulder Mountain Park. Golden eagles, red-tailed hawks, turkey vultures, prairie falcons, and peregrine falcons.

🦉 Comanche National Grassland, canyon areas south of La Junta. Golden eagles, red-tailed hawks, turkey vultures, prairie falcons, American kestrels, common barn owls, and great horned owls.

GREAT HORNED OWLS

No matter where you live in Colorado, a pair of great horned owls is probably nesting within a couple of miles of your house. These adaptable predators can breed almost anywhere, preferring abandoned hawk or magpie nests but also using cliff ledges, caves, tree hollows, building ledges, and mine shafts. They prey on just about anything that moves, including birds, snakes, mice, rabbits, prairie dogs, skunks, muskrats, and house cats. They take no prisoners when it comes to defending nesting territories or driving away competitors.

Although great horned owls hoot throughout the year, their calls become more frequent and ardent during December and January as mating fervor peaks. By mid-February, most pairs breeding at lower elevations have selected a nest site. Owls do not build nests, so they must take advantage of what nature, or other birds, have provided. In Colorado great horned owls frequently recycle red-tailed hawk, American crow, or black-billed magpie nests. After making some minor improvements, the female lays one to five eggs. The eggs hatch within about a month, and the young begin walking around on neighboring tree branches or ledges about six weeks later.

Often the young owlets fall or flutter to the ground, where they waddle around helplessly for days, attracting the attention of red foxes, coyotes, and other predators. If a predator comes too close, the adult owls will defend their young, squawking, screaming, and lashing out with their talons. Sometimes an adult coaxes the grounded chicks up onto a low branch or a stump, where they can perch safely until strong enough to fly.

The young stay with their parents throughout the summer and into the fall. On autumn nights we sometimes hear all four or five members of a family hooting at

COLORADO'S NESTING OWLS

SPECIES	WHEN AND WHERE	VOCALIZATIONS
COMMON BARN OWL	March–October; western valleys and eastern plains.	Hisses and rattles.
EASTERN SCREECH-OWL	March–June; riparian and urban areas, plains north of Palmer Divide.	High trill or ghostly, horselike whinny.
WESTERN SCREECH-OWL	March–June; western valleys and southeastern plains.	4 to 20 short hoots on same pitch, like bouncing Ping-Pong ball.
GREAT HORNED OWL	February–May; plains to subalpine forest.	Low, resonant hoots: "wh-whoo, whoo-whoo."
FLAMMULATED OWL	May–July; midelevation ponderosa pine and aspen.	Soft, resonant hoot, single or in threes: "hoot, hoot, wh-wh-hoot."
NORTHERN PYGMY-OWL	March–June; coniferous forests, mesas, foothills, and mountains.	High, hollow whistles, sometimes paired; "toot-toot, toot, toot, toot-toot."
BURROWING OWL	May–July; rodent colonies, western valleys and eastern plains.	A soft "coo-cooooo" or a jaylike rattle.
SPOTTED OWL	April–July; southwestern canyons near Mesa Verde National Park.	3 or 4 low-pitched, cadenced notes: "who, who-whoo, whooo."
LONG-EARED OWL	March–July; dense thickets in low- to midelevation riparian and coniferous forests.	A resonant hoot, loud squawks, moans, and squeals.
SHORT-EARED OWL	April–July; grasslands and wetlands, San Luis Valley and eastern plains.	Low-pitched series of cooing or "boo" notes, 2 to 5 per second, reminiscent of a distant steam engine.
NORTHERN SAW-WHET OWL	April–June; mostly coniferous forests, foothills, mesas, and mountains.	High, hollow whistles, two or three notes higher pitched than pygmy and seldom paired: "toot-toot-toot-toot."
BOREAL OWL	March–June; spruce-fir forests above 9,500 feet.	A short series of rapid, hollow "hoo" notes, reminiscent of winnowing snipe.

These calls appear on two readily available tapes and CDs, *Peterson's Field Guide to Western Bird Songs* and *Voices of New World Owls*. Both can be ordered from the Cornell Laboratory of Ornithology in Ithaca, New York, or from your local Wild Bird Center. See also *North American Owls*, by Paul Johnsgard, for more call descriptions.

once. The adult male's basso profundo (wh-whoo, whoo-who) falls three to four notes lower than the female's slightly more complex contralto (who-wh-wh-whoo, wh-whoo-who). The youngsters' voices seem to range slightly higher.

As the next breeding season approaches, adult owls become intolerant of their offspring and chase them away. Within a year or two, the young owls establish their own nesting territories, where they may remain for the rest of their lives.

Great horned owls inhabit every Colorado ecosystem except the alpine tundra, and they thrive in and around human settlements. Nesting populations in the Front Range urban corridor have increased dramatically since the early 1900s. Meanwhile, populations of some less adaptable and less cosmopolitan owls have plummeted. The long-eared owl, a close competitor once considered common throughout much of eastern Colorado, has vanished from many of its historic Front Range haunts. Biologists don't know whether the great horned owls are eating the long-eared owls, chasing them away, or simply outcompeting them for prey and nest sites.

Where To Go

On the eastern plains and in western valleys look for the heads and tail feathers of incubating great horned owls poking out over the rims of large, flat-topped nests in cottonwoods and other deciduous trees, February through May. In mountain forests, listen for hooting owls and look for pellets—oblong masses of regurgitated bones, fur, and feathers—at the bases of nest and roost trees. The following places usually support at least one nesting pair:

෯ Walker and Horsethief Canyon State Wildlife Areas, Colorado River west of Grand Junction.

෯ La Garita Creek and Monte Vista wildlife refuges, near Alamosa.

෯ Comanche National Grassland—Carrizo, Cottonwood, and adjacent canyons—south of La Junta.

෯ Pueblo Reservoir.

෯ Chatfield Reservoir, south of Denver.

෯ Fort Collins Greenbelt.

෯ Bonny Reservoir, north of Burlington.

FIRST SPRING MIGRANTS—THE BLUEBIRDS

If Emily Dickinson had lived in Colorado, the mountain bluebird might have been the one that inspired her line: "Hope is a thing with feathers."

It's the northward migration of the bluebird, not the appearance of robins (year-round Colorado residents), that signals spring, bringing a burst of happiness to those who spot bluebirds between winter's rages. However, in the contest for state bird, the bluebird lost to the lark bunting, a late May arrival (see pp. 101–103, May, for details on this contest).

Both eastern and western bluebirds occur in Colorado, delighting us with their deep blue and robin-red color combination. But it's the brilliant cerulean mountain bluebird (*Sialia currucoides*) that makes our hearts soar and occasionally lose a beat—just like the bird's rising and dipping flight. Even the somber female is accented with a pale blue tail, rump, and primaries.

The Paiute Indians tell a story about this color. The Great Spirit painted all the birds and animals but one. The forgotten bird flew up into the sky to protest his drab coat. Bits of the sky stuck to his feathers, and he became our mountain bluebird.

Early migrants arrive in February but may be pushed back south by storms. Larger flocks, sometimes numbering more than one hundred individuals, arrive in March and occasionally linger at lower elevations until May, when they pair and move up to the foothills and mountains for nesting.

These cavity-nesters use old woodpecker holes in aspen and other trees and readily accept birdhouses if the hole is 1 9/16 inches in diameter. This seems like a curious number and differs from many earlier recommendations. Although a bluebird will use larger holes, this size is too small for a starling. In *Birds of Colorado*, Alfred Bailey and Robert Niedrach relate some strange nest sites: a coupler on a freight car, a cliff swallow's nest, a chipmunk hole, and a ledge at 12,000 feet on Loveland Pass.

Concern about decreasing populations started as early as 1914, when two bird-watchers (quoted by Bailey and Niedrach) wrote, "In the early days of Colorado Springs the Bluebird bred readily in houses put up for it, but now days it has no show against the omnipresent English Sparrow." Now it also faces competition from starlings and suffers from habitat destruction, especially the removal of the dead snags it needs for nesting.

To help bluebirds recover, many people are placing and monitoring bluebird nesting boxes. The Denver Audubon Society and the Division of Wildlife are collaborating on the Colorado Bluebird Trail, which will eventually cover 826 miles in Colorado with about ten boxes per mile. Sherry Chapman, project coordinator, says that during the 1996 nesting season 603 mountain bluebirds, 202 western bluebirds, and 1 eastern bluebird were fledged from these boxes. Bluebirds (or their descendants) often return to the same box year after year. Denver teacher Kenneth Lane has had blue-birds nest in his box every season since 1972, even though the box "was crude to say the least," with no two joints fitting.

In summer and early fall mountain bluebirds often hover above 14,000-foot peaks, taking advantage of the lavish supply of bugs that undergo a population explosion during the brief but abundant growing season above timberline.

Although a few bluebirds may stay around for winter, expanding their insect diet to include berries and other fruits, most gather in huge flocks before heading to Texas and Mexico in October.

Where To Go

The Colorado Bluebird Trail meanders throughout the state, starting in the northeast corner where eastern bluebirds have nested. This is not a hiking trail, but an auto route with nesting boxes mounted on posts along the roadsides. Look for bluebirds and nesting boxes as you drive segments of the following route: Hwy. 6 Sterling to Fort Morgan; Hwy. 144 Fort Morgan to Orchard to Hwy. 34; Hwy. 34 to Estes Park; Hwy. 7 Estes Park to Raymond; Hwy. 72 Raymond to Nederland; Hwy. 119 Nederland to Hwy. 6 in Clear Creek Canyon; Hwy. 6 to I-70; I-70 to El Rancho; Hwy. 74 El Rancho to Conifer; Hwy. 285 Conifer to Johnson Village; Hwy. 24 Johnson Village to Buena Vista; Rd. 306 Buena Vista to Taylor River Rd.; Taylor River Rd. to Almont; Hwy. 135 Almont to Gunnison; Hwy. 50 Gunnison to Hwy. 149; Hwy. 149 to South Fork; Hwy. 160 South Fork to Durango; Hwy. 550 Durango to Montrose; Hwy. 90 Montrose to Hwy 141; Hwy. 141 to Hwy. 50; Hwy. 50 to Grand Junction.

PASSION IN THE SNOW

Was Valentine's Day invented because we need the flame of love during winter's icy embrace? It could have been invented for frolicking foxes, which reach the height of their breeding season between January and March.

The four species of foxes that occur in Colorado have similar habits and timeta-bles for breeding and bearing young. Red foxes mate during January and February; gray foxes, during February and March; swift and kit foxes, from late December through February. Pairs stay together to rear the young. Many mate for life, though they separate in autumn until their foxy fancy brings them together again.

All are opportunistic feeders, catching prey ranging from rabbits to rodents, grouse to grasshoppers. They can hear a mouse squeaking from more than 100 feet and can follow the scent of bait for more than a mile.

Now is a good time to see adult foxes because you can follow their tracks in the snow. Sometimes you can even sniff out dens (which have multiple entrances) as a faint, skunklike aroma permeates the area. Although foxes tend to be nocturnal, they spend more time hunting during daylight in winter than they do in summer. It's worth getting out at dawn to catch a flash of red flame against white snow. According to Apache folklore, the red fox is so colored because, in order to steal fire for mankind, he stuck his tail into the flames tended by the gods.

The fact that red foxes (*Vulpes vulpes*) are not always red makes you wonder about the color sense of taxonomists. The most common color phase of the red fox is reddish-orange with white underparts. "Silver" foxes are black with silver tips on the hair (though some black forms lack the silver tips), and "cross" foxes are usually a pale red with black hair forming a cross on their shoulders and back. All these color phases belong to the same species. The bushy white-tipped tail (did he dip it into the fire's ashes?) is the diagnostic feature to look for when trying to identify our most common fox.

Gray foxes (*Urocyon cinereoargenteus*), smaller and daintier than their red relatives, can easily be mistaken for domestic cats. Gray on top, white underneath, this fox's elegant attire is embellished with red streaking on ears, neck, and legs and finished off with a black-tipped tail.

Swift foxes (*V. velox*), small and buffy colored with black-tipped tails and black facial marks, are much less common than either red or gray foxes.

Kit foxes (*V. macrotis*) resemble tiny swift foxes with huge ears and are very rare in Colorado. Division of Wildlife surveys show there may be fewer than one hundred left in the state.

Where To Go

❧ Red foxes are found throughout the state, usually near a water source, except in the extreme southeast. They prefer an area with a mixture of vegetation types but have adapted to all sorts of habitats. They even thrive above timberline and in areas as urbanized as Denver, where they are frequently seen in cemeteries and greenbelts. Several color phases at Wheat Ridge Greenbelt have become quite tame.

❧ Gray foxes prefer shrublands and piñon-juniper and ponderosa pine forests on the eastern side of the Continental Divide. They also are found at lower elevations on the Western Slope. Though not seen as often as red foxes, they are fairly common and sometimes investigate suet feeders in the foothills.

Swift foxes inhabit the shortgrass and midgrass prairies of the eastern plains. Look for them in Pawnee and Comanche National Grasslands.

Kit foxes live in semidesert shrublands and canyonlands and at the edge of piñon-juniper forests on the Western Slope. According to *Mammals of Colorado*, one population exists near Delta, and others have been reported from northwestern Colorado.

COYOTE LOVE

If the day should ever come when one may camp and hear not a note of the coyote's joyous stirring song, I hope that I shall long before have passed away, gone over the Great Divide.

—*Ernest T. Seton*

On cold midwinter mornings, courting coyotes race through the woods and wrestle playfully in the snow. During tender moments, the female may lick the corner of her mate's mouth, or he may lay his head gently on her shoulders. Several males sometimes vie for the attentions of a single estrus female. Once she chooses her partner, the pair hunts together and sets to work enlarging their den, typically a burrow in an embankment or under a rock or log.

The female gives birth to two to twelve helpless, hairless, and blind pups about two months later. The pups subsist on milk for about two weeks and then feed on regurgitated bits of food brought to the den by both adults. The pups stimulate regurgitation by licking the corners of their parents' mouths. Families usually stay together throughout the summer. In fall, the full-grown pups head out to find their own niche in a world that sometimes tolerates, but rarely welcomes, coyotes.

It's no accident that, while wolves have been extirpated from most of North America, coyotes have proliferated. Wolves traveling in packs and preying on domestic livestock made easy targets for hunters, trappers, and ranchers. Coyotes, who hunted singly or in pairs and preyed mostly on rodents and insects, learned to avoid people while taking advantage of the tidbits civilization had to offer.

Coyotes learned to steer clear of traps and stay just out of rifle range. They developed a taste for human garbage, melons and other cultivated crops, and the occasional chicken or lamb. When local populations were depleted by hunters or trappers, females produced larger litters, quickly repopulating the range. With their main competitors—the wolf, mountain lion, and grizzly bear—mostly eradicated, coyotes expanded eastward, crossing the Mississippi River and working their way into New England and the Atlantic Coast states. Most experts believe today's North American coyote population exceeds that of the early nineteenth century.

In Colorado, these resilient and intelligent canids grace every life zone and every ecosystem, from the grasslands and deserts to the tundra. Coyotes skulk through our cities and camp out in our backyards, mocking our efforts to control their numbers. With luck, they'll continue to howl up the moon long after we're gone.

BUTTERFLIES FLUTTER BY IN WINTER?? YES!!

Although most butterflies live only a few weeks as adults, a few hardy species overwinter as adults in Colorado. Mourning cloak and Milbert's tortoiseshell butterflies creep into crevices in bark or find sheltered spots in caves or under leaves where they hibernate away the winter. But either species may awaken and take flight during a February thaw. Even when no flowers are blooming, they find nourishment from sap oozing from aspen and other trees and from bird droppings.

Somber dark wings trimmed in ivory give *Nymphalis antiopa* the name "mourning." However, when the sun hits the spread dorsal side of the wings, bright blue spots highlight the ivory border, and the brown wings shimmer with hints of purple. With wings closed, the butterfly almost disappears into its background. Several broods may emerge during the summer at lower elevations, but only one brood

Mourning cloak butterfly.

typically appears at higher elevations, usually in late August and September. The caterpillars (black with red spots on the back and several rows of bristles) feed on willow, aspen, hackberry, elm, and cottonwood.

In *Butterflies of the Rocky Mountain States,* Clifford Ferris and F. Martin Brown

MILBERT'S
TORTOISESHELL

MOURNING
CLOAK

write that Milbert's tortoiseshells (*Aglais milberti*) can be seen "flitting over ski slopes" on a sunny midwinter day. When the wings are spread, a bright orange to yellow band almost shouts for attention, but when the irregular-edged wings are folded, tortoiseshells could pass for bark or dead leaves. Like mourning cloaks, they may produce several broods during the summer season. The spiny caterpillars— black with a yellow band and green side stripes—feed chiefly on nettles.

Both species belong to a large family known as "brush-footed butterflies" because of their reduced forelegs. Unless you look closely, the brush-footed butter- flies seem to break the rule that insects have six legs.

43

Where To Go

Mourning cloaks and Milbert's tortoiseshells thrive in a variety of habitats from desert canyons to the tundra. See the distribution maps in the back of Clifford Ferris and F. Martin Brown's *Butterflies of the Rocky Mountain States* for detailed location information.

FEBRUARY EVENTS

MAMMALS

❧ Deer lose their antlers and begin to grow new ones.

❧ Raccoons mate in February and March and may usurp your chimney for a nursery.

❧ Foxes, coyotes, and wolves mate between January and March.

BIRDS

❧ Bluebirds arrive.

❧ Great horned owls and golden eagles nest.

❧ Canyon wrens, meadowlarks, red-winged blackbirds, and house finches begin to sing.

OTHER CRITTERS

❧ Mourning cloak and Milbert's tortoiseshell butterflies appear during warm spells.

PLANTS

❧ Early wildflowers (filarees, Easter daisies, creeping mahonia, and spring beauties) bloom if the weather cooperates.

❧ First crocuses bloom in urban gardens.

In the Sky

❅ "Crust of Snow Moon" (Ojibwa). Other peoples called it "Wolf Moon" and "Hunger Moon."

❅ Candlemas, the approximate halfway point between the Winter Solstice and the Vernal Equinox, is celebrated on February 2. This festival, a precursor to Groundhog Day and Valentine's Day, honors the stirrings of new growth and passion that accompany the waxing light of late winter.

❅ Taurus, "The Bull," is almost directly overhead at 9:00 P.M. Taurus contains the spectacular star cluster known as the Pleiades, or "Seven Sisters," and the red giant, Aldebaran.

Migrating sandhill cranes grace the sky over the San Luis Valley.

3

March

We shall live again,

We shall live again,

The sun's beams are spreading out—He'e'yo!

The sun's yellow rays are spreading out—Ahi'ni'yo'!

—ARAPAHO

AS THE SUN'S warmth increases, lakes and ponds start to thaw, and wetlands throughout the state quicken with life. We examine the melting mud for tracks of muskrats, raccoons, and beavers and listen for the song of meadowlarks, the clamor of yellow-headed blackbirds, the chorusing of frogs, and the snipe's winnowing call. We watch for migrating sandhill cranes who stop over by the thousands to feed in wet fields. Green cattail shoots appear, and rainbow trout spawn.

Pygmy and saw-whet owls establish territories, and red-tailed hawks nest. Babies are born to prairie dogs and to badgers and foxes, who must now hunt more diligently than ever. Creeping mahonia and yellow violets sprinkle tan hillsides with drops of gold—a promise of more splendor to come.

With the northward-turning sun, abundant life has come again.

	Grand Junction (4,824 ft.)	Steamboat Springs (6,760 ft.)	Alamosa (7,536 ft.)	Berthoud Pass (11,310 ft.)	Denver (5,282 ft.)	Lamar (3,620 ft.)
Ave. high (°F)	56	41	49	29	52	59
Ave. low (°F)	31	14	16	6	26	26
Max. high (°F)	81	67	73	50	84	92
Min. low (°F)	5	–34	–20	–24	–11	–26
Ave. prec. (in.)	0.90	2.04	0.45	4.11	1.28	0.90
Max. prec. (in.)	2.36	4.38	1.62	6.72	4.56	4.67
Ave. snow (in.)	4.0	24.2	7.0	57.9	12.8	5.5
Max. snow (in.)	14.9	62.8	29.2	92.8	30.5	25.5

Some of Colorado's heaviest snowstorms occur as the jet stream sags over the state, enabling Arctic air masses to mix with subtropical moisture sucked up from the Gulf of Mexico. During March 1970 Boulder received more than 56 inches of snow. This seems paltry compared to the 249 inches that blanketed the Ruby mining camp, near Crested Butte, in March 1899. Nearly 12 feet of snow fell on Ruby during a single three-day storm. In contrast, the Arkansas Valley town of Holly sweltered at 96 degrees in March 1907.

See "Colorado Climate Summary" (p. 1) for information on averages, extremes, and sources.

march ecosystem

Awakening Marshes

Ducks begin to congregate at Monte Vista National Wildlife Refuge, in the lower San Luis Valley, in early March. First to arrive are mallards, pintails, green-winged teal, American wigeons, common goldeneyes, and common mergansers, who have wintered nearby along ice-free stretches of the Rio Grande and its tributaries. They paddle around in small openings on the ponds' mostly frozen surfaces, quacking, whistling, and grunting in subdued tones.

In mid-March thousands of sandhill cranes glide into the agricultural fields and pastures bordering the refuge. Soon after, the long distance migrant ducks—redheads from Central America, gadwalls from southern Mexico, cinnamon and blue-winged teal from South America—add their numbers to the growing multitudes. By the end of the month, several hundred thousand ducks, geese, and other

"Spring" in Boulder County!

water birds will gather in the marshes, sloughs, and rivers of the lower San Luis Valley.

By early April flocks of migrating shorebirds patrol the mudflats and shallows bordering the refuge's ponds and sloughs. Spotted sandpipers who have flown up from Central and South America give their shrill, two-note call while skittering along the shoreline. Russet-breasted American avocets, recently arrived from the Gulf Coast, sweep their long upturned beaks through the nutrient-rich waters. Mixed flocks of lesser and greater yellowlegs wheel in tight formation over the mudflats and shallows. Killdeer scream out warnings as they race across the alkali flats and saltgrass meadows.

Within a couple of weeks, many of the ducks and shorebirds have passed on to the north. But the activity level in the marsh continues to build as chorus frogs chirp, mice and voles scurry through the dry vegetation, muskrats and beavers refurbish their lodges, and songbirds noisily advertise their nesting territories.

Male common snipe fly in circles over their nesting areas. Every few seconds, they swoop earthward, making a high, quavering "winnowing" sound as the wind whistles through their tail feathers. When perched on the ground, snipes emit a slow, sharp "wheek-a-wheek-a-wheek-a" that can be heard from several hundred yards away. The female nests on the ground, usually in a shallow scrape close to water.

Marsh wren males chatter metallically as they zip through the cattails searching for nesting material. They weave spherical nests from cattail leaves, cattail fluff (seeds), and other plant material. They attach their nests to the previous year's stalks, a foot or two above water. Each male may build as many as ten "dummy nests" to confuse predators.

Red-winged and yellow-headed blackbirds attach their cup-shaped nests to two or more dead cattail stalks. The red-wing males advertise nesting territories by singing and croaking raucously and flashing the bright red epaulets (shoulder patches) on their wings. The song and display tell other males to keep away. In one study, scientists captured territorial males and covered the epaulets with nontoxic black paint. These males had great difficulty defending nesting territories.

Pied-billed grebes build floating nests anchored to reeds, rushes, or cattails. Shortly after hatching, the young hop onto their mother's back and catch a free ride to open water, where small fish abound. When she dives, they hold on tight or shake free, bobbing on the surface like fluffy yellow corks.

When feeding, Wilson's phalaropes look like red and white tops spinning on the water. The spinning motion apparently stirs up invertebrate-laden sediment from the bottom. These medium-sized shorebirds nest in a shallow scrape among sparse vegetation. In a breeding arrangement known as polyandry, the brightly colored females lay the eggs, but the less colorful and smaller males incubate them. Wilson's phalaropes generally practice monogamous polyandry (one nest per female). In other phalarope species, females may lay several clutches, turning each one over to a different mate.

Muskrats often construct their haystacklike lodges from cattails. Propelled along by slightly webbed hind feet and using their tails as rudders, they swim effortlessly through the marsh seeking out tender stems and roots of young plants and occasionally preying on a frog, salamander, fish, or duckling. Their sleek, waterproof fur keeps them warm as they forage under the ice in winter. When fresh food is scarce, they subsist on caches stored in their lodge or munch away at the lodge itself.

The activities of these large microtine (volelike) rodents create habitat for an array of marsh species. By harvesting large quantities of cattails, muskrats create clearings where invertebrate life flourishes, attracting foraging ducks and shorebirds. Canada geese sometimes nest on top of muskrat lodges. Other birds perch on the lodges or harvest the swarms of insects that share the muskrats' often fetid quarters.

Cattails

Cattails convert solar energy into plant material with remarkable efficiency. In a Kansas study, Wayne Hoffman determined that cattails growing in flooded pools can produce more than 20 pounds of organic matter on every square yard of surface during the growing season. This rate of production compares favorably to that of corn and other domesticated grains.

Since cattails require standing water or saturated soil to survive, they may not have occurred naturally over much of Colorado's eastern plains, where the drought cycle causes most ponds to dry up every few years. Since settlement by Europeans, reservoirs and irrigation ditches have provided cattails a more permanent source of water.

Cattails spread rapidly and quickly take root. A single stalk can produce more than 200,000 seeds. The seeds can float for miles on the wind. Each plant also produces hundreds of clones, which fan out across the marsh on rapidly growing roots and rhizomes. The broad-leaved cattail (Typha latifolia) has spread throughout much of Eurasia, North Africa, North America, and South America. The narrow leaved cattail (T. angustifolia) occurs throughout North America. Both species grow in Colorado wetlands from about 4,000 to 8,000 feet.

Muskrat young, along with eggs and fledglings of ground-nesting birds, provide nourishment for the mink, a sleek, secretive predator that inhabits marshes throughout Colorado. This 1- to 3-pound member of the weasel family spends much of the day sleeping in its den under a pile of brush, in a hollow log, or in an abandoned beaver or muskrat house. At night it swims and scurries through the marsh, preying on small mammals, fish, insects, and birds. Mink young are usually born in April or May.

Occupying the top of the food chain, minks, along with coyotes, red foxes, northern harriers, and other predators, benefit from the wealth of animal life in freshwater marshes. These animals, in turn, owe their existence to the abundant plant life in these nutrient rich environments.

Only a small percentage of marsh plants are consumed directly by animals. The bulk of plant material decomposes or settles to pond bottoms, where bacteria and invertebrates convert it into the slimy ooze characteristic of marshes. Anaerobic organisms living in this muck provide food for invertebrates, such as crayfish and bloodworms, who in turn nourish amphibians, birds, and small mammals. The anaerobic organisms produce byproducts of methane gas, hydrogen sulfide, and ammonia, which give the marsh its characteristic rotten-egg smell.

Pungent odors notwithstanding, marshes are cleansing environments. When pesticides, commercial fertilizers, and other toxins enter these ecosystems, marsh bacteria convert them to less harmful substances. Colorado ecologists create artificial wetlands below toxic mine sites to reduce the impacts of their pollutants on streams and rivers.

In *Cheyenne Bottoms: Wetland in Jeopardy*, ecologist John Zimmerman describes the stench of a marsh as "... a seductive smell ... of organic richness." He adds, "Sewers and rotten eggs alone do not smell good; but a marsh smells good. I sometimes wonder if the appeal of the odor of the marsh is not some sort of atavistic recall in the biochemical essence of our being, since marshes smell like the whole world must have smelled during the first billion or so years after life began."

Where To Go

The term *freshwater marshes* encompasses an array of ecosystems, ranging from prairie potholes on the plains to willow thickets in the high mountains. Colorado's largest marshes generally occur in the mountain parks and around large reservoirs on the eastern plains.

- Browns Park National Wildlife Refuge, northwest of Craig.
- Arapaho National Wildlife Refuge, near Walden.
- Monte Vista and Alamosa National Wildlife Refuges, near Alamosa.
- Lower Latham Reservoir, south of Greeley.
- Barr Lake State Park, northeast of Denver.
- Nee Noshe and Nee Granda Reservoirs, north of Lamar.
- Bonny Reservoir, north of Burlington.

FLIGHT OF THE SNOW GEESE

My ears would resound with the cries of the wild geese and, when I closed my eyes [at] night, I saw them still, their strong wings flashing in the sunlight, their immaculate bodies projected against the azure sky. They were my criterion of beauty, my definition of wildness, my vision of paradise.
—Paul Johnsgard, *Song of the North Wind*

With the first glimmer of spring in early March, waves of snow geese stream across the Great Plains. They fly northward from northern Mexico and the Gulf Coast in a series of 500- to 1,000-mile "hops," eventually reaching their Arctic breeding grounds in early June. Once there, they have no more than eighty days in which to build their nests, incubate their eggs, raise their young, and molt before beginning the southward migration in late August or early September.

About a half million snow geese stop over in Nebraska's Rainwater Basin, south of the Platte River, in March. Throughout the month the basin's farmlands and wetlands explode with a sexually charged cacophony. The snows, along with several

Snow geese at Nee Noshe Reservoir in southeastern Colorado.

hundred thousand white-fronted and Canada geese, a half million sandhill cranes, and several million ducks honk, trumpet, and quack as they sense spring's approach and feel the urge to fly northward.

Smaller groups of snow geese pass through Colorado on their way north. Among the ten thousand or so snows that stop over at NeeNoshe, Bonny, and Julesberg Reservoirs are some that have wintered along the Arkansas River in southeastern Colorado and others that have wintered in New Mexico, southwestern Texas, and northern Mexico. Other flocks fly over western Colorado on their way to a massive staging area in the wetlands surrounding the Great Salt Lake.

Snow geese travel in family groups. If parents become separated from their young, they swoop over the flock, which may number tens of thousands of wildly honking compatriots, until they hear their offsprings' distinctive voices. Adults tenaciously defend their nests from Arctic foxes, gyrfalcons, and other predators, and many females die each summer from starvation while incubating their eggs.

Geese that survive the harsh Arctic summers must weave their way through a gauntlet of hunters as they fly southward each fall. Nevertheless, North American populations have increased steadily over the last several decades. By nesting in the

COLORADO SWANS AND GEESE

SPECIES	COLORADO STATUS
TUNDRA SWAN	Rare spring and fall migrant, rivers, lakes, and mountain parks. Very rare winter resident near eastern foothills.
TRUMPETER SWAN	Very rare fall and early winter migrant on eastern plains.
GREATER WHITE-FRONTED GOOSE	Rare spring and fall migrant and winter resident on eastern plains. Very rare migrant and winter resident in western valleys.
SNOW GOOSE	Fairly common spring and fall migrant in eastern third of state. About 5,000 winter on southeastern plains in Arkansas Valley area.
ROSS' GOOSE	Rare to uncommon spring and fall migrant and winter resident in western valleys, in the San Luis Valley, and on the eastern plains.
CANADA GOOSE	Common resident statewide. Abundant spring and fall migrant on eastern plains.

Brants (three records) and black brants (five records) have also been seen within the state during migration.
Source: Robert Andrews and Robert Righter, *Colorado Birds,* pp. 29–36.

sparsely populated Arctic, snow geese have escaped the fate of many North American waterfowl, whose numbers have diminished as wetlands have been drained, paved over, or converted to agriculture. Now biologists are becoming concerned about overpopulation of snow geese in the Arctic. In some areas, nesting geese have denuded the landscape, threatening the viability of the tundra ecosystem. Many conservationists advocate lengthening the fall hunting season to control snow goose populations.

Where To Go

‰ Arkansas River Valley from La Junta to Holly.

‰ Nee Noshe Reservoir, north of Lamar. Here some 5,000 to 10,000 snow geese congregate in March and early April. Some may overwinter.

‰ Julesburg (Jumbo) Reservoir, near Julesburg. Several hundred to a few thousand snow geese in March and early April.

‰ Bonny Reservoir, north of Burlington; March or early April.

‰ Runyon/Fountain Lakes SWA, near Pueblo; March and April.

DANCING CRANES

Take a bird with a 7-foot-wide wing span and a weird, wild voice that seems to come from everywhere at once like an amplified turkey gobbler. Put thousands of them in the sky. Add a river valley bordered by 14,000-foot snow-capped peaks, and you have a spectacle like the Monte Vista Sandhill Crane Festival. About twenty thousand sandhill cranes stop over in the Monte Vista Wildlife Refuge each spring, starting in February, peaking in mid-March, and continuing through early April.

For thousands of years these stunning birds have been migrating along the Rio Grande through the San Luis Valley, stopping for several weeks to fatten up on grains, insects, toads, and snakes before the breeding season. In anticipation of mating, they often engage in a graceful courting dance. From the valley, they continue north, stopping briefly at other Colorado wetlands and nesting in Idaho, Nebraska, and Utah. They pass through Colorado again in September and October for a shorter visit on their way to winter in Mexico and New Mexico.

About forty pairs nest in the northwestern corner of Colorado in marshes and willow-lined drainages. This breeding population was formerly considered endangered but was recently downlisted to threatened by the Colorado Division of Wildlife. The courtship dance of sandhill cranes is a strange yet dignified minuet. The huge, ungainly birds lift their wings and gracefully waft themselves a few feet off the ground. They caper and leap and bow and toss grass into the air, accompanying themselves with a song that writer Aldo Leopold, in *A Sand County Almanac,* called "the trumpet in the orchestra of evolution" and that Roger Tory Peterson rendered as "garooo-a-a-a . . . tuk-tuk—tuk-tuk—tuk-tuk" in his *Field Guide to Western Birds.*

This eerie cry emanates from a 4-foot windpipe that coils up in the keel of the breast. Long-legged and long-necked, sandhills weigh about 12 pounds and stand about 4 feet high. Their brownish-gray plumage is saved from drabness by a bright red cap.

Cranes were important symbols to many American Indians, who pictured them in petroglyphs, imitated their dance, and wove wonderful stories about them, such as this Cree story about how the sandhill crane got his red cap: Once upon a time, Rabbit yearned to fly to the moon. He asked all the great birds to take him there, and all refused . . . until he came to Crane. Crane told Rabbit to hold onto his legs and they would fly to the moon. However, Rabbit was very heavy, causing Crane's legs to stretch out farther and farther. When they reached the moon, Rabbit touched Crane's head and gave him a dazzling red headdress in reward. If you look when the moon is full, you still see Rabbit riding on the moon, and Crane's legs remain long and straight, and his head is forever red.

Where To Go

🦆 Monte Vista National Wildlife Refuge.
🦆 Red Lion and Jumbo Reservoir State Wildlife areas, near Sterling.

✿ North Platte River near Lewellyn, Nebraska.

✿ The Lillian Annette Rowe Bird Sanctuary along the Platte River near Kearny, Nebraska, is only a few hours drive from the northeast corner of Colorado and is well worth the drive. As many as 500,000 sandhills plus a few whoopers stop over at this National Audubon Society refuge in late March. In the early 1990s this flock was jeopardized when Colorado proposed constructing Two Forks Dam, which would have altered the flow of the Platte River and destroyed sandbars needed by cranes for nighttime roosting.

WHOOPING CRANES OVER COLORADO

The U.S. Fish and Wildlife Service used sandhill cranes to raise whooping cranes in an experiment starting in 1975. Biologists took whooping crane eggs from nests in Wood Buffalo Park in Canada (the only breeding ground for wild whoopers) and from captive whooping cranes. Usually only one of the chicks survives, so taking one egg from a two-egg clutch did not hurt the wild population. The eggs were placed in sandhill crane nests at Grays Lake National Wildlife Refuge in Idaho, the nesting grounds for most sandhill cranes that pass through Monte Vista.

The purpose of the project was to insure that if a catastrophe wiped out the Wood Buffalo flock, another flock, with a different migratory route, would still survive. By 1985 the experimental flock numbered thirty-three birds. Unfortunately, the mortality rate was high, and none of the foster-parented whoopers bred because they were sexually imprinted on sandhill cranes. In 1989 the project was discontinued. By March 1997, only three whoopers returned through Colorado plus one sandhill-whooper hybrid.

However, several captive-reared whooping cranes may lead the way to new horizons for their species. In October 1997, an ultralight aircraft led these inexperienced youngsters from Idaho through Colorado to Bosque del Apache in New Mexico. Rancher and pilot Kent Clegg taught the whooper chicks to fly behind his ultralight. First the chicks learned to follow behind him as he ran. Then they progressed to flying behind a vehicle and, finally, to flying behind the plane. In early 1998, the two surviving "ultralight cranes" were socializing with two older whoopers from the original experiment and had begun to dance. If all goes well, this method may be used to establish wild whooping crane flocks in different locales with different migratory routes.

PYGMY- AND SAW-WHET OWLS

At dusk the breathy whistles of northern pygmy-owls and northern saw-whet owls float through the conifers like whispers on the wind. The sound is easy to miss or to file away as something imagined. Once the call has been clearly identified and located, the source usually remains hidden even to patient and practiced eyes. Many early naturalists referred to these owls as "ventriloquial." The truth is that they are so tiny and blend so perfectly into their surroundings that they can go where they wish without much fear of being detected by our pathetic excuse for night vision.

Of the two, the 8-inch-high northern saw-whet is by far the most elusive. Entirely nocturnal, saw-whets spend the day perching silently in the boughs of conifers or, occasionally, in branches of large deciduous trees. They respond to predators by remaining motionless. An injured saw-whet will perch comfortably on your finger, as if that were the most natural place in the world to roost.

At night saw-whets swoop silently down on voles, mice, and insects. They nest in a woodpecker hole in a ponderosa pine, piñon pine, lodgepole pine, aspen, or cottonwood. They vocalize most frequently from mid-March to early May and will respond readily to any approximation of their territorial call, including human whistles. In Colorado, northern saw-whet owls nest primarily in coniferous forests from about 5,000 to 10,000 feet.

In winter northern pygmy-owls sometimes show up at urban bird feeders and in low-elevation river drainages. By early March most have moved back up into the foothills and mountains, where they nest in woodpecker holes, usually in ponderosa pines or aspens. They hunt most actively at dawn and dusk, preying on songbirds, mice and other small rodents, reptiles, and insects.

Northern pygmy-owls often perch on the tips of bare branches, about 15 feet off the ground, attracting the attention of angry chickadees, jays, and robins intent on driving the predator away from their nesting or foraging areas. Two false eye spots on the back of the pygmy-owl's head may serve to frighten away mobbing songbirds. Though measuring only 6.5 inches from head to tail tip, pygmy-owls can kill birds several times their own weight, including rock doves and young grouse. They have been known to chatter at and strafe humans who stared too long at their nesting cavities.

Listen and look for northern pygmy-owls in low- to mid-elevation coniferous forests throughout the state. Peak vocal activity occurs from early March to mid-April. Once females begin incubating, both pygmy and saw-whet owls usually cease calling. A small owl that sings too much, though not running a great risk of being seen by humans, may end up in the stomach of a goshawk, Cooper's hawk, or great horned owl.

Where To Go

🦆 Douglas Pass, north of Grand Junction. Pygmies and saw-whets.

🦆 Colorado National Monument, near Grand Junction. Listen for calling saw-whets in piñon-juniper woodlands.

🦆 Great Sand Dunes National Monument, northeast of Alamosa. Saw-whets nest in piñon-juniper woodlands surrounding the dunes.

🦆 Castlewood Canyon State Park, south of Denver. Listen for calling saw-whets in the ponderosa pines and junipers.

🦆 Mount Falcon Park, west of Golden. Nesting saw-whets and pygmies.

🦆 Boulder Mountain Park. Saw-whets and pygmies nest on Green Mountain.

🦆 Rocky Mountain National Park. Saw-whets and pygmies nest in Horseshoe Park, Moraine Park, Beaver Meadows, and Wild Basin areas.

BIRD SONG

Heightened levels of testosterone stimulate males of most species to begin singing in early spring. Males sing to attract females and to discourage other males from invading nesting territories. Most birds also utter a variety of "calls"—short chips, cries, and rasps—to indicate alarm or to keep in contact with others of their species. A few species sing throughout the year; Townsend's solitaires and northern mockingbirds sing in winter to keep conspecifics away from foraging territories.

Some songbirds (birds that utter a succession of musical notes to advertise nesting territories) are born with an innate ability to sing a complete territorial song. However, most learn to sing complete songs only after listening to adult males of their species. The "auditory template hypothesis," developed by ornithologists who have studied vocal development in songbirds, holds that each male is born with a neurological model of its song and develops the song by matching the vocalizations it hears with the auditory template in its brain.

Some birds incorporate a variety of sounds, including songs of other species, into their vocal repertoires. Northern mockingbirds will imitate squeaking gates, car horns, alarms, dog barks, and human whistles, along with the songs of most of their neighbors. You can compile a fairly accurate list of birds breeding in a given area by listening to a single northern mockingbird. Ornithologists believe that mimicry in mockingbirds, thrashers, catbirds, and starlings serves as a means of acquiring a rich or varied repertoire rather than as a device to scare off other species. In most instances, the mimicry is not good enough to fool even a human ear. Studies of brown thrashers have determined that those males with the most complex songs have the highest chance of attracting a mate.

Bird songs vary geographically and throughout the year. Lazuli buntings nesting in adjacent drainages often sing entirely different songs, and the vocalizations of each group change every few weeks. This variation is one reason why learning to identify birds by ear is so difficult. *The Peterson Field Guide to Western Bird Songs* and the Peterson *Birding by Ear* tapes and CDs are good learning aids. However, there is no substitute for local knowledge. Some of the species on the Peterson tapes sing with a decidedly eastern accent!

A good way to learn bird songs is to keep a monthly record of which species are singing in your neighborhood. In March listen for the rich, melodic phrases of western meadowlarks, house finches, and robins; the sweet, downslurred whistles of canyon wrens; and the complex, sustained warbles of Townsend's solitaires.

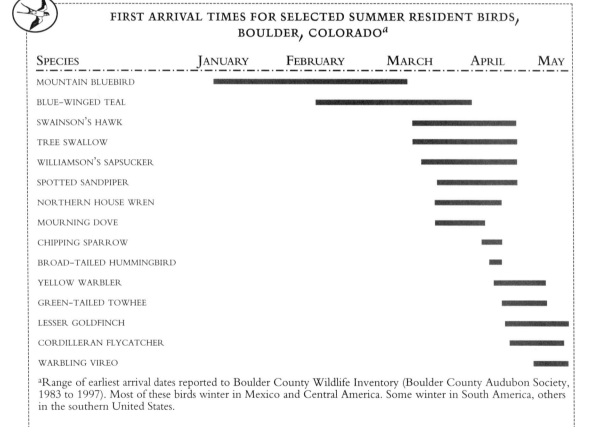

FIRST ARRIVAL TIMES FOR SELECTED SUMMER RESIDENT BIRDS, BOULDER, COLORADO[a]

SPECIES	JANUARY	FEBRUARY	MARCH	APRIL	MAY
MOUNTAIN BLUEBIRD	▬▬▬▬▬▬▬▬▬▬▬▬				
BLUE-WINGED TEAL		▬▬▬▬▬▬▬▬▬▬			
SWAINSON'S HAWK			▬▬▬▬▬▬▬		
TREE SWALLOW			▬▬▬▬▬▬▬		
WILLIAMSON'S SAPSUCKER			▬▬▬▬▬▬▬		
SPOTTED SANDPIPER			▬▬▬▬▬▬		
NORTHERN HOUSE WREN			▬▬▬▬▬		
MOURNING DOVE			▬▬▬		
CHIPPING SPARROW				▬▬	
BROAD-TAILED HUMMINGBIRD				▬	
YELLOW WARBLER				▬▬▬▬	
GREEN-TAILED TOWHEE				▬▬▬▬	
LESSER GOLDFINCH				▬▬▬▬▬	
CORDILLERAN FLYCATCHER				▬▬▬▬▬	
WARBLING VIREO					▬▬

[a]Range of earliest arrival dates reported to Boulder County Wildlife Inventory (Boulder County Audubon Society, 1983 to 1997). Most of these birds winter in Mexico and Central America. Some winter in South America, others in the southern United States.

BEAVERS AT WORK

During winter, beavers subsist on the bark of saplings stored underwater near their lodges. Each lodge has one or more underwater entrances, so the beavers can swim to and from their sapling cache without exposing themselves to predators. Inside the well-insulated lodge, the family, consisting of the adults, yearlings, and kits, remains warm and cozy. In a Canadian study, the average minimum winter temperature inside beaver lodges was 34°F higher than the average minimum outdoor temperature. Naturalists have reported seeing steam rising from beaver lodges in winter and hearing these sociable rodents chattering away contentedly throughout the day.

As the ice thaws in spring, engineering work begins. After a period of playful exploration of their domain, the beavers set about repairing and reconstructing their dams. Dams must be strong enough to withstand the spring runoff and high enough to provide underwater access to favored feeding areas. Canals dug outward from the main pond allow the beavers to expand their foraging area without exposing themselves unduly to terrestrial predators.

Another essential spring activity is the building and marking of scent mounds. These mounds, constructed from gobs of mud and organic material and anointed with musk from the beaver's castor or anal glands, serve notice to other beavers that the territory is occupied. Two-year-olds, who are chased away by their parents with the birth of the year's young in April or May, use the scent mounds as olfactory road maps steering them away from occupied territories.

French scientist Françoise Patinaude watched a family of wild beavers prepare for the birth of new kits. Working together, the beavers plastered the inside walls of their lodge with mud, gnawed away protruding branches, and covered the floor with fresh grass. After the young were born, the father, mother, and one yearling formed a protective triangle around them. The newborn kits looked like "miniature adults" and began walking and swimming within a few minutes after birth.

In *Lily Pond*, naturalist Hope Ryden described the "coming out party" of a pair of Catskill Mountain beaver kits: "Every member of the family was present to accompany the two youngsters up and down . . . the little ones swam like corks and frequently clambered onto handy backs. To my delight over the next two weeks, this performance was repeated many times. Whenever the kits emerged from the lodge, beavers converged from all directions and seemed to compete with one another for the privilege of shepherding them about the pond."

Beavers thrive in wetlands throughout Colorado from about 4,000 to 11,500 feet. They perform an essential task of altering riverine and wetland habitats so that other species, including aspen, willows, and aquatic animals, can survive. The Colorado Division of Wildlife estimates that today's statewide population equals or exceeds that of the pretrapping era.

BIRTHING TIMES AND LOCATIONS FOR COLORADO CARNIVORES

SPECIES	WHEN	WHERE
COYOTE	May–June	Burrow near water: **WS, MT, PL.**
RED FOX	March–June	Burrow in earthen mound or bank; **WS, MT, PL.**
SWIFT FOX	March–April	Burrow in ground; **PL.**
KIT FOX	March–April	Burrow in ground; **WS.**
GRAY FOX	March–June	Burrow or hollow log in heavy brush; **WS, PL.**
BLACK BEAR	November–March	Caves, rock crevices, burrows; **WS, MT.**
RINGTAIL	May–June	Rock crevices, hollow trees, stumps, and logs; **WS.**
RACCOON	April–May	Hollow tree or burrow; **WS, MT, PL.**
MARTEN	March–May	Log, rock pile, or stump; **MT.**

BIRTHING TIMES AND LOCATIONS FOR COLORADO CARNIVORES (CONT'D)

SPECIES	WHEN	WHERE
LONG-TAILED WEASEL	March–May	Burrow lined with grass and hair; **WS, MT, PL.**
SHORT-TAILED WEASEL	April–May	Burrow under rock or tree; **WS, MT.**
MINK	April-May	Hollow log, burrow, beaver or muskrat house; **WS, MT, PL.**
WOLVERINE[a]	March–April	Thicket or rock crevice; **MT.**
BADGER	March–May	Burrow; **WS, MT, PL.**
SPOTTED SKUNK	April–June	Hollow log or burrow; **WS, MT.**
STRIPED SKUNK	May–July	Under rocks or buildings, in hollow logs; **WS, MT, PL.**
HOG-NOSED SKUNK	April–May	Den in rocky crevice; **PL.**
RIVER OTTER	March–April	Stick nest in bank burrow; **WS, MT.**
MOUNTAIN LION	All year, most often in midsummer	Rock shelters, caves, eroded banks; **WS, MT.**
CANADA LYNX[a]	April–June	Hollow log, rock shelter, fallen tree; **MT.**
BOBCAT	All year, peaks May–June	Hollow log, rock shelter, fallen tree; **WS, MT.**

MT: Mountains above 7,500 feet; **PL:** Plains and eastern foothills to about 7,500 feet; **WS:** Western Slope valleys and plateaus to about 7,500 feet.
[a]Rare species, poorly documented in Colorado.
Sources: James Fitzgerald, Carron A. Meaney, and David M. Armstrong, *Mammals of Colorado;* John O. Whitaker and Robert Elman, *Audubon Field Guide to North American Mammals.*

TROUT THRILLS

Romance is in the air—or rather, in the water—as cutthroat and rainbow trout start to spoon—or rather, spawn—at lower elevations. Using her tail, the female trout sweeps out a small depression in the shallows, often heading upstream or into tributaries to find a suitable spot. Simultaneously she releases eggs, and the dominant male deposits "milt," or sperm, over them.

The female then "dances" over the spot, possibly rounding up stray eggs, before swimming upstream a short distance and sweeping a thin layer of sand and gravel over the egg pocket, called a "redd," with her tail. The fish repeats these actions several times, creating a series of light-colored circles in the gravel. "Anglers with any consciousness at all religiously avoid stepping on the redds because we know they hold the source of all our future angling dreams," fly-fishing writer Ed Engle says.

When the eggs hatch, the free-swimming young are called "alevins" and are nourished by protein-rich yolk sacs attached to their bellies. After absorbing the yolk, the young fish (now called "fry") emerge from the protective gravel to begin feeding on their own. If they survive predators, these trout will begin the cycle anew in about three years, when they are ready to spawn.

Stretches of the Blue River and of the South Platte River below Spinney Mountain Reservoir are two places to see the rainbow spawning run in March when, in the words of Ed Engle in his newspaper column, "the big males glow like a soft red neon light."

Although rainbow trout are one of the most popular sport fish in Colorado, they are not natives. Only three native trout still exist in the state: the greenback cutthroat—a subspecies found only in Colorado and our official state fish since 1994—and two other subspecies, the Colorado River cutthroat and the Rio Grande cutthroat. A crimson slash on either side of the throat explains their apt name. At this time of year they are even more colorful than usual, as the males turn bright red all over.

Before Colorado was settled, four native cutthroat trout subspecies lived in state waters. The yellowfin became extinct, and the others hybridized with rainbows. The natives suffered from competition with rainbows and other introduced species, and their numbers dropped. By 1935 they were all thought to be extinct.

When two small populations of greenbacks were discovered in the South Fork of the Cache la Poudre River and in Como Creek near Nederland, the Division of Wildlife and the U.S. Fish and Wildlife Service began raising the fish in hatcheries and releasing them into high mountain lakes inaccessible to nonnative trout. By 1978 greenbacks had recovered sufficiently to be downlisted from endangered to merely threatened. A similar success story applies to Rio Grande and Colorado River cutthroats, which have also made great leaps toward recovery.

But now, whirling disease, caused by a tiny parasite that attacks cartilage before it can harden into bone, threatens trout with disaster. The microscopic spores of the parasite can lie dormant for decades before infecting an intermediate host, the tubifex worm.

Symptoms in fish with advanced whirling disease include bulging eyes, a deformed spine, and frenzied whirling. The disease affects only young salmonids (trout, kokanee, and whitefish) and does not strike bass, catfish, walleyes, and other species. Even with trout, different species have different tolerances to the disease, and the affliction does not change the health or edibility of adult fish.

This scourge was introduced into the United States in 1957 when infected frozen trout from Denmark were ground up and fed to trout in a Pennsylvania hatchery. It first appeared in a private Colorado hatchery in 1987. When infected trout were stocked in the wild, whirling disease spread rapidly throughout the state.

March is not the only month for fish infatuation. Trout and walleyes continue spawning into April and May, and most fish do it when waters become warmer in May and June. Brown and brook trout spawn in fall.

MARCH EVENTS

MAMMALS

᪥ Snowshoe hares and long-tailed weasels begin their prevernal molt. From now through April they gradually turn from white to brown.

᪥ Black-tailed prairie dogs are born. They leave their parents in about ten weeks and attain full size in about six months.

᪥ Fox and badger babies are born.

BIRDS

᪥ Meadowlarks and canyon wrens start to sing.

᪥ Most bald eagles leave for nesting areas farther north.

᪥ Red-tailed hawks nest.

OTHER CRITTERS

᪥ Chorus frogs start to sing.

᪥ Greenback cutthroat and rainbow trout spawn.

PLANTS

᪥ First pasqueflowers, creeping mahonia, and yellow violets usually bloom in the wild, and daffodils bloom in towns.

᪥ Willow stems turn red or gold, an especially colorful display in the Grand Valley, where globe and weeping willows are abundant.

᪥ Winter wheat, planted in the fall, greens up on farms in the eastern part of the state.

IN THE SKY

᪥ "Sore Eyes Moon" (Sioux).

᪥ The Vernal Equinox occurs around March 21 when days and nights are of approximately equal length. Most modern calendars designate this as the first official day of spring.

᪥ Leo ("the Lion") lies high in the eastern sky just above the ecliptic at 9:00 P.M. The head and neck of the lion, also known as "the Sickle," form a distinctive, backward question mark. The first-magnitude star Regulus lies at the bottom of the question mark.

Dome Rock in Mueller State Park. (Photo by Glenn Cushman.)

4

April

As my eyes

    search

    the prairie

    I feel the summer in the spring.

—CHIPPEWA

PASQUEFLOWERS OPEN PALE lavender petals to reveal centers as gold as the sun that steadily melts April's snow. In between snatches of summer, the wet storms of spring bring winter back for encores. But after each storm, mustards, violets, and other hardy flowers bloom, and the wind feels less chill.

Cottonwoods and willows are budding, and asparagus is popping up along fencerows. Prairie chickens, ready for romance, strut and boom. Prairie dog babies appear above ground. Raptor migration reaches its peak, and we welcome Swainson's hawks back from Argentina. River otters frolic in rivers now freed from ice, diving for fish and for fun. Appearing more serious about their fishing, a few bald eagles and osprey, slowly recovering from the DDT years, perch atop newly constructed nests.

In the spruce-fir forests winter still reigns, and boreal owls continue to call. But we know that summer is curled up, waiting to unfurl in the buds of April.

APRIL WEATHER

	Grand Junction (4,824 ft.)	Steamboat Springs (6,760 ft.)	Alamosa (7,536 ft.)	Berthoud Pass (11,310 ft.)	Denver (5,282 ft.)	Lamar (3,620 ft.)
Ave. high (°F)	66	53	59	36	62	70
Ave. low (°F)	39	24	24	14	35	38
Max. high (°F)	89	79	80	57	90	98
Min. low (°F)	11	−15	−6	−12	−2	9
Ave. prec. (in.)	0.75	2.18	0.49	4.43	1.71	1.15
Max. prec. (in.)	1.95	4.39	1.72	7.42	4.17	5.71
Ave. snow (in.)	1.0	13.7	4.0	54.6	9.0	1.8
Max. snow (in.)	14.3	31.5	16.4	93.0	28.3	9.0

Pacific storms and Arctic fronts continue to bring rain to the western valleys and heavy snows to the mountains and eastern foothills. A total of 95 inches of snow fell during a thirty-two-hour period at Silver Lake, west of Ward, on April 14 and 15, 1921. The April 14 total of 76 inches stands as a national twenty-four-hour record. (In January 1997, a small community in western New York State reported 77 inches in twenty-four hours, but their claim to a new record was disqualified owing to measuring irregularities.)

April is one of seven months during which at least one Colorado weather station has recorded a temperature of 100 degrees or higher. Las Animas, in the Arkansas Valley near La Junta, reached 100 degrees on April 21, 1989.

See "Colorado Climate Summary (p.1) for information on averages, extremes, and sources.

april ecosystem

Greening Woodlands

As the ground thaws and the days lengthen, cottonwoods and willows spring to life. At lower elevations, the terminal flower buds of cottonwoods begin to open in early April. The flowers on male trees look like red chenille tassels, whereas the flowers on female trees resemble strings of pale green beads. Soft catkins of tightly bunched male and female flowers adorn the willows that grow along the riverbanks. As if on cue, songbirds begin singing. Song sparrows buzz and trill in the willows. Robins chirrup melodically. Belted kingfishers chatter, swooping from one

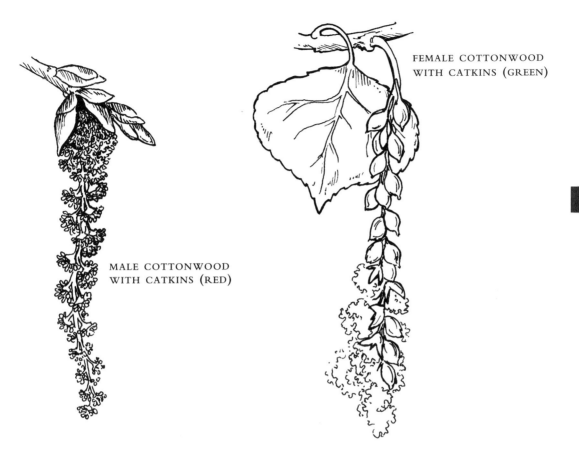

FEMALE COTTONWOOD
WITH CATKINS (GREEN)

MALE COTTONWOOD
WITH CATKINS (RED)

streamside perch to another. Common flickers hammer away at the cottonwood bark and pierce the air with their shrill calls.

By the end of the month, lowland cottonwoods and willows begin to leaf out. A horde of ants, beetles, caterpillars, and other insects emerges to feed on the new growth. The warblers come flying in, from Brazil, from Costa Rica, from Chiapas and Chihuahua. They flit through the fresh green canopy, flashing bits of bright yellow and cerulean blue, singing their sweet, breathless songs.

Yellow-rumped warblers, a few of whom winter in Colorado, appear first. By the end of the month, they are joined by flocks of Virginia's and orange-crowned warblers that have wintered in Central America and Mexico. Later on, usually during the first week of May, yellow-breasted chats; common yellowthroats; and MacGillivray's, Wilson's, and yellow warblers arrive from as far south as the Brazilian Amazon. Mixed in with these flocks are oddities and accidentals—northern parulas and Cape May, Nashville, and Tennessee warblers—who have strayed west on their journey from their wintering areas in the tropics to nesting areas in North American deciduous forests.

By mid-May most of the transients have moved along, and most of the Colorado resident warblers have made their way up into the foothills and mountains. Only three warbler species—yellow warbler, common yellowthroat, and yellow-breasted chat—typically nest in lowland riparian ecosystems (see table below).

Bullock's orioles arrive in early to mid-May and promptly set to work weaving pendulous nests from plant fibers, bark strips, grass, plant down, and hair. The nests, so conspicuous when dangling from bare cottonwood branches in winter, dissolve into the sea of fresh green foliage. So do the colorful orioles, but their ratchety song resonates through low-elevation cottonwood groves from Grand Junction to Burlington.

On April nights, screech-owls call from the branches of the silvery-barked

COLORADO'S NESTING WARBLERS

SPECIES	NESTING HABITAT	ABUNDANCE
ORANGE-CROWNED WARBLER	Shrublands, aspen forest, and riparian woodland.	Fairly common on Western Slope; rare in mountains.
VIRGINIA'S WARBLER	Shrublands and low- to mid-elevation coniferous forest.	Common on mesas and foot-hills; **WS, MT, PL.**
YELLOW WARBLER	Lowland and foothills riparian woodlands.	Fairly common, low to mid elevations; **WS, MT, PL.**
CHESTNUT-SIDED WARBLER	Foothills riparian shrublands.	Rare in eastern foothills; **MT, PL.**
YELLOW-RUMPED WARBLER	Coniferous forests and aspen forests.	Fairly common in mountains; **WS, MT.**
BLACK-THROATED GRAY WARBLER	Piñon-juniper woodlands.	Fairly common, mesas, west and southeast; **WS, PL.**
GRACE'S WARBLER	Ponderosa pine forests.	Uncommon, southwest only; **WS.**
AMERICAN REDSTART	Riparian forests and urban woodlands.	Rare in foothills canyons; **PL.**
OVENBIRD	Riparian thickets and coniferous forest understory.	Rare in foothills canyons; **PL.**
MACGILLIVRAY'S WARBLER	Riparian shrublands and aspen forests.	Fairly common, low to mid elevations; **WS, MT, PL.**
COMMON YELLOWTHROAT	Cattail marshes and riparian shrublands.	Fairly common, low to mid elevations; **WS, MT, PL.**
WILSON'S WARBLER	Willow thickets and wet meadows.	Fairly common near tree line; **MT.**
YELLOW-BREASTED CHAT	Lowland and foothills shrublands and woodlands.	Fairly common in mesas and foot-hills; **WS, PL.**

Black-throated blue warbler (one nesting record) and bay-breasted warbler (one nesting record) also have nested in the state. **MT:** Mountains above 7,500 feet; **PL:** Plains and eastern foothills to about 7,500 feet; **WS:** Western Slope valleys and plateaus to about 7,500 feet.
Sources: Robert Andrews and Robert Righter, *Colorado Birds,* pp. 304–338; Hugh Kingery, ed., *Colorado Breeding Bird Atlas.*

Eastern screech-owl chick surveys its world.

cottonwoods. Eastern screech-owls nest in natural cavities and woodpecker holes in cottonwoods and other deciduous trees in northeastern Colorado, usually east of the foothills and north of the Palmer Divide. Western screech-owls breed in lowland riparian and piñon-juniper woodlands in western and southeastern Colorado. Screech-owls feed on birds, small mammals, snakes, lizards, fish, and crayfish. They usually begin nesting in April and fledge their young in June.

The Colorado Division of Wildlife estimates that 95 percent of the state's birds and mammals depend on lowland riparian ecosystems during at least part of their life cycle. Mammals that thrive in cottonwood-willow woodlands include deer mice, western harvest mice, meadow voles, muskrats, fox squirrels, beavers, Virginia oppossums, raccoons, striped skunks, red foxes, long-tailed weasels, and white-tailed deer.

Raccoons, which spend much of the winter sleeping in a burrow, culvert, or hollow log, become much more active in early spring. Females usually give birth in April or May. The helpless young do not open their eyes or ears for about twenty days and do not leave the den for almost two months. On summer evenings the young raccoons follow their mother along the stream banks and through adjacent woods as she forages for berries, fruits, garden and field crops (especially corn), crayfish, fish, snakes, birds, eggs, and small mammals.

Striped skunks, which occur throughout the state, have denning and feeding habits similar to those of raccoons. In winter skunks sometimes den communally in an underground burrow, sleeping, but not hibernating. They usually mate in February or March, when some males form harems of receptive females. Young are born in late spring and usually appear above ground by mid-June.

The Virginia oppossum is one of many mammals and birds that have recently extended their ranges westward into Colorado along the South Platte and Arkansas River drainages. Oppossums now range as far west as Denver, and a separate population has been introduced in the Grand Valley. Other creatures that have followed river corridors into eastern Colorado include fox squirrels, white-tailed deer, great crested flycatchers, blue jays, and cardinals.

These range extensions by species with affinities for eastern deciduous forests may reflect a change in the structure of cottonwood-willow ecosystems in the South Platte and Arkansas River drainages. During the early years of European settlement, long stretches of the South Platte contained few or no cottonwoods. In her 1849 recollections of the California Gold Rush, Sarah Royce (*A Frontier Lady*) described a 200-mile stretch along the Platte River in present-day Nebraska where only a single cottonwood tree grew. The town of Orchard, near Fort Morgan, may have been named for its grove of cottonwoods, one of the few between Denver and Julesburg.

Elimination of natural flooding, prairie fires, and bison, along with deliberate cultivation of deciduous trees, led to a proliferation of cottonwoods along rivers and streams during the twentieth century. However, plains cottonwoods (*Populus deltoides*), which require some flooding to germinate, are not regenerating in many areas. Cattle grazing, along with invasion of Russian olives, tamarisk, and other nonnative shrubs, has disrupted natural shrub growth along many streams. The cottonwood-willow ecosystems we see today, though still vital for wildlife, are unnatural creations with an uncertain future.

Where To Go

Cottonwood-willow woodlands thrive at low to mid-elevations (3,600 to 8,000 feet) throughout the state.

- Yampa River State Wildlife Area, west of Hayden.
- Walker and Horsethief Canyon State Wildlife Areas, Grand Junction.
- Animas River, north of Durango.
- La Garita Creek Riparian Demonstration Area, near Alamosa.
- Fort Collins Greenbelt.
- Tamarack Ranch and Red Lion State Wildlife Areas, near Sterling.
- Bonny Reservoir and South Republican River State Wildlife Areas, north of Burlington.
- Arkansas River State Wildlife Area, Holly.

COTTONWOODS

Four native species of *Populus* (cottonwoods, aspen, and poplars) grow in Colorado. Plains cottonwoods (*Populus deltoides*) occur at lower elevations on the eastern plains and in the western valleys. Quaking aspen (*P. tremuloides*), balsam poplar (*P. balsamifera*) and narrowleaf cottonwood (*P. angustifolia*) grow at higher elevations.

Westering pioneers and Plains Indians scraped cottonwood twigs for a sweet pulp called "cottonwood ice cream." Horses grazed on the young saplings and on cottonwood bark. Plains Indians ate the trees' young buds in the spring and made yellow dye from them. They used the buds and the bark as pain relievers (both contain salicin and populin, which are related to acetylsalicylic acid, the primary ingredient in aspirin). Children made toy tepees from the heart-shaped leaves, and many Pueblo peoples still carve the wood into drums and sacred kachinas. The Navajo made prayersticks, tindersticks, looms, ceremonial duck effigies, and dice from cottonwood wood.

In his book, *The Thunder Tree,* Robert Pyle tells the Arapaho legend about how stars in the sky really come from the earth. The stars move up through the roots of cottonwoods into the branches and wait till the night spirit asks the wind spirit to provide more stars. In the ensuing gale, twigs break off and release stars from their nodes. If you snap off a twig that's neither too old nor too young, you will see a starburst at the node.

Cottonwoods live for only about 100 to 150 years, but they can become enormous. A tree growing along Crane Hollow Road in northern Boulder County (near the town of Hygiene) stands 105 feet high and measures more than 35 feet in circumference. According to the National Register of Big Trees, this is the largest cottonwood in the United States. Call the Boulder County Parks and Open Space Department (303-441-3950) for more information.

APRIL WILDFLOWERS

Walking through April reveals a new species of wildflower in bloom almost every day at lower elevations. Here we describe several flowers in detail and list some other favorites to look for. If you find the right habitat and if the weather cooperates, these flowers bloom throughout the eastern prairies, the foothills, and the Western Slope. Remember that south-facing rocky slopes are prime habitat for spring bloomers.

Pasqueflowers

Pasqueflowers are the quintessential spring flower. Although they look fragile, they thrive in gravelly soil from 4,000 to 10,000 feet and have even been found above tree line. Pasqueflowers lead spring up the mountains, blooming in warm microclimates in March and in the mountains in June.

The pasqueflower's popularity is proven by the many names, both common and scientific, that it goes by. Sometimes called prairie smoke, wild crocus, wild

EARLY SPRING WILDFLOWER SAMPLER

SPECIES	DESCRIPTION	HABITAT
ADOBE MILKWEED *Asclepias cryptoceras* Milkweed family	Low-growing plant with broad leaves and cream-colored, purple-tipped flowers.	Clay or shale knolls; **WS.**
FLEABANE DAISY *Erigeron* spp. Sunflower family	Narrow white ray flowers with yellow centers on slender stems.	Exposed hillsides, meadows, and prairies; **WS, MT, PL.**
CHIMING BELLS *Mertensia* spp. Borage family	Bright blue, bell-shaped flowers in nodding clusters on 6-inch to 4-feet tall leafy stalks.	Grasslands, meadows, forests, and tundra, lower elevations in April; **WS, MT, PL.**
BLUE MUSTARD[a] *Chorispora tenella* Mustard family	Fields of small, 4-petaled purple flowers on slender stems; cilantro-like odor.	Abundant weed in fallow fields; **WS, PL.**
WALLFLOWER *Erysimum* spp. Mustard family	Ball-like clusters of 4-petaled yellow-orange flowers on 12- to 18-inch spikes.	Mostly grasslands and sunny slopes; **WS, MT, PL.**
WILD CANDYTUFT *Noccaea montana* Mustard family	Delicate white 4-petaled flowers in cluster atop 10-inch stem, clasping leaves.	Shady sites, foothills to alpine; **WS, MT.**
WHITE MILK VETCH *Astragalus drummondii* Pea family	Tall, erect legume with leafy stems and numerous white flowers.	Dry grasslands on plains and mesas and occasionally in western valleys; **WS, PL.**
SHORT'S ASTRAGALUS *A. shortianus* Pea family	A low-growing, spreading legume with deep pink flowers.	Mesas and dry foothills, east; sagebrush hillsides, west; **WS, PL.**
GOLDEN BANNER *Thermopsis* spp. Pea family	Showy yellow flowers on leafy, pale green stalks.	Grasslands and meadows, plains to alpine; **WS, MT, PL.**
SAND LILY *Leucocrinum montanum* Lily family	White, 6-petaled, star-shaped flowers among long, slender leaves growing low to ground.	Dry, sandy slopes on eastern foothills and eastern plains; rare on Western Slope; **WS, PL.**
SPRING BEAUTY *Claytonia rosea* Purslane family	Small white to pinkish, 5-petaled flowers on slender stems, bearing 2 to 4 leaves.	Moist meadows and open forests at low to mid elevations; **WS, MT.**
PASQUEFLOWER *Pulsatilla patens* Buttercup family	Pale lavender, 6-sepaled flowers with yellow centers on hairy, leafless stalks.	Meadows, fields, open woods, sagebrush, and tundra; **WS, MT, PL.**
YELLOW VIOLET *Viola nuttallii* Violet family	Small, yellow, nodding flowers among long-stalked leaves with pointed tips.	Grasslands and forest borders, rocky areas plains to subalpine; **WS, MT, PL.**

MT: Mountains above 7,500 feet; **PL:** Plains and eastern foothills to about 7,500 feet; **WS:** Western Slope valleys and plateaus to about 7,500 feet.
[a]Nonnative.

White pasqueflowers

tulip, hartshorn, windflower, and Easter flower, it has been widely known as pasqueflower, meaning Easter flower, since John Gerard's *The Herbal or General History of Plants* was published in 1597. In *Rocky Mountain Flora—Eastern Slope,* William Weber places it in the Ranunculaceae (buttercup family) and names it *Pulsatilla patens,* subspecies *hirsutissima.*

Appropriately, *hirsutissima* means *hairy.* The soft, silky gray hairs that cover the buds and stems are thought to protect the flower from the intense rays of the sun by reflecting light and providing shade. They also protect it from dehydration by reducing wind velocity. The flower buds rise from a buried root crown before the lobed leaves unfurl. Western American Indians made poultices for rheumatism from the leaves.

Nuttall's Violets

Violets may be even shyer than their reputation. The pansylike flowers that bloom in spring seldom bear seeds. Instead, self-fertile, greenish flowers lacking petals produce seeds later in the season. These inconspicuous, seed-bearing flowers bloom underground and never open. Ants disperse the seeds, which have evolved an irregular growth on the side, enabling ants to carry them.

Unlike most violets, *Viola nuttallii* is bright yellow and thrives along dry, beaten paths and in disturbed soil, especially alongside rocks. The unviolet-like leaves are long and lanceolate. Named for Thomas Nuttall, an eccentric botanist who explored the western plains in the early 1800s, this plant grows at lower altitudes on both the eastern and western slopes. Although many violet species are edible, the yellow ones are said to have purgative effects.

Spring Beauties

These delicate white or pinkish flowers with deep pink veins have been found in January but are at their peak from April to mid-May at lower altitudes. The small, five-petaled flowers are aptly named "spring beauties." They belong to the Portulacaceae (purslane family) and are related to rock moss, so popular in rock gardens. Two species (*Claytonia* spp.) grow under Front Range ponderosa pine–Douglas-fir forests and in Western Slope oak woodlands and sagebrush uplands and seem to like the protection of low shrubs, such as mountain mahogany. Other species grow in the moist, rich soil of mountain parks and alpine meadows and on rocky tundra slopes, where they bloom from June to September.

American Indians ate the tubers, which are said to taste like radishes when raw and potatoes when boiled. However, in today's heavily populated world, eating tubers and roots of wild plants may be detrimental to the future of the plants.

Mustards

Mustards, which bloom throughout the spring and summer, are among the easiest wildflowers to identify. All have four-petaled flowers that are radially symmetrical, forming a cross. The flowers mature into two-chambered fruit pods (also known as siliques), distinctly shaped in each species. If you've been frustrated by plant keys in botanical guides, try keying out a mustard; the pod shape leads you directly to the genus.

Mustards provide many of our common foods. Amazingly, kale, brussels sprouts, cabbage, broccoli, cauliflower, and kohlrabi are all variations of a single mustard species, *Brassica oleracea*. White and black mustard also come from the genus *Brassica.*

Two Colorado mustards, Bell's twin pod (*Physaria bellii*) and *Draba grayana,* grow nowhere else in the world. Bell's twin pod blooms in April on dark shales at the base of the Front Range foothills between Boulder and Ft. Collins. You can see its bright yellow flowers, arranged in a halo around a rosette of dull green leaves, on both sides of the North Foothills Highway (US 36) between Boulder and Lyons. *Draba grayana* blooms in midsummer on rocky slopes and summits above tree line.

Several species of wallflower (*Erysimum* spp.) bloom at lower elevations throughout the state in April and May. These 1- to 2-foot tall mustards sport colorful clusters of yellow-orange flowers. Their pods are long and narrow. The Lakotas called the western wallflower "wahca'zi s'ica'man," meaning "bad-smelling yellow flower." Nevertheless, they used it as a remedy for stomach cramps and rubbed a wallflower concoction on the skin to relieve headaches and prevent sunburn. A 6-inch-high, striking magenta wallflower blooms in the tundra in early summer.

The False Flower

For years we puzzled over a small, mustard-gold flower, one of the first to appear in coniferous forests in spring but not in any guidebook. And then the mystery was revealed. It's not a flower at all but a rust fungus that invades rock cress

(*Arabis holboellii*), causing the cress to send up a "floral" shoot, double its leaves, and add swirls to the rosette at its base. The fungus exudes a sweet fluid, so the plant not only looks like a flower but smells and tastes like one to insects. Barbara Roy, who studied the phenomenon at the Rocky Mountain Biological Laboratory at Gothic, reports that the insects get ten to one hundred times the sugar from the fake flowers as from real ones nearby. In return, the insects redistribute sex cells, enabling the fungi to reproduce sexually.

CHICKEN STRUT

Prairie chickens and grouse hop, dance, stomp, and square-off on booming grounds, or leks, throughout Colorado. Males of most species arrive on booming grounds by early April. The females stroll in a week or two later, and as the season progresses they gradually show more and more interest in the males' bizarre activities. After a month or so of strutting and booming, the fittest males finally attract mates, who disperse into the tall grass or shrubbery to lay their eggs in shallow, grass-lined depressions.

Leks are usually located on low rises or flats affording unobstructed views of the surrounding shrublands and grasslands. Many leks around the state are accessible to automobiles and open to public viewing.

The Bureau of Land Management provides access to sage grouse leks east of Gunnison and north of Craig, and there are additional sage grouse leks at Arapaho National Wildlife Refuge, near Walden. You have to arrive well before dawn and stay in your car until the grouse have finished dancing an hour or two after sunrise. It's well worth the trouble. The males' mechanical, often comical, courtship antics, accompanied by an eerie hooting or popping as they inflate their large throat sacs, seem almost surreal.

Male sharp-tailed grouse extend their wings, raise their tails, and stomp their feet while performing a mesmerizing dance that was often imitated by Plains Indians. From time to time, the dancers cackle loudly and jump several feet into the air. Sharp-tailed grouse once inhabited most of eastern Colorado. Hunting, farming, and urbanization have reduced their populations to a few hundred birds, all in Douglas County, where remaining habitat is rapidly yielding to encroaching suburbia. Habitat alteration has also reduced populations in northwestern Colorado, where a few thousand sharp-tails breed in oak and sagebrush shrublands.

Greater prairie chickens make a low, resonant "whoom" sound while dancing on leks in northeastern Colorado's tallgrass and sand-sage prairies. Greater prairie chickens were listed as endangered in Colorado in 1973 when statewide populations dropped to below 1,000 individuals. Reintroduction programs carried out by the Colorado Division of Wildlife, along with habitat preservation through

GREATER PRAIRIE CHICKENS

SAGE GROUSE

BLUE GROUSE

improved grazing management, have contributed to their recovery in northeastern Colorado, where populations have increased to 3,000 to 6,000 birds. Leks are located on private ranch land, but both the Colorado Division of Wildlife and The Nature Conservancy arrange tours by appointment.

Instead of "whooming," lesser prairie chickens emit a high, turkeylike call as they puff out two rose-colored throat sacs. Lesser prairie chickens were so abundant during the nineteenth century that millions were shipped back east and served as delicacies in the finest restaurants. Today, about twenty thousand remain in the midgrass prairies of southeastern Colorado, southwestern Kansas, and western Oklahoma.

Blue grouse, which are fairly common residents of Colorado's coniferous forests, do not gather at leks. Instead, males display individually on dispersed territories. They make a soft, very low drumming sound by rapidly fluttering their wings, or they inflate their magenta-colored air sacs and produce a breathy note similar to the sound of someone blowing across an empty cider jug.

While strutting, testosterone-charged grouse and chickens have trouble focusing on anything else. Sometimes a hawk dives into their midst, kills one of their numbers, and perches there, casually munching on the dead carcass while the remaining males continue their frenzied, ritualized dance. Hikers on the Mesa Trail west of Boulder have been attacked by blue grouse that were defending individual displaying areas. One hiker, after being pecked on the hand until bloodied, picked up the high spirited bird and heaved it off into the forest. The grouse came running back, like a windup toy, and continued the attack.

Where To Go

🦆 Sage Grouse Leks, north of Craig, mid-March to mid-May.

🦆 Arapaho National Wildlife Refuge sage grouse leks, 5 miles south of Walden, early April to late May.

🦆 Greater Prairie Chicken Leks, north of Wray, early April to late May.

🦆 Lesser Prairie Chicken Lek, 30 miles southeast of Springfield, mid-March to mid-May.

🦆 Crescent Lake National Wildlife Refuge, sharp-tailed grouse viewing blind, 30 miles north of Oshkosh, Nebraska, early April to mid-May.

HAWKS IN FLIGHT

Migrating eagles, hawks, and falcons soar northward on warm air currents, or thermals, rising up over the foothills and mountains. At the Morrison Hogback Hawk Watch Site, you can see as many as fifty raptors per hour, but almost any ridge or pass running north-south attracts migrating raptors.

The spring flight usually begins in mid-March with the eagles and large hawks and peaks in early April as thousands of smaller forest hawks, or accipiters—Cooper's hawks, sharp-shinned hawks, and goshawks—pass through. In most areas hawk watching is best around midmorning, when strong thermals begin to develop. Later in the day, the raptors may vanish into the blue, a mile or more up.

Migrating raptors depend on updrafts to give them the "lift" necessary to cruise for miles without flapping their wings. By soaring, rather than flapping, they conserve energy. Migrating raptors typically avoid oceans, where thermals are weak, and often follow ridge tops, where updrafts are strongest. Narrow strips of land between oceans and high mountains create "bottlenecks," where raptors concentrate. As many as a million raptors a day pass through one such location, near Vera Cruz, Mexico, during spring and fall migration.

Some migrating raptors traverse 5,000 miles or more, others only a few hundred miles. Swainson's hawks traveling in flocks of several hundred wing their way northward from Argentina to nest on the prairies of eastern Colorado. Rough-legged hawks that winter on the Colorado prairies fly all the way to the Arctic tundra to breed. In contrast, many of the golden eagles that nest in Colorado don't migrate at all.

Where To Go

☣ Poncha Pass, south of Poncha Springs, mid-March to late April.

☣ Morrison Hogback Hawk Watch Site, south of Golden, mid-March to mid-April. Volunteers are often present to help with identification.

☣ Rabbit Mountain Open Space, west of Longmont, mid-March to mid-April.

☣ Pawnee Buttes, Pawnee National Grassland, mid-March to late April. Golden eagles and prairie falcons nest here as well.

BOREAL OWLS

On starry nights in the high country, a series of crystal clear, rapidly rising "hoo" notes pulses hypnotically over the snowy landscape. To hear this rare and enchanting song, you have to go hiking, skiing, or snowshoeing in the spruce-fir forest, home of the 10-inch-high boreal owl.

Boreal owls usually begin singing shortly after sundown, when males advertise their territories for a brief time before gliding off into forest clearings to hunt voles and other small mammals. Around the nest, both sexes emit an improbable assortment of ghostlike cries and wails, including an alarm call that sounds like a laser gun in a Star Wars movie. Boreal owls call most actively in March and April while establishing nesting territories and choosing nest sites in woodpecker holes.

During early spring, moonlight skiers in Colorado spruce-fir forests probably have about a fifty-fifty chance of hearing a boreal owl, though the likelihood of ever seeing one is minuscule. By day the owls are virtually invisible as they roost in heavy foliage close to the trunk of a large conifer. At night, when they become active, they dissolve into the darkness.

So elusive are boreal owls that no one knew for sure whether they nested in Colorado until the mid-1980s. Biologists at Colorado State University, knowing that these owls inhabited spruce-fir forests in Canada, began searching for them on spring nights in the Cameron Pass area, west of Fort Collins. In 1984 these scientists located thirty-six singing males and found the first boreal owl nest ever documented in the state. Since then, researchers and bird-watchers have encountered boreal owls throughout the high mountains of Colorado.

Where To Go

۸ Grand Mesa, east of Grand Junction, March to May.

۸ Cumbres Pass, west of Antonito, March to May.

۸ Cameron Pass, west of Fort Collins, March to May. Listen for the owls from the roadway, near the top of the pass.

۸ Red Rock Lake, west of Ward, March to May. Hike or ski toward Left Hand Reservoir or Brainard Lake.

FISH EAGLES: NESTING BALD EAGLES AND OSPREY

In early spring it's not unusual to see bald eagles flying around with large sticks in their beaks or constructing flimsy nests on top of cottonwoods or conifers. Pre-migratory nest building by wintering bald eagles is a ritualistic behavior that helps bond pairs together before they fly north to breeding areas in the Pacific Northwest and southeast Alaska. Only a tiny fraction of Colorado's wintering balds actually breeds in the state.

But numbers of nesting balds are growing steadily. In 1974 a single pair nested in Colorado. About thirty pairs nested in 1997. One nest, at Barr Lake State Park only 8 miles from Denver International Airport, has fledged young in seven of the last nine years.

The bald eagle's recovery in North America has been attributed largely to the banning of DDT in 1972. The insecticide that accumulated in the fatty tissues of fish and other prey species was ingested by the eagles and disrupted their calcium metabolism, causing them to lay eggs with thin, breakable shells. The osprey, another fish-eating raptor known popularly as the "fish eagle," was similarly affected.

Colorado's nesting osprey population has more than doubled during the past decade. Most of the state's forty or so active osprey nests are situated in mountain wetlands in and around North Park and Middle Park. Wildlife agencies have constructed artificial nest platforms in the Dolores River Canyon, the Fort Collins Greenbelt, and at Boulder Reservoir, where migrating osprey visit each April. A pair nested in Fort Collins in 1997, and two pairs nested at Boulder County reservoirs in 1997. These were the first nestings ever documented in those areas of the state.

Where To Go

❧ Yampa Valley State Wildlife Area, Hayden. Nesting bald eagles, April to July.

❧ Shadow Mountain Reservoir, south of Grand Lake. You can observe nesting ospreys with a spotting scope or binoculars from the Pine Beach Picnic Area. May to September.

❧ Valmont Reservoir, east of Boulder. Ospreys visit in April and October and sometimes nest on power poles near the Public Service plant.

❧ Barr Lake State Park, northeast of Denver. A bald eagle nest is visible from a gazebo viewing area. Volunteer naturalists are on hand with telescopes, April to July.

FRESHLY MINTED PRAIRIE DOGS

Black-tailed prairie dog pups gaze out cautiously at April's greening landscape. During their first few weeks above ground, they huddle at the burrow entrance, rarely venturing more than a few yards from the doorstep. Their instincts are right; golden eagles, ferruginous hawks, red-tailed hawks, great horned owls, red foxes, swift foxes, coyotes, and badgers all prey on young prairie dogs.

Black-tailed prairie dogs produce only one litter per year. They breed in February or March and give birth about a month later. The young are born blind and naked and do not emerge from the burrow until four to seven weeks old. They usually pop up around the end of April, when prairie grasses and wildflowers begin to sprout.

Through play, food sharing, wrestling, and mock fighting, young prairie dogs gradually become integrated into the colony's complex social system. Each colony can be divided into several geographical units, known as wards. Each ward contains

Black-tailed prairie dog at its burrow.

several kinship units, known as coteries. A coterie consists of a dominant male, several subdominant males and females, and the year's young. Coteries control territories of about .25 acres to 1 acre. The males patrol territorial boundaries, while the females care for the young. Prairie dogs throughout the colony communicate using a variety of visual cues and vocalizations, including the distinctive "alarm bark" and a wheezy "all clear" signal delivered while leaping into the air.

The popular images of prairie dogs as either cute, cuddly pets or plague-infested ravagers of grazing lands do not stand up to scrutiny. When confined in close captivity, male prairie dogs sometimes fight one another to the death. In the wild, females occasionally slip into neighboring burrows to eat the young of their sisters and cousins. Most studies of prairie dog grazing impacts have concluded that, in natural settings, their grazing does alter the species composition of the prairie, suppressing native grasses and making room for other plants, but does not reduce the total amount of plant mass. In fact, one study found that cattle actually preferred to graze in pastures containing prairie dogs, presumably because these areas produced a higher quality of forage than did the pastures that contained no prairie dogs.

In urban settings, where prairie dogs are often confined to small areas of previously overgrazed or disturbed land, they can strip away almost all the remaining vegetation, creating miniature dust bowls susceptible to erosion and weed infestation. Plague, a flea-borne disease brought to the New World by humans, affects prairie dogs, often decimating their populations, but is rarely transferred to humans.

Black-tailed prairie dogs inhabit Colorado's eastern plains, usually below 6,000 feet. Populations have declined precipitously since the mid-nineteenth century, when some colonies stretched more than 10 miles across, and the high plains population probably exceeded one billion individuals. Currently, less than 1 percent of public land in the Pawnee and Comanche National Grasslands contains active prairie dog colonies. Black-footed ferrets, now extinct in Colorado, along with swift foxes, ferruginous hawks, golden eagles, burrowing owls, and badgers, have all been hurt by the poisoning and plowing under of prairie dog colonies.

PRAIRIE DOGS AND PLAGUE

Prairie dogs and many other wild rodents harbor fleas that sometimes carry a bacterium, *Yersinia pestis,* that causes plague. Plague, known as Black Death during the Middle Ages, was probably introduced to North America from Asia around 1900. It was first reported in Colorado in 1941. It now occurs in rock squirrels, fox squirrels, prairie dogs, wood rats, other species of ground squirrels, chipmunks, and cottontails throughout the state. Humans can be exposed to plague when they pick up dead animals or handle pets who have been in contact with plague-infested rodents. Typical symptoms, which occur after two to six days, include fever and chills, severe headache, muscle aches, nausea, and vomiting. The disease responds to antibiotics if treated promptly.

From 1957 to 1996, the Colorado Department of Health reported forty-one human cases and seven deaths from plague. Plague outbreaks in 1984 and 1985 and 1993 through 1995 obliterated hundreds of prairie dog colonies between Denver and Fort Collins. To control the spread of plague, wildlife biologists and health department officials recommend dusting rodent holes with flea-killing pesticides, but they do not recommend killing the rodents, as this only causes the fleas to disperse into the environment. Contact with rock squirrels poses the greatest threat to humans, because the plague-carrying fleas on rock squirrels are more aggressive and less host specific than the fleas on prairie dogs and most other rodents.

White-tailed prairie dogs inhabit grasslands and shrublands of western and northwestern Colorado. Their populations appear to be stable or increasing slightly. Gunnison's prairie dogs inhabit grasslands and shrublands in central, southern, and southwestern Colorado. Plague and poisoning have greatly reduced their numbers throughout much of their Colorado range.

OTTER ODYSSEY

Five subspecies of river otter once cavorted in Colorado's waterways. Though never abundant, they were widespread until mountain men trapped them out along with beaver. When the Colorado Division of Wildlife reintroduced them in 1976, no otters had been sighted in almost fifty years.

Three pups from Oregon were released in Cheesman Reservoir, near Deckers. Later, others were released in isolated parts of the state. The reintroduction, largely funded by the nongame tax checkoff on state income tax forms, succeeded. Though still endangered, otters again swim, mate, and play in Colorado rivers. No hunting or trapping is allowed.

Colorado was not the only state to extirpate otters. During the early decades of the twentieth century, river otters disappeared from most of their watery turfs throughout the country, victims of trapping, water pollution, and habitat destruction. Reintroduction programs, habitat restoration, and protective legislation are bringing them back.

Weighing about 20 pounds and measuring about 4 feet long, *Lutra canadensis* is a member of the weasel or Mustelidae family. Otters sport sleek, dark brown pelts that formerly doomed many to a future as a fur coat. Their powerful tails act as rudders when they swim and as props when they stand. Their stiff but sensitive whiskers help in locating prey (crustaceans, mollusks, amphibians, and water insects as well as fish) along the river bottom. Although they occasionally take trout, their usual fish dinner consists of crayfish and nongame species such as carp.

In winter otters continue to swim under ice but shift from quiet water to moving water when possible. Congregations are sometimes seen around waterfalls, rapids, and springs.

In April one to five pups are born and remain in the den for about three months. Soon after the birth of one litter, the female mates again, an activity that usually takes place in water and may last for twenty minutes. Otters are one of the few animals to undergo delayed implantation. Although the egg is fertilized in the spring, it doesn't begin to develop until late fall. Also in April, yearling pups usually disperse from the mother's home range and may travel many miles from their birthplace. Under good conditions, otters live ten to twenty years.

"A pint-sized mermaid with a mustache" is how writer Ronald Rood described these web-footed creatures that are famous for their *joie de vivre* (*National Wildlife* 13 [August 1975]:20–24). They slide down muddy hills and snowbanks, sometimes pushing with a hind foot like a boy on a scooter. They juggle pebbles, sticks, and other objects of importance to an otter. They play hide-and-seek and tussle with one another. In short, they are otter delight.

Showy Grasshoppers

The first grasshoppers to emerge in spring are usually the speckled range grasshoppers whose bright orange wings flash like fritillary butterflies; another early grasshopper has wings like a mourning cloak butterfly.

Canoe trips on remote stretches of water provide opportunities for sightings. Even if you see no otter, look for their sign—slides, tracks, and scat—in snow or in mud.

Where To Go

🦆 Shadow Mountain Reservoir, near Grand Lake.

🦆 Gunnison River.

🦆 Dolores River Canyon, north of Cortez.

🦆 Piedra River, west of Pagosa Springs.

🦆 Rocky Mountain National Park, especially the Kawuneeche Valley.

🦆 Fort Collins gravel ponds.

APRIL EVENTS

MAMMALS

🦆 Otters, minks, long-tailed weasels, beavers, raccoons, foxes, and porcupines are born.

🦆 Baby prairie dogs appear above ground.

🦆 Black bears begin to leave dens, though many females and cubs will not emerge until May.

BIRDS

🦆 Golden eagle chicks hatch.

🦆 Swainson's hawks return from Argentina, and burrowing owls return from Mexico and the Southwest.

🦆 Broad-tailed hummingbirds pass through the lowlands en route to nesting sites.

🦆 Goldfinches and meadowlarks transmute drab winter plumage into gold.

OTHER CRITTERS

🦆 Bull snakes mate.

🦆 Early butterflies—cabbage whites, sulphurs, skippers, Melissa blues, red admirals, and painted ladies—appear.

🦆 Water striders, sometimes called Jesus bugs, skate across water surfaces feeding on small insects.

❧ Ticks latch on to hikers. Some may be out as early as March; continue "tick checking" until the hot, dry weather of late summer.

PLANTS

❧ Cottonwoods produce flowers that look like tassels and beads.

❧ Pasqueflowers, yellow violets, and spring beauties reign over the wildflower parade as chickweed, mertensia, candytuft, and various species of vetch and mustard join the ranks.

❧ Ferns unfurl.

❧ In towns, fruit trees bloom and rhubarb is harvested.

IN THE SKY

❧ The Lyrid meteor shower occurs in the northeast around April 20.

❧ The Gemini Twins (Castor and Pollux) are high in the western sky around 9:00 P.M., MDT. Look along the ecliptic about halfway between Orion and Ursa Major (the Big Dipper). The ancient Egyptians referred to these two stars as the Two Sprouting Plants, and Hindus called them the Twin Deities.

Stately Pawnee Buttes, on the state's northeastern prairie.

5

May

Spring is opening.
I can smell the different perfumes
    of the white weeds used in the dance.

       —PAWNEE

MAY IS SWEET with perfume. Antelope brush, wild plum, and apple blossoms scent the balmy air, and we bury our noses in ponderosa pine bark to inhale intoxicating clouds of vanilla.

Humans are not the only ones to dance as spring arrives. Little blue butterflies dance above creek crossings, and Abert's squirrels chase each other through the ponderosas in mating bouts that appear choreographed. We visit the prairie to hear the intricate songs of lark buntings and to see their spiraling courtship displays, more graceful than ballerinas.

Warblers, orioles, lazuli buntings, and other songbirds return from the tropics. Flammulated owls hoot softly. Great horned owlets fledge. Great blue herons, who returned several months ago, are now busy feeding fish to noisy newborns. Even lumbering porcupines are gently nursing babies.

May is a month for song and dance, for courting and for giving birth, for savoring fragrances. It's a month when we open up our hearts with the opening of spring.

MAY WEATHER

	Grand Junction (4,824 ft.)	Steamboat Springs (6,760 ft.)	Alamosa (7,536 ft.)	Berthoud Pass (11,310 ft.)	Denver (5,282 ft.)	Lamar (3,620 ft.)
Ave. high (°F)	76	64	68	45	71	78
Ave. low (°F)	48	31	33	23	44	48
Max. high (°F)	95	87	85	62	96	102
Min. low (°F)	26	12	11	−3	22	26
Ave. prec. (in.)	0.87	2.11	0.64	3.85	2.40	2.50
Max. prec. (in.)	2.74	5.66	1.85	6.88	7.31	7.38
Ave. snow (in.)	0.1	2.9	1.8	37.2	1.7	0.1
Max. snow (in.)	5.0	20.5	13.5	69.6	13.6	3.5

Cyclonic storms carrying Pacific and Gulf moisture can produce heavy flooding on the eastern slope. Flood waters swept through downtown Boulder on May 31, 1894, after continuous rains drenched the mountains west of town for three days. A similar storm in 1969 dropped up to 10 inches of rain on Denver suburbs, causing serious flooding along the South Platte River. Denver's all-time record twenty-four-hour rainfall of 6.53 inches fell in May 1876. Holly set a May state record high of 107°F in 1996.

See "Colorado Climate Summary" (p. 1) for information on averages, extremes, and sources.

THE LAST SPRING FREEZE

Some parts of Colorado never experience a "last spring freeze." Subfreezing temperatures are common on the highest peaks throughout June, July, and August.

CITY	ELEVATION (FT.)	AVERAGE DATE OF LAST SPRING FREEZE
COLORADO SPRINGS	6,008	May 5
CORTEZ	6,201	May 27
CRAIG	6,186	June 5
DENVER	5,282	May 2
DURANGO	6,523	June 4
GLENWOOD SPRINGS	5,763	May 24
GRAND JUNCTION	4,597	April 21
GREELEY	4,664	May 6
JULESBURG	3,477	May 9
LAMAR	3,620	April 30
TRINIDAD	6,025	May 12

Source: Colorado Climate Center (Fort Collins), *Colorado Climate* 19 (April–May 1996): 4.

The table (bottom previous page) shows the average last freeze dates for selected low- to mid-elevation Colorado cities. During any given year, the last spring freeze may occur as many as forty days before or after the average date. That's why long-term Denver residents often recommend leaving tomato plants indoors until after the Memorial Day weekend.

may *ecosystem*

Under the Ponderosa Pines

Western bluebirds dart in and out of tiny nest cavities. Abert's squirrels scamper through the tree canopy. Lavender pasqueflowers and penstemons, golden arnicas, sky-blue harebells and mertensia carpet the grassy meadows and clearings. The vanilla-scented air carries melodious songs of warbling vireos, western tanagers, and black-headed grosbeaks.

Each chip or song comes from a slightly different location, reflecting the birds' particular foraging strategies. Pygmy nuthatches ("peep-peep, peep") walk upside down on the slender outer branches, nabbing ants, spiders, and beetles. The slightly larger red-breasted nuthatches ("ink, ink, ink") hop around on the main branches, usually in the upper third of the tree canopy. The still larger white-breasted nuthatches ("yank-yank-yank") scurry head first down the trunks, probing the textured bark for insects and seeds. Brown creepers (a high-pitched "seeee, see-see-see") spiral their way up the trunks. Mountain chickadees ("chick-a-dee-dee") cling to the cones. Hairy woodpeckers ("peeek") hammer away at the bark. Dark-eyed juncos and chipping sparrows hop around on the ground.

Specialized feeding strategies enable birds of various species to "partition" the forest's resources in this way and avoid direct competition. The same principle applies to nesting (see table on p. 92). At the bottom of the nesting ladder are the western bluebirds and house wrens, who lay their eggs in woodpecker holes a few feet off the ground. At the top are the tanagers, yellow-rumped warblers, and pine siskins, who usually nest in the canopy, safely out of view of predators and most bird-watchers.

Now and then a sharp-shinned hawk dodges through the trees. These small accipiters

Bumblebees

The big bumblebees gathering pollen and nectar in early spring are the queens that overwintered, the only bumblebees to survive the winter. Now they are feeding the first brood of the new colony, but soon they will be pampered in turn by newly hatched sterile females. Throughout the summer the queen's only job will be to lay eggs. Finally, toward autumn, new queen bees will be produced from specially fed larvae, and these queens will carry on the life cycle as the old queen dies.

COMMON NESTING SONGBIRDS OF PONDEROSA PINE AND DOUGLAS-FIR FORESTS

SPECIES	SONG
Shrub and Lower Tree Canopy Nesters	
MOURNING DOVE	A mournful "coowoo-ooo-woo-oo"
BROAD-TAILED HUMMINGBIRD	High-pitched trill made with wings
WESTERN WOOD-PEWEE	Sings rarely; call a soft "zhee-yer"
HERMIT THRUSH[a]	Flutelike, descending whistles
AMERICAN ROBIN	Loud, rich "cheery-cheer-up-cheerio"
PLUMBEOUS VIREO	Loud, abrupt "chu-wee, cheerio"
WARBLING VIREO	Rich, syncopated "I am a vireo vireo"
VIRGINIA'S WARBLER	Breathy "swee-swee-swee, see-s-s-see"
CHIPPING SPARROW	Monotonic trill of dry "chip" notes
DARK-EYED JUNCO	Monotonic trill of bell-like notes
LESSER GOLDFINCH	Song varied and musical; call a plaintive "tee-yee"
Tree Cavity Nesters	
VIOLET-GREEN SWALLOW	Call a series of quick "chip" notes
MOUNTAIN CHICKADEE	Harsh, breathy, "chick-a-dee-dee"
PYGMY NUTHATCH[b]	Rapid "beep, beep, beep-beep, beep"
RED-BREASTED NUTHATCH	Nasal "ink, ink, ink"
WHITE-BREASTED NUTHATCH	Nasal "yank, yank, yank-yank-yank"
HOUSE WREN	Rich and bubbly, with buzzes
WESTERN BLUEBIRD	Brief, clear notes, "few few fawee"
Mid to Upper Canopy Nesters	
HAMMOND'S FLYCATCHER	A thin "sillit tsurrp shrillit"
YELLOW-RUMPED WARBLER	Breathy "see-see-see see-see-see"
WESTERN TANAGER	Robinlike, but harsher and shorter
PINE SISKIN	Rich, sustained musical warble; call a harsh, ascending "tzhreeet"

[a]Primarily Douglas-fir.
[b]Primarily ponderosa pine.

feed on songbirds, squirrels, and other small rodents. Their stick nests, high in the treetops, are easily missed, but their piercing screams or the presence of a bloodied, carrion-littered stump may betray a nest site. Other high-pitched cries overhead may belong to a Cooper's hawk, northern goshawk, prairie falcon, or golden eagle. In all, fifteen species of hawks, eagles, falcons, and owls nest in Colorado's ponderosa pine forests or on adjacent cliffs.

If you sit quietly in the forest in May, you'll eventually see a troupe of Abert's squirrels dashing from limb to limb in a madcap mating frenzy. The estrus female takes the lead, with several ardent admirers close on her tail. The chase order corresponds roughly to the proximity of the males' home ranges to that of the estrus female. When one male "cuts in line," other males may wrestle him to the ground, scratching and biting until the interloper submits and reassumes his proper position in the chase hierarchy. Young are born in May or June and spend the first few weeks of their lives in a massive, round, stick nest high in the canopy.

With their long, wispy ears, bushy tails, and sleek black or gray fur, Abert's (or "tassel-eared") squirrels rank among the most beautiful of North American mammals. They live almost exclusively in mature ponderosa pine forests of the central Rockies and southwestern United States. The lives of Abert's squirrels and ponderosa pines have evolved mutualistically and competitively over tens of thousands of years. The squirrels feed on pine nuts and on the soft inner bark of the twigs, sometimes damaging the trees to the point where they become weak and die. The trees "respond" by producing semitoxic monoterpenes (which give the forest its characteristic vanilla scent) and by producing subaverage cone crops every few years. When seeds are scarce, the squirrels scour the forest floor for mushrooms, including those that develop their fruiting bodies underground. These "false truffles" grow symbiotically with ponderosa roots, fixing nitrogen. By harvesting the false truffles, squirrels benefit the ponderosas by spreading fungi spores throughout the forest.

When alarmed, Abert's squirrels freeze motionless on a low branch, stamp their feet angrily, or race up to the top of the tallest pines. Since they occupy stable home ranges of about 40 acres throughout the year, you can return to the same spot and get to know a squirrel on a first-name basis. After a while it's easy to become possessive and protective of these personable rodents who depend on mature, undisturbed ponderosa forests for their survival.

Most Colorado ponderosa pine forests have been severely altered by human activities such as logging, wildfire management, and development. Ponderosa pine forests require frequent low- to moderate-intensity fires to remove litter from the forest floor, thin out the smaller trees, and provide bare ground where seeds can germinate. Since the late nineteenth century, fire suppression in the central Rockies has created sickly, crowded forests that are ripe for insect infestation and catastrophic fires that destroy large areas of the forest. No one knows how much of Colorado's presettlement ponderosa pine forests were old growth. Most biologists agree that the ponderosa pine forest belt in the central Rockies was probably a mosaic of old-growth and younger forests. This mosaic changed constantly as fire, wind, lightning, floods, and drought destroyed some stands and rejuvenated others.

Today, only a few small pockets of old-growth remain. These old-growth remnants often occur in remote canyons cutting through the Front Range foothills and Western Slope mesas between about 6,000 and 8,500 feet. Look for open forests with large-diameter trees (more than 3 feet), large standing dead trees, and a mixture of younger trees and seedlings.

Where To Go

🦆 Piedra River north of Chimney Rock (Pagosa Springs area).

🦆 Rocky Mountain National Park, especially Copeland Meadows, Beaver Meadows, and Moraine Park.

🦆 Boulder Mountain Park.

🦆 Mt. Falcon Park, west of Morrison.

🦆 Manitou Park, northwest of Colorado Springs.

🦆 Picketwire Valley, Purgatoire River west of Trinidad.

WILD ORCHIDS

The very word *orchid* conjures up visions of the rare and exotic, of jungles and flamboyant flowers. Yet in Colorado twenty-five orchid species thrive, most of them in habitats far removed from a florist's hothouse. They range from the showy yellow lady's-slipper (*Cypripedium parviflorum*) to the inconspicuous white adder's-mouth (*Malaxis brachypoda*), Colorado's rarest orchid. Herbalist John Gerard focused on the orchid's most important attribute in 1597 when he wrote in *The Herbal or General History of Plants:* "They are chiefly regarded for the pleasant and beautifull floures wherewith Nature hath seemed to play and disport her selfe."

All orchids share the same basic flower structure: three sepals, which usually resemble colorful petals; three petals; and a column (stamens and stigma fused together), all of which attach above the ovary. A hand lens reveals the true elegance of the smaller species. The two upper petals are symmetrical, but the lower one, called the lip, is specialized so as to attract pollinators and act as a landing platform. It's often shaped like a pouch or shoe—hence the common names "lady's-slipper," "fairyslipper," "brownie lady's-slipper," and "moccasin flower" and the scientific name of one genus, *Cypripedium,* which means "Aphrodite's sandal." The family name, first used some three hundred years B.C., comes from the Greek word *orchis,* meaning "testicle," because many species have swollen twin bulbs. (Castration is still called an "orchidectomy.")

Many orchids also contain a nectar-producing spur at the base of the lip and emit a delicate, sweet fragrance. In fact, one of the common names for white bog orchid (*Limnorchis dilatata albiflora*) is "scent bottle." Next time you find a clump, kneel down, ignore the wetness, and inhale! Edwin Way Teale writes in *North with the Spring* that some orchids give off a different scent by day than by night. One species, he says, smells like vanilla in the morning and narcissus at night. Commercial vanilla is actually obtained from the cured seed pods of an orchid in Central and South America.

The blooming season varies according to species and elevation. Fairyslippers (*Calypso bulbosa*) and coralroots (*Corallorhiza* spp.) usually begin in May or June, and Ute ladies'-tresses (*Spiranthes diluvialis*) and rattlesnake plantains (*Goodyera oblongifolia*) in August.

In Colorado most orchids grow at elevations of from 5,500 feet to 12,000 feet, with the majority in the montane and subalpine zones—a habitat that seems alien for a plant that more often grows suspended in air from tropical trees. Most Col-

A good look at the structure of a fairy-slipper orchid. (Photo by Glenn Cushman.)

orado species prefer north-facing slopes or cool, moist ravines in coniferous forests. Some bog orchids even flourish at or above timber line. Lower elevations are usually too dry for orchids. However, the rare Ute ladies'-tresses like moist meadows in the Denver-Boulder area, and the giant helleborine (*Epipactis gigantea*) grows in springs and seeps of Western Slope canyons.

In *Colorado Flora: Eastern Slope,* William Weber writes: "Paradoxically, the orchid family is the second largest family in numbers of species, and it probably contains more rare and endangered species than any other family." For this reason it is especially important not to pick the flowers or disturb the plants.

Where To Go

If you search the right habitat, watching where you step, you are likely to find orchids in many locations throughout the state, including:

℘ Big Creek Lakes Trail northwest of Walden (insectivorous sundews as well as brownie lady's-slipper and coralroots, June).

❀ Dolores River Canyon and Unaweap Seep south of Grand Junction (giant helleborine, hooded ladies'-tresses, and other rare species, June).

❀ Piedra River north of Chimney Rock (giant helleborine and bog orchids in June).

❀ Poncha Springs (giant helleborine in the runoff from the hot springs below the old resort, southeast of the present town, late June).

❀ Rocky Mountain National Park (fairyslippers, coral roots, bog orchids, and brownie lady's-slippers are especially good along the trail to Ouzel Lake and near Bear Lake, late May and June).

LATE SPRING WILDFLOWER SAMPLER

COMMON NAME	SCIENTIFIC NAME	FAMILY	HABITAT
Western Valleys (4,000–7,500 feet)			
BLADDER-POD	*Lesquerella ludoviciana*	Mustard	Arid hills
CLARET CUP	*Echinocereus triglochidiatus*	Cactus	Dry sites
SEGO LILY	*Calochortus nuttallii*	Mariposa	Adobe hills
COMMON HAREBELL	*Campanula rotundifolia*	Bellflower	Dry mountainsides
MILK VETCH	*Astragalus* spp.[a]	Pea	Varied
LAMBERT'S LOCOWEED	*Oxytropis lambertii*	Pea	Grasslands
SAND-VERBENA	*Abronia elliptica*	Four-o'clock	Adobe hills
WHITE STEMLESS EVENING-PRIMROSE	*Oenothera caespitosa*	Evening-primrose	Bare and dry ground
Mountain Forests and Meadows (7,500–10,000 feet)			
FIELD MOUSE-EAR	*Cerastium strictum*	Pink	Throughout
GROUNDSEL	*Senecio integerrimus*	Sunflower	Moist meadows
WILD CANDYTUFT	*Noccaea montana*	Mustard	Throughout
FALSE SOLOMON'S SEAL	*Maianthemum* spp.	Mayflower	Moist forests
FAIRYSLIPPER	*Calypso bulbosa*	Orchid	Moist forests
SPRING BEAUTY	*Claytonia rosea*	Purslane	Pine forests
PASQUEFLOWER	*Pulsatilla patens*	Buttercup	Throughout
CINQUEFOIL	*Potentilla* spp.	Rose	Throughout
Eastern Foothills and Plains (3,600–7,500 feet)			
WILD ONION	*Allium* spp.	Onion	Dry places
WAVYLEAF DANDELION	*Nothocalais cuspidata*	Sunflower	Dry slopes
DRUMMOND MILK VETCH	*Astragalus drummondii*	Pea	Dry slopes
GOLDEN BANNER	*Thermopsis divaricarpa*	Pea	Throughout
LAMBERT'S LOCOWEED	*Oxytropis lambertii*	Pea	Grasslands
LARKSPUR	*Delphinium nuttallianum*	Hellebore	Meadows and woods
YELLOW STEMLESS EVENING-PRIMROSE	*Oenothera howardii*	Evening-primrose	Dry or bare soil
ONE-SIDED PENSTEMON	*Penstemon secundiflorus*	Figwort	Dry, sandy areas

[a]About fifty species of milk vetch bloom on the Western Slope.

LOCOWEEDS AND MILK VETCHES

One of Colorado's most spectacular wildflower displays begins in early April as the magenta flowers of Lambert's locoweed (*Oxytropis lambertii*) unfurl on shale slopes in the Front Range foothills. In late May the display spreads to the tablelands surrounding Black Mesa and Mesa de Maya, in southeastern Colorado, and to shales, grasslands, and sagebrush hills on the Western Slope. By early June, these showy locos begin blooming in mountain meadows, where they hybridize with a purple-white loco, *Oxytropis sericea,* creating a breathtaking color show.

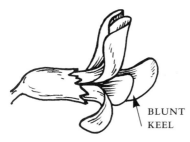

ASTRAGALUS DRUMMONDII
(DRUMMOND MILK VETCH)

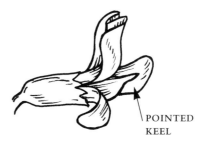

OXYTROPIS LAMBERTII
(LAMBERT'S LOCOWEED)

Locoweeds (the common name often given to peas in the genus *Oxytropis*) and milk vetches (peas in the genus *Astragalus*) thrive on selenium-rich soils. This poisonous element accumulates in the plant tissues and, when ingested by livestock, causes "blind staggers" or "alkali disease." Lambert's locoweed is extremely poisonous.

More then sixty species of *Astragalus* and about ten of *Oxytropis* occur in Colorado. Though species can be difficult to identify, the two genera are easy to separate. In flowers of *Oxytropis,* the lowermost petal, known as the keel, is distinctly pointed; in flowers of *Astragalus,* the keel is blunt or rounded. Other genera of the pea family include lupine (*Lupinus*), clover (*Trifolium*), and vetch (*Vicia*).

Plains Indians harvested the round seedpods of the groundplum milk vetch (*A. crassicarpus*) and ate them raw, cooked, or pickled. The Blackfeet dug up the roots and stems of Canada milk vetches (*A. canadensis*) in the spring and ate them after boiling. The Lakota pulverized Canada milk vetch roots and chewed them to relieve chest and back pains. They referred to this milk vetch as *peju'ta ska hu,* meaning "white stem medicine." The slender milk vetch (*A. gracilis*), known as *peju'ta sku ya* (sweet medicine), was thought to promote milk production in nursing mothers. However, all milk vetches have the potential to be poisonous, and we do not recommend their consumption.

Look for locos, milk vetches, lupines, and other members of the pea family in sandy soils, shales, grasslands, and mountain meadows throughout the state in May, June, and July. For more information on Native American uses of legumes and other wild plants, see *Medicinal Wild Plants of the Prairie* and *Edible Wild Plants of the Prairie,* both by Kelly Kindscher.

FLAMMULATED OWLS:
ELFIN DENIZENS OF ANCIENT FORESTS

It was on a hillside in the North St. Vrain Canyon, west of Lyons, that we first heard the hoots of flammulated owls. Shortly after sunset, a bat-sized form flitted overhead and disappeared into the foliage of a tall ponderosa pine. For a moment there was only the sound of water trickling down below and the distant, flutelike song of a hermit thrush. Then came the hoots. Deep and resonant, they floated out across the canyon and echoed off the granite cliffs on the opposite side. The statuesque old ponderosa loomed in the moonlight, but the little owl remained invisible.

A few weeks later, we camped in a meadow near the place where we first heard the owl. All night long the owl hooted from the ponderosas that towered above our campsite. Sometimes the hoots came singly, about a second apart. More often they came in threes or fours: "Wh-wh-whoot, wh-wh-whoot-wh, wh-wh-whoot." At dawn the hooting stopped, and there was no trace of the owl.

The following summer, Lyons naturalists Raymond Davis and Laurie Sirotkin told us of a flammulated owl nest in a remote canyon of the Boulder Mountain Park. We visited the site an hour before sunrise and listened for the hissing sound young owls make when begging for food. The loud hisses and rasps led to a scrawny aspen surrounded by much larger ponderosas and Douglas-firs. The sound came from a 2-inch-diameter hole about 20 feet up. An adult came flying in with a moth flopping in its talons. The hissing grew louder for a moment and then subsided as the owl fluttered off into the forest.

When you hear a flammulated owl, you know you're in a wild place. While searching for these owls, we've seen wild turkeys, black bears, and elk and heard the screams of mountain lions and northern goshawks. A little like northern spotted owls in the Pacific Northwest, flammulated owls favor old-growth and near old-growth forests. In Colorado they nest predominantly in mid-elevation ponderosa pine–Douglas-fir forests or aspen groves. Richard Reynolds and Brian Linkhart, who have studied these owls for more than ten years in the Manitou Park area northwest of Colorado Springs, have determined that the owls typically choose large-diameter conifers for roosting and large, dead ponderosas for nesting. Since the owls feed predominantly on moths and other insects, they frequent sites with relatively dense undergrowth, often along small streams. In a Boulder County Nature Association study, volunteers found singing flammulated owls in sixteen of twenty roadless foothills canyons between Lyons and Golden.

The word *flammulated* describes the inconspicuous fiery-orange feathers on the owls' rumps. However, their most distinguishable physical features are their small size (about 6.5 inches from head to tail tip), square body shape, and coal black eyes. They respond readily to human hoots or tape playbacks of territorial calls from mid-May to early July, when they are establishing nesting territories. When we use the tapes, we play them softly for short periods of time, so as not to frighten or overly stress nesting pairs.

Sometimes these little owls respond to our hoots by flying to within a few feet, perching on a low branch, and swiveling their heads around to find the intruder. Most of the time we only hear them, calling from somewhere off in the forest, but we leave contented with the knowledge that they and the old trees still have a place in our crowded world.

Where To Go

❧ Piedra River north of Chimney Rock (Pagosa Springs area).
❧ North, Middle, and South St. Vrain Canyons, west of Lyons.
❧ Boulder Mountain Park.
❧ Mount Falcon Park, west of Morrison.
❧ Manitou Park, northwest of Colorado Springs.

GREAT BLUES

The hunched-over great blue heron stands immobile and almost invisible against the shoreline. Sometimes it stalks through shallow water in exaggerated slow motion. Suddenly its coiled neck strikes forward. Its stiletto bill disappears into the water and emerges with dinner.

However, these stately wading birds are not always so eFISHient. Once we watched when a great blue failed to get his fish. He turned suddenly, dashed into a nearby prairie dog village, grabbed a baby prairie dog, and swallowed it whole. In 1840, John James Audubon wrote of a great blue who captured a fish so large it dragged the heron for several yards: "When, after a severe struggle, the heron

disengaged itself, it appeared quite overcome, and stood still near the shore, his head turned from the sea, as if afraid to try another such experiment" (*North American Birds*).

Usually a heron seizes a fish crosswise and then tosses it into the air, catching it lengthwise so it slips easily down the bird's long throat. If the fish is too large to manipulate, the heron may bash it against the water or take it ashore to kill it.

A few great blue herons overwinter in Colorado near open water, but most head south. They return in late February and March, when they begin repairing old nests made from sticks and twigs. They usually return to the same colony each year. Many heronries have been used for decades. Watch for courtship and mating antics on the nests in April. In late April up to five pale blue eggs are laid at intervals of several days. By May the adults are noisily rearing young in rookeries that can number over a hundred birds. One cottonwood tree may hold ten or more bulky nests.

Both parents share nest building, incubation, and child rearing. They take turns guarding the nest and hunting for fish, frogs, snakes, crustaceans, and other tidbits that they regurgitate into the chick's beak. The adults raise their plumes and arch their necks in an elaborate greeting ceremony on returning to the nest.

Mortality for chicks is high. Adults will abandon nests if sufficiently disturbed by humans, dogs, or predators. Birders can help by watching from a distance through binoculars. Great blues and other herons also suffer from habitat destruction, as development frequently swamps their swampy homes.

Other birds that may nest in great-blue heronries include black-crowned night herons, double-crested cormorants, great egrets, and snowy egrets.

Where To Go

Most rookeries are in mature cottonwood stands along streams, rivers, ponds, and shallow reservoirs, usually below 8,000 feet.

🦆 Confluence Park, Delta.

🦆 La Garita Creek Riparian Demonstration Area, near Alamosa.

🦆 Barr Lake State Park northeast of Denver.

🦆 Chatfield State Park, south of Denver (this heronry has been used since about 1900).

🦆 John Martin Reservoir State Wildlife Area, east of La Junta.

🦆 Empire Reservoir, west of Fort Morgan.

THE LARK BUNTING: OUR FAIR WEATHER STATE BIRD

Most Coloradans have never encountered our state bird because it seldom ventures into the cities or into the mountains. It's a fair weather friend, arriving in the state each year in late April and leaving by mid-September before blizzards blanket its shortgrass prairie home.

Why, then, did Colorado designate a half-time eastern effete arriviste as the official state bird? It was primarily because Roy Langdon of Fort Collins fought for its adoption in the early 1930s and then packed the legislative galleries with 121 high school students on the day of debate. How could brave legislators possibly vote for the bluebird or the meadowlark or the dodo (nominated by a Denver newsman) in the face of a multitude of teenagers cheering for the bunting, a middling-sized member of the Fringillidae family and related to finches and sparrows?

Langdon won out in a three-way battle that also included Charles Hutchins of Boulder, who whistled the mating song of the bluebird in support of his candidate, and Katherine Craig, state superintendent of schools, who was armed with 41,504 schoolchildren's votes for the meadowlark.

On April 29, 1939, just as the birds were staking out their territories, Gov. Billy Adams signed a bill making *Calamospiza melanocorys* the state bird. Lest you think the mountainous part of the state has been neglected, consider what Denver ornithologist Hugh Kingery points out: Our state flower, the blue columbine, grows only in the mountains, so "between the state bird and the state flower, we cover the entire state."

In May large flocks of twenty to forty lark buntings may be seen on the plains. Kingery estimates that there is at least one pair per acre at Pawnee National Grassland, and on May 18, 1968, he tallied a grand total of 1,167 individuals. He

LARK BUNTING
AND YUCCA

frequently sees 500 or more during a day of bunting watching. However, as the shortgrass prairie disappears, losing out to urban expansion and agriculture, the buntings are declining. The Colorado Bird Observatory reports their numbers have decreased by 53 percent over twenty-four years of observation.

The male lark bunting is about 7 inches long, the size of a mountain bluebird. His summer coat is glossy black with broad white wing patches and white edging on the wings, under the tail, and on the outer tail feathers. The comparatively drab female is a streaked gray-brown with buff wing patches. In winter males lose their elegant attire and resemble their mates in color and markings.

In spring this nondescript female elicits a torrent of whistles and trills from the flashy male, who sometimes sings from the tip of a weed stalk, sometimes from a fence post, and most often as he ascends and descends in rapturous courtship flights. When he was researching his M.A. thesis in 1981, wildlife photographer Bill Ervin discovered a surprising fact that goes against traditional bird lore: "The windier it is, the longer the song and display," he found. Usually birders have low expectations on windy days because birds (other than hawks) tend to hunker down and seek protection. "But," said Ervin, "conventional wisdom doesn't hang together on the prairie." And so, the lark bunting uses the wind to save energy by orienting into it. Consequently, on windy days the bunting has a shorter ascent but a much longer glide during which he sings longer than on a calm day. There is nothing on the prairie to block the sound so "downwind you can hear it for miles." Ervin said that the ideal wind speed is 15 to 20 miles per hour and that song-flights are most frequent in morning.

In June the buntings build soft nests of grasses, rootlets, and weeds in depressions in the ground under a protective clump of weeds or under a shrub or cactus, where the female lays four to five pale blue eggs. Gregarious buntings may nest within 100 feet of each other. If a bird erupts almost from under foot, you may have found its artfully hidden nest.

The young are fed grasshoppers, other insects, weed seeds, and grain by both parents. When daylight hours grow short, the entire family migrates south, deserting Colorado for southern California, Nevada, Arizona, New Mexico, Texas, and Mexico. Undoubtedly, they carry on their official business there, promoting the beauties of Colorado to other feathered transients.

Where To Go

🦆 Pawnee National Grassland, northeast of Greeley.
🦆 Barr Lake State Park, northeast of Denver.
🦆 Bonny State Recreation Area, north of Burlington.
🦆 Comanche National Grassland, south of La Junta.
🦆 Along back country roads in eastern plains, especially along U.S. 36 from Byers to Idalia.

VANISHING MIGRANTS?

You hear the same complaint everywhere: The spring songbird migration isn't what it used to be. Bird-watchers describe times, long ago, when you could expect to see a dozen species of warblers in a single day, when there was a warbler on every tree branch. Are migrating songbirds disappearing from Colorado, or is nostalgia overcoming reason?

In *Where Have all the Birds Gone?* Princeton biologist John Terborgh documents a frightening decline in nesting populations of neotropical migrants (songbirds that winter in the tropics and nest in the northern temperate zone) along the Eastern Seaboard. He attributes the decline mainly to fragmentation of nesting habitat in the North rather than to destruction of rain forests in the South. In fact, a long-term study of breeding birds in Great Smoky Mountains National Park, where nesting habitat has remained unfragmented, showed little change in nesting populations from the late 1940s to the mid-1980s.

Populations of deciduous forest nesting species, including red-eyed vireos, scarlet tanagers, and ovenbirds, have plummeted in areas where large tracts of deciduous forest have been broken up into smaller tracts. These species may fare poorly in fragmented forests because they have not evolved defenses against forest-edge predators, such as raccoons, jays, and crows, or against brood parasites (birds that dump their eggs in other birds' nests), such as brown-headed cowbirds. In urbanized portions of Delaware, Maryland, New Jersey, and New York, many forest-nesting species have vanished completely.

The story is somewhat different in the Rocky Mountain region. Available studies, though incomplete, indicate that populations of most neotropical migrants have remained stable in the Rockies during the past thirty years.

Since 1966, the U.S. Fish and Wildlife Service has sponsored a continent-wide breeding bird survey (BBS). Volunteers drive 24.5-mile survey routes each spring, stopping every .5 miles to watch and listen for three minutes. According to BBS data, the following species showed "statistically significant" changes (based on BBS criteria) in Colorado breeding populations from 1966 to 1994:

❦ Increasing populations: broad-tailed hummingbird, western kingbird, cliff swallow, barn swallow, mountain bluebird, black-headed grosbeak, common grackle, brown-headed cowbird.

❦ Decreasing populations: northern mockingbird, Brewer's sparrow, lark bunting, western meadowlark.

The increasers include species that nest on bridges, barns, or other human structures (cliff swallow, barn swallow, and mountain bluebird) and species that thrive around human settlements (western kingbird, common grackle, and brown-headed cowbird). All of the decreasers nest in grasslands or shrublands, where expanding agriculture probably has encroached on nesting habitat.

The relative stability of neotropical migrant nesting populations in the central Rockies, compared to populations in the Eastern Seaboard, probably stems from two factors. First, nesting habitats in our region are less fragmented than habitats in the more heavily populated eastern United States. Second, few of our breeding species winter in tropical rain forests, and only a handful fly as far south as the Amazon Basin, where rain forest destruction is proceeding most rapidly.

The Breeding Bird Survey data, though our best source of information, are hardly the last word on Colorado's nesting songbird populations. There are not enough breeding bird survey routes in Colorado (only about one hundred in 1997) to adequately sample all, or even a majority, of our neotropical migrants. There have not been enough observations of most rare or hard to find species to draw conclusions about their population status. More comprehensive breeding bird studies will be needed to determine what is really happening to our songbirds.

Local surveys indicate that several other species that nest in Colorado and migrate to the tropics are in jeopardy. American bitterns, northern harriers, burrowing owls, red-headed woodpeckers, and brown thrashers have disappeared from large areas of the state. Piping plovers, which nest in the Platte and Arkansas river drainages, have been placed on the Federal Endangered Species List. As urbanization of Colorado continues and more wild habitats are compromised, more species will become threatened or endangered.

If you are experienced at identifying birds both by sight and sound and would like to participate in the North American Breeding Bird Survey, write regional representative Hugh Kingery, P.O. Box 584, Franktown, CO 80116.

Where To Go

The following places are particularly good for seeing neotropical migrants, especially warblers:

- Yampa River State Wildlife Area, Hayden.
- Escalante State Wildlife Area, Delta.
- Billy Creek State Wildlife Area, north of Ouray.
- Boulder Mountain Park, Gregory and Skunk Canyons.
- Wheat Ridge Greenbelt.
- Pueblo Greenway.
- Crow Valley Campground, Pawnee National Grassland, northeast of Greeley.
- Cottonwood and Carrizo Canyons, Comanche National Grassland, south of La Junta.
- Bonny Reservoir, north of Burlington.

For more places to go, see "Cottonwood-Willow Woodlands" in April.

PADDING ALONG WITH PORCUPINES

Young porcupines enter the world with their eyes open. Within a few hours they're able to crawl out of the den—under a log, shrub, or rock—and follow their mother off into the forest.

During their first few weeks of life, the young (usually one per female) feed on their mother's milk and on the more palatable items in the forest: flowers and flower stems, willow catkins, mushrooms, and pond lilies. Many of these food items are at their peak in both succulence and abundance in late spring, when baby porcupines are born. Tree-climbing lessons begin early, and by the age of six weeks most youngsters can scramble up aspen and conifer trunks behind their mothers, using their long claws and padded feet for gripping and their stout tails for anchoring. Babies stay with their mothers for only a few months, going their separate ways in late summer or early fall.

Porcupines spend most of the daylight hours roosting in a tree or in a secluded den. At night they follow set routes to favored feeding areas. The inner bark of conifers and deciduous trees makes up a major portion of their diet, but a porcupine cannot subsist on bark alone. Though porcupines remain active throughout the winter, they lose weight and must fatten up on herbs, mushrooms, and other delicacies each spring to make it through the year.

Watch for porcupines and listen for their childlike wails in coniferous forests throughout Colorado and in riparian woodlands in the western valleys and on the eastern plains. Porcupines typically occupy home ranges of less than 100 acres, so once you find one's haunts, you can return time and again to observe its behavior. Areas of stripped bark dripping with sap indicate recent feeding activity. The scats are cylindrical and often filled with bark and berries.

We like to watch from a discreet distance as porcupines make their evening rounds. With their well-armored bodies, they have little fear of predators, including us. They move slowly and purposefully through the woods, sniffing their way from tree to tree, stopping every now and then to nibble on a mushroom or wildflower. Theirs is a calming presence that helps us to slow down and appreciate the sights, smells, and sounds of the forest.

SPRINGTIME BLUES

Mud puddles in May attract some of our smallest but brightest butterflies, the "little blues," which are about the same size, shade, and shape as two fallen petals of blue flax. These butterflies probe the mud for minerals with a long proboscis, a tube curled up against the face that can be unfurled and used like a drinking straw.

Lepidopterists (people who study butterflies) call this sipping behavior, which is common to many butterfly species, "puddling." Sometimes we find so many little blues at stream crossings that by waving our arms, we can direct their movements like a conductor with an orchestra.

In *The Audubon Society Field Guide to North American Butterflies,* Robert Pyle devotes sixteen pages to photos of the various species of this group and look-alikes. The little blues, collectively called the "Polyommatinae blues," are a subfamily of the Lycaenidae. Sixteen species regularly breed in Colorado, including the colorful orange-bordered blues, dotted blues, emerald-studded blues, greenish-blues, spring azures, and silvery blues (the first to emerge in spring). The Xerces Society, devoted to the conservation of invertebrates and their habitats, is named in honor of the Xerces blue, which became extinct in 1943 when its last stronghold fell to a military facility near San Francisco.

Vladimir Nabokov, a famous lepidopterist as well as author, studied the mountain blues. In his novel, *Lolita,* he writes of the main character's "fine, downy limbs"—a phrase taken from a technical description of the butterflies.

Unless you look closely, the blues look very much alike. The upper side of the male's wings are a shimmering blue with iridescent overtones of lilac, silver, and green, depending on species. The underside of the wings is grayish and patterned with dots and sometimes with orange bands or accents. The pattern of dots along the wing margin distinguishes the various species. The drabber females are usually brownish above and grayish below. One characteristic of all members of this subfamily is the four-branched radial vein in the forewing.

Polyommatinae caterpillars feed mostly on members of the pea and buckwheat families, with lupine a favorite for many species. Some caterpillars in the Lycaenidae family are "milked" by ants for honeydew, a sugary waste product secreted from their bodies.

Where To Go

Look for little blues at mud puddles and stream crossings and in fields of lupine, vetch, or alfalfa, throughout the state. Various species occur from spring through late summer. See the distribution maps in the back of Clifford Ferris and F. Martin Brown's *Butterflies of the Rocky Mountain States* for detailed location information.

MAY EVENTS

MAMMALS

🦨 Spotted skunks, striped skunks, Colorado chipmunks, and white-tailed deer are born in May or June.

🦨 Short-tailed weasels breed in May or June, but because of delayed implantation, young are not born until the following April or May.

🦨 Abert's squirrels engage in mating bouts.

🦨 Female black bears and their cubs emerge from dens.

BIRDS

🦨 Blue grouse "drum" and display throughout coniferous forests, starting in late April.

🦨 Many species of birds mate and nest.

🦨 Migration and bird song reach peak.

🦨 Great horned owl young fledge.

OTHER CRITTERS

🦨 Cecropia and polyphemous moths hatch from cocoons spun on deciduous trees the previous fall.

🦨 Miller moths pass through on their way to mountain breeding areas; sometimes huge irruptions occur.

🦨 Tent caterpillars emerge from their cobwebby tents.

PLANTS

🦨 Orchids, milk vetches, locoweeds, wild clematis, and pink-flowering cacti begin to bloom.

🦨 Wild asparagus tempts us to nibble.

🦨 Conifers release great clouds of golden pollen in late May and throughout June.

🦨 Lilacs and fruit trees blossom in urban areas.

IN THE SKY

❄ "Moon of Budding Plants" (Ojibwa).

❄ The Eta Aquarid meteors peak around May 3.

❄ May Day (May 1) traditionally marked the approximate halfway point between the Vernal Equinox and the Summer Solstice and celebrates the blossoming of flowers and the arrival of warm days.

❄ The pentagon-shaped constellation Auriga (the charioteer), though not particularly well known, is prominent in the low northwestern sky around 9:00 P.M. MDT. The first-magnitude star Capella is actually a binary system with the two suns orbiting around a common center of mass. They complete one orbit in 104 days.

May

The greening tundra on Uncompahgre Peak (elev. 14,309) in the San Juan Mountains.
(Photo by Glenn Cushman.)

6

June

Flitting white-fire insects!

Wandering small-fire beasts!

Wave little stars about my bed!

Weave little stars into my sleep!

—OJIBWA

FIREFLIES CAN TURN a midsummer night to magic. But then, the entire month of June is magic. Wildflowers burgeon in the grasslands early in the month and on the tundra by month's end. Waterfalls, swollen with spring runoff, put on their most impressive show of the year, and tiny dippers nest behind rainbows in the spray.

June can be a month of delightful paradox as nature confounds our preconceived ideas. For instance, some "sea birds," such as white pelicans, arrive to nest on island havens in inland Colorado, and one owl, the burrowing owl, nests in a hole in the ground.

June is also the month for babies. Aspen trees become condo dwellings for a multitude of bird species and their fledglings. Young badgers emerge from dens in the grasslands at about the time babies are born to pronghorns, bighorn sheep, elk, and deer. A truly magic moment is to find a dappled fawn blending into shadows on the grass.

June's magic show is marred, however, by a disappearing trick. Amphibians are vanishing, and no one knows why.

JUNE WEATHER

	Grand Junction (4,824 ft.)	Steamboat Springs (6,760 ft.)	Alamosa (7,536 ft.)	Berthoud Pass (11,310 ft.)	Denver (5,282 ft.)	Lamar (3,620 ft.)
Ave. high (°F)	88	75	78	54	81	88
Ave. low (°F)	57	36	41	32	52	58
Max. high (°F)	105	96	95	70	104	108
Min. low (°F)	34	20	24	11	30	36
Ave. prec. (in.)	0.50	1.52	0.67	2.23	1.79	2.19
Max. prec. (in.)	2.07	4.31	2.58	5.16	4.69	7.54
Ave. snow (in.)	0.0	0.1	0.0	11.8	0.0	0.0
Max. snow (in.)	0.0	5.6	0.2	44.0	0.3	0.0

Eastern Colorado's tornado season begins as violent thunderstorms, fueled by the mixing of warm, moist Gulf air and cold mountain air, build up over the sun-baked foothills and plains. On June 3, 1981, three tornadoes touched down in the Denver area, destroying eighty-seven homes in Thornton. A twister that blew through southeastern Colorado in 1977 produced estimated winds of 260 miles per hour. A June 13, 1984, thunderstorm dumped hailstones as large as grapefruits on Denver, causing a half billion dollars worth of damage. Colorado lies on the western edge of the world's most active thunderstorm belt. The high peaks of the Sangre de Cristo mountains receive more than one hundred thunderstorms per year.

See "Colorado Climate Summary" (p. 1) for information on averages, extremes, and sources.

june ecosystem

A Sea of Grass

If spring breaks just right—if rains come in time, if summer heat waves don't arrive too soon, and if June thunderstorms bring enough moisture to keep things growing—Colorado's grasslands become a tapestry of color. Thunderheads billow up over rolling green hills and chalk cliffs. Magenta-colored locoweeds, lavender phlox, and yellow evening-primroses burst into bloom. Golden eagles and prairie falcons soar overhead. In the evening, rainbows frame the darkening sky, and sunlight reflects off the receding clouds, setting the grasses aglow.

For ten months of the year the shortgrass prairie's dominant grasses, blue grama

Shortgrass prairie at Cottonwood Canyon in Comanche National Grassland.

and buffalograss, lie dormant. In the dry, windy climate, these grasses grow only a few inches high, while their root systems extend 6 feet or more underground, drawing minerals and precious water from the soil. With the arrival of the spring rains and the first extended stretches of warm weather, the grasses spring to life.

Miracles unfold. Inside the bell-shaped, creamy white flowers of the yucca plant (*Yucca glauca*), a small gray moth prepares to raise her family. She pierces the flower's ovary with her sharp ovipositer and lays an egg inside. Then she takes a wad of pollen from behind her head and stuffs it down the flower's style. The fertilized ovary will produce hundreds of seeds to feed her young. No other insect can pollinate yucca flowers. No other flower can support pronuba moth larvae. Should pronuba moths disappear, so would the yuccas. The prairie would change irrevocably, for yuccas act as soil stabilizers that help other colonizing plants gain a foothold on barren ground and sand hills.

Nearby a scarab dung beetle rolls a marble-sized ball of dung across the gravelly soil and over tufts of grama grass. The female beetle digs a hole and deposits the dung, which contains her eggs, just below the ground surface. The dung also contains grama grass seeds that will take advantage of their nitrogen-rich environment to germinate. In experiments conducted on an indoor prairie at the University of Wyoming, only those blue grama seeds that had been rolled up and planted by scarab dung beetles managed to sprout and grow.

A spadefoot toad sleeps several feet underground. When she hears thunder rumbling overhead, she digs her way back up to the surface to search for a mate. Puddles of standing water provide the perfect nursery for her eggs, which soon hatch into tiny tadpoles.

A western horned lizard follows a scent trail from one harvester ant colony to another. At each colony it stops long enough to lap up a few juicy ants, but not long enough to trigger a mass uprising among the harvester community. It stops from time to time to rest, disappearing into its surroundings as it crouches motionless on the pebbly ground.

A mountain plover sits patiently on her nest, a shallow scrape lined with a few pieces of grass and cow dung. A hundred yards away, her mate huddles over a pair of downy chicks who have just fought their way free of a second clutch of eggs that he has incubated for four weeks. A badger shuffles across the prairie. The male plover races away from the hatchlings, dragging a wing, running in circles, jerking spasmodically. The badger, distracted from the baby birds, follows for a short distance and then continues on its way.

Shortgrass prairie covers most of eastern Colorado. In a smattering of relatively moist areas where annual precipitation exceeds 14 inches, it gives way to midgrass prairie, dominated by wheatgrasses, needle-and-thread grasses, little bluestem, and side-oats grama, and to tallgrass prairie, dominated by big bluestem, Indiangrass, switchgrass, and prairie cordgrass. Scattered throughout the grasslands are small groves of stunted ponderosa pines and junipers, usually growing on rocky outcrops or escarpments. A limber pine woodland growing near the Pawnee Buttes may be a remnant of a much more extensive forest that covered much of eastern Colorado during the last glacial period.

Although much of Colorado's shortgrass, midgrass, and tallgrass prairies have been plowed under or grazed into oblivion, many relatively natural areas remain, if you are willing to accept cattle as a reasonable substitute for bison. On a summer evening, when coyotes howl and pronghorns stand silhouetted against the fiery sky, it's easy to appreciate nineteenth-century artist George Catlin's description of the shortgrass prairie as a place of ". . . soul melting scenery . . . where heaven sheds its purest light and lends its richest tints."

Where To Go

⌘ Pawnee National Grassland, northeast of Greeley.
⌘ Beecher Island Battle Ground, south of Wray.
⌘ South Republican River State Wildlife Area, north of Burlington.
⌘ Two Buttes Reservoir, north of Springfield.
⌘ Comanche National Grassland, south of La Junta.

MILKWEEDS

The strong perfume of showy milkweed (*Asclepias speciosa*) smells like lilacs or jasmine. Nineteenth-century settlers collected the morning dew from this plant's pink and white, ball-shaped flowers and spread it on their pancakes. They also rubbed the white sap on their skin to remove warts. Plains Indians ate the young shoots, flowers, buds, and immature green fruit pods of this and several other species of milkweed. Some of the Omahas and Pawnees referred to cabbage as "white man's milkweed." Beware, however, if you decide to sample milkweed: Some milkweeds are quite poisonous, and even "edible" species contain toxins and should be boiled several times, changing the water, before eating.

Monarch butterflies, which lay their eggs on milkweeds, use the plant's toxicity to their advantage. The cardiac glysocides, resinoids, and alkaloids ingested by monarch caterpillars render them unpalatable to birds. When they hatch into adults, they retain these toxins in their system.

About a dozen different milkweeds bloom in Colorado during spring and summer. Dwarf milkweed (*A. asperula*) grows only 3 inches high and is easily overlooked in grasslands and coniferous woodlands east of the Continental Divide. Adobe milkweed (*A. cryptoseras*), with its cream-colored petals crowned with purple hoods, is one of the showiest early spring flowers in western valleys. Showy milkweed grows 3 to 4 feet tall along fencerows and irrigation ditches at lower elevations throughout the state.

Milkweed flowers resemble no others. Often the petals point downward, away from the flower center. Between the five petals and the five stamens lies a whorl of five united, petallike parts, known as a corona. Each segment of the corona is called a hood; in many species these hoods support protruding hornlike structures. The stamens are united to the style, and the pollen sacs are embedded in the style. To remove them, an insect has to catch the spines of its feet on threadlike structures, called translators, that connect the pollen sacs. When the insect takes off, it yanks the pollen sac free, sometimes losing a leg in the process. In *Wildflowers of the Western Plains*, Zoe Kirkpatrick writes that "a milkweed flower is clearly an unusual-looking creation, with a center full of fusion and confusion, but once learned, never forgotten."

EARLY SUMMER WILDFLOWER SAMPLER

COMMON NAME	SCIENTIFIC NAME	FAMILY	HABITAT
Western Valleys (4,000–7,500 feet)			
PRINCE'S PLUME	*Stanleya* spp.	Mustard	Adobe flats
LUPINE	*Lupinus* spp.	Pea	Throughout
AMERICAN VETCH	*Vicia americana*	Pea	Meadows
SCORPION WEED	*Phacelia heterophylla*	Waterleaf	Meadows and open ground
WILD ROSE	*Rosa* spp.	Rose	Throughout
PAINTBRUSH	*Castilleja* spp.	Figwort	Throughout
PENSTEMON BARBATUS	*Penstemon barbatus*	Figwort	Rocky canyonsides
PENSTEMON STRICTUS	*Penstemon strictus*	Figwort	Meadows and sagebrush
Mountain Forests and Meadows (7,500–11,000 feet)			
HEART-LEAVED ARNICA	*Arnica cordifolia*	Sunflower	Moist, shady areas
CHIMING BELLS	*Mertensia* spp.	Borage	Moist areas
LODGEPOLE LUPINE	*Lupinus argenteus*	Pea	Meadows and open woods
WILD GERANIUM	*Geranium* spp.	Geranium	Dry meadows
SPOTTED CORALROOT ORCHID	*Corallorhiza maculata*	Orchid	Conifers and aspens
SHOOTING STAR	*Dodecatheon pulchellum*	Primrose	Shady, wet places
PAINTBRUSH	*Castilleja* spp.	Figwort	Throughout
MOUNTAIN BLUE VIOLET	*Viola adunca*	Violet	Meadows and aspen groves
Tundra (above 11,000 feet)			
ALPINE FORGET-ME-NOT	*Eritrichum aretioides*	Borage	Dry meadows
WALLFLOWER	*Erysimum capitatum*	Mustard	Dry meadows
WILD CANDYTUFT	*Noccaea montana*	Mustard	Dry meadows
ALPINE CAMPION	*Gastrolychnis* spp.	Pink	Meadows
AVALANCHE LILY	*Erythronium grandiflorum*	Lily	Melting snowbanks
ALPINE PHLOX	*Phlox* spp.	Phlox	Meadows
ALPINE PRIMROSE	*Primula angustifolia*	Primrose	Meadows
SNOW BUTTERCUP	*Ranunculus adoneus*	Buttercup	Melting snowbanks
Eastern Foothills and Plains (3,600–7,500 feet)			
SHOWY MILKWEED	*Asclepias speciosa*	Milkweed	Moist meadows
BLANKET FLOWER	*Gaillardia* spp.	Sunflower	Throughout
PRINCE'S PLUME	*Stanleya* spp.	Mustard	Adobe flats
PRICKLY PEAR CACTUS	*Opuntia* spp.	Cactus	Arid grasslands
SPIDERWORT	*Tradescantia occidentalis*	Spiderwort	Gravelly areas
PURPLE PRAIRIE CLOVER	*Dalea purpurea*	Pea	Grasslands
WHITE LARKSPUR	*Delphinium virescens*	Hellebore	Dry hillsides
BLUE FLAX	*Adenolinum lewisii*	Flax	Arid grasslands
PRICKLY POPPY	*Argemone polyanthemos*	Poppy	Grasslands

PELICANS ON THE PRAIRIE

Fifty years ago a white pelican in Colorado would have been something to write home about. Now these graceful waterbirds seem common on the eastern plains, where they skim in tight formation over lakes and reservoirs and soar high above the prairie.

White pelicans breed on predator-free islands in the center of large lakes or reservoirs. The first Colorado breeding colony began nesting on an island in Riverside Reservoir, east of Greeley, in 1962. Now 500 to 1,000 pairs breed there each year. A second colony began nesting at Antero Reservoir in South Park in 1990, and a third colony became established in North Park in 1991.

However, you don't have to drive to these sites to see white pelicans. Nearly every medium to large reservoir on the eastern plains supports a summer population, and a few wanderers appear along the Colorado and Gunnison Rivers each year. Many of these pelicans are one-year-olds not yet ready to breed. Others are adults who have flown 50 miles or more from their breeding grounds to catch fish.

White pelicans often fish cooperatively, gathering into tight lines to herd or

White pelican.

encircle their prey. When they dip their bills and open their mouths, up to 4 gallons of water flow into their expandable pouches. The pelicans then lift their heads, empty the water from their pouches, and swallow the fish in one gulp. When adults return to the nesting colony, the young stick their long bills down the parents' throats, stimulating the adults to regurgitate bits of fish.

With a wingspan of 9 feet or more and weighing in at 10 to 17 pounds, white pelicans dwarf all other Colorado birds, including bald eagles. Although they often fly in V-formation, like ducks and geese, their long, lazy wing flaps and their habit of flapping and gliding in unison easily distinguish them from other waterbirds.

Only about fifteen colonies totaling about thirty-five thousand birds remain in the world. In the past, DDT poisoning endangered white pelican populations. Today, accidental shooting and nest disturbance by humans probably pose the greatest threats. When a boat approaches a nesting colony, the adults often take flight, exposing the young to sunstroke or predation by gulls.

Where To Go

🦆 Antero Reservoir, south of Fairplay.

🦆 Russell Lakes State Wildlife Area, near Saguache.

🦆 Barr Lake State Park, northeast of Denver.

🦆 Riverside Reservoir, east of Greeley. Restricted access trail provides distant view of nesting colony.

🦆 Adobe Creek Reservoir State Wildlife Area, near Las Animas.

🦆 Bonny Reservoir State Wildlife Area, north of Burlington.

BURROWING OWLS

When the first extended heat waves bake lowland prairies and shrublands, young burrowing owls begin to appear above ground. During the relatively cool mornings and evenings, they stand around on the burrow mound waiting for their parents to bring them bits of grasshopper, beetle, mouse, or vole. From time to time they hiss and rasp, begging for food, or twist their heads around nearly upside down to peer at a curious object. They occasionally join in games of chase with young prairie dogs or jostle among themselves over a favored perch. When danger approaches in the form of a coyote or bird-watcher, they scramble back into the burrow.

Burrowing owl.

At about ten weeks of age, the chicks disperse to individual burrows within the rodent colony. They continue to beg for food and follow their parents around until September, when the whole family heads south for Texas, New Mexico, Arizona, or Mexico. Few return to Colorado the following spring: Of 326 adults and juveniles banded at the Rocky Mountain Arsenal in 1990 and 1991, only 28 returned to nest in 1992 or 1993.

No one knows what happens to the owls that don't make it back. Many may succumb to predators or insecticide-laced insects. Some are killed by automobiles. Those that do return face a rapidly fragmenting landscape where successful nesting becomes more difficult each year. As people poison or plow under prairie dog towns and clutter prairie landscapes with highways, shopping malls, and housing developments, Colorado's burrowing owl populations steadily decline. Although burrowing owls are capable of digging their own nest chambers, most depend on previously excavated rodent burrows.

These owls have vanished from all of Boulder County and from large areas of Larimer, Adams, Douglas, El Paso, Montezuma, and Dolores Counties. Once considered common on the eastern plains, they now breed in scattered colonies separated by miles of wheatfields and sanitized (prairie dog–free) grasslands.

In Zuni folklore, burrowing owls acted as high priests who looked out for prairie dogs, controlling the weather and the growth of green plants. In exchange, the prairie dogs provided comfortable and secure homes for the owls. One species could not live without the other, and the chain of all life depended on both. Today burrowing owls remind us of the astonishing variety of wildlife that westering pioneers encountered when they reached the High Plains: badgers, black-footed ferrets, elk, bighorn sheep, grizzly bears, endless herds of bison. Should we lose the owls or their prairie dog companions, along with the previously extirpated species, we will have destroyed the heart and soul of the prairie.

Where To Go

❀ Grand Valley, around Grand Junction.
❀ Sand Wash Basin, near Maybell.
❀ Rocky Mountain Arsenal, near Denver.
❀ Pawnee National Grassland, northeast of Greeley.
❀ Comanche National Grassland, south of La Junta.
❀ John Martin Reservoir State Wildlife Area, east of La Junta.
❀ Bonny Reservoir and South Republican River State Wildlife Areas, north of Burlington.

A TON OF WATER, AN OUNCE OF BIRD

Tons of water crash over the precipice. More than enough, one would think, to crush any living thing below. Yet a gray, wrenlike bird weighing only a few ounces bobs up and down on a rock. It dives into the torrent, walks under the water nibbling tasty insect larvae, and eventually flies through the falls to its nest, a mossy ball perched precariously behind a raging cataract or under a bridge.

Often it stops to sing a bubbling cadenza of melody that seems to imitate the cascade itself. This intrepid bit of fluff is the American dipper, so called for its dipping movement. It's often called affectionately by its older name, water ouzel, and is a bird that stays with us through the winter, making short vertical migrations and singing throughout the year. During its underwater forays it closes a membrane (an action called "nictitating") over its eyes and a flap over its nostrils.

Cinclus mexicanus occurs only in the western United States, ranging from the Aleutian Islands to Panama, from the foothills to the tundra. Each pair of dippers occupies from .5 to 1 mile of territory along a stream. If there is a spirit of waterfalls, a water sprite, it must be the dipper, which raises its young in June when waterfalls are at their rambunctious best.

The sheer grandeur of most waterfalls inspires awe. But frequently it is the small, almost overlooked minutiae, like the dipper, that make the sight memorable. For instance, there was our first sight of Hanging Lake and its waterfalls. After a gorgeous gorge hike up from Glenwood Canyon, we came around a small ledge and found perfection: white ribbons of water falling over pale pink travertine walls into deep blue-green pools surrounded by yellow columbine. As if this were not delight enough, the trail continued up another hundred yards or so to Spouting Rock. Here water gushed from a hole high in the rock wall. Behind the waterfall

Cascade Creek Falls near Lone Eagle Peak. (Photo by Glenn Cushman.)

was a water shrew swimming in a small seepage and a nest of dippers in the grotto-pocked cliff.

In 1894 John Muir wrote the following about what he called "the mountain streams' own darling": "No cañon is too cold for this little bird, none too lonely, provided it be rich in falling water. Find a fall, or cascade, or rushing rapid, anywhere upon a clear stream, and there you will surely find its complementary ouzel flitting about in the spray, diving in foaming eddies, whirling like a leaf among beaten foam bells...."

Where To Go

Waterfalls and dippers are common throughout the mountainous areas and into the foothills. To make your own discoveries, check topographic maps for waterfall symbols. Or visit the spectacular falls listed below.

✗ Bridal Veil Falls. This must be the all-time favorite name for waterfalls, as we have at least three so named in Colorado:

✗ Bridal Veil Falls and Spouting Rock above Hanging Lake in Glenwood Canyon.

✗ Bridal Veil Falls in Rocky Mountain National Park.

✗ Bridal Veil Falls in Telluride (365-foot drop).

✗ Crystal Mill and Falls (one of the most photographed spots in the state) on Crystal River, near Marble.

🎝 North Clear Creek Falls in San Juan Mountains above Santa Marie Reservoir.

🎝 Treasure Falls on U.S. 160 southwest of Wolf Creek Pass. Black swifts nest behind the falls.

🎝 Alberta Falls above Glacier Gorge Junction in Rocky Mountain National Park (farther up the trail are Glacier Falls, Timberline Falls, and Ribbon Falls).

🎝 Boulder Falls in Boulder Canyon.

See pp. 22–24 (January) for additional waterfalls.

CAVITY CONDOS

In June many birds live in an avian equivalent of a high-rise condo. An old aspen trunk may be punctuated with a dozen holes. Once we watched as a pygmy nuthatch, a house wren, and a common flicker all erupted from the same tree. Other cavity-nesting birds found in aspen trees include bluebirds, sapsuckers, woodpeckers, flycatchers, brown creepers, chickadees, swallows, and flammulated owls.

As unlikely as it may seem, some ducks nest in tree cavities. Barrow's goldeneyes favor dead trees standing in high elevation lakes in central and northern Colorado. In the late nineteenth century this duck was considered numerous in Colorado, but by 1965, when Alfred Bailey and Robert Niedrach published *Birds of Colorado,* Barrow's goldeneyes were listed as rare winter stragglers. Now they are on the rise again.

The flamboyant wood duck chooses a hole in a dead tree near a stream for its nest. Bush pilot Norm Hughes reported the first account of wood duck nesting in the state in 1952. He watched as a mother duck coaxed three fledglings to drop from a hole 10 feet up in a dead aspen. The babies bounced off the soft understory debris and toddled off to nearby water.

Most cavity-nesters are not equipped with bills capable of gouging out a hole. Instead, they rely on woodpeckers and sapsuckers, who usually excavate a fresh one each year. These "primary cavity nesters" prefer trees infected with heart rot fungus, because the soft interior is easy to drill.

Many other bird species nest in the aspen canopy, the shrub understory, and on the ground beneath the aspen. Once we even found a hummingbird nest tucked into the bark of a dead aspen. Most nesting birds seem to prefer open, mature stands with abundant understory vegetation as opposed to dense stands of small trees with little undergrowth. In 1973, Utah graduate student Janet Young counted 20 breeding species with 6 pairs per acre in a mature aspen stand, but only 14 species with 3 pairs per acre in a crowded stand. Researchers have also found that shrubs and herbaceous plants, which provide additional cover and food, increase the diversity of bird species.

PRONGHORNS IN THE GRASS

It doesn't seem possible. You're walking along on the prairie, alert and minding your own business, when suddenly you trip over a pronghorn. It's happened to us a couple of times in the Comanche National Grassland. On each occasion a hiking boot was about to descend on the recumbent fawn when the youngster jumped to its feet and sprinted off toward its mother, who pranced back and forth on a nearby rise, snorting her disapproval.

How can a white and tan animal the size of a small collie blend so well into a background of short green grass? It must have something to do with the improbability of the situation. We don't expect to stumble upon a pronghorn lying out in the open, so our eyes don't register its presence. Predators also have trouble locating the motionless and odorless fawns, although clever coyotes may be able to estimate the fawn's location by observing the angle of a bluffing doe's retreat (the does tend to head in the same direction, relative to the fawn and the coyote, when trying to lead the coyote away).

When a coyote or bobcat finds a fawn lying in the grass, mothers respond aggressively. In the Comanche we watched a doe chase a coyote back and forth across the prairie for ten minutes before the predator finally trotted off with its tail between its legs. When the doe returned to the spot she had been defending, three pint-sized pronghorns popped up to greet her.

Pronghorn females wander off by themselves to give birth to their young (usually one or two) from late May to early July. Fawns spend the first two to three

A YOUNG PRONGHORN

123

weeks of their lives "lying out" motionless. Three to six weeks after birth, fawns and their mothers rejoin the summer herd, a "nursery band" consisting mostly of does and their offspring. Younger males form bachelor bands in summer, while older, more dominant males remain solitary.

In the fall does gravitate toward territories of dominant males. Bucks mate with individual does or form small harems on their territories. Mating usually occurs in September and October. In winter all sexes and ages congregate in large herds that roam over the open prairies and shrublands, browsing and grazing on shrubs, forbs, and, occasionally, grasses. Both male and female pronghorn have horns, but the males' horns are significantly larger.

Pronghorns are the only surviving member of the family Antilocaparidae, which is unique to North America. They are more closely related to the European chamois than to the African antelope. They evolved during the Pleistocene, when cheetahs still stalked the North American savannahs. This fact may partially explain the pronghorns' remarkable speed. Over short distances, pronghorns have been clocked at 60 miles per hour. Their leg bones are incredibly strong, and their large fore feet have cartilaginous pads that serve as shock absorbers. Enormous lung capacity and oversized hearts enable them to run for miles without tiring. They can go for days without water.

As many as 50 million pronghorns may have ranged throughout the western United States, western Canada, and northern Mexico prior to European settlement. Today's population stands at around 1 million, with 50,000 to 60,000 in Colorado. Look for pronghorns on the eastern plains, in western valleys, and in mountain valleys from about 3,600 to 9,000 feet.

Where To Go

- Sand Wash Basin, near Maybell.
- Dinosaur National Monument, north of Rangely.
- Kremmling pronghorn viewing site.
- Upper San Luis Valley, Villa Grove area.
- Fort Carson, south of Colorado Springs.
- Pawnee National Grassland, northeast of Greeley.
- Piñon Canyon, southwest of La Junta.
- Comanche National Grassland, south of La Junta.

BADGERS: BULLDOZERS WITH AN ATTITUDE

"Thoroughly misanthropic . . . more antisocial than shy" is how mammalogist David Armstrong describes this member of the weasel (Mustelidae) family (in *Rocky Mountain Mammals*). Although badgers probably get their name from the white stripe or badge on their forehead, the word has come to mean *harass*. However, it's questionable whether the badger was the "harasser" or the "harassee." Until 1850 badgers were persecuted in England, where they were often driven into a barrel and forced to fight a pack of dogs. Dachshunds were specially bred for this "sport."

Many dogs must also have been killed, because short, squat badgers have heavy claws up to 2 inches long, powerful jaws and teeth, and muscular front legs. It's hard for anything else to get a grip on a badger because its loose-fitting hide permits it to turn inside its own skin. Even bears are reluctant to tangle with this fighter that writer John Madson described as "a bowlegged, pigeon-toed doormat that sweeps the ground with its trailing end" (quoted in Les Line, "The Benefits of Badgers," *National Wildlife* [Dec.-Jan. 1996]:20).

> ### Badger, the Folk Hero
>
> Badgers frequently star in American Indian folk tales. In one story Badger is methodically placing stars into constellations when impatient Coyote comes along and flings the remaining stars out at random into the sky, forming the Milky Way. In another story Badger takes pity on Coyote when Coyote loses his skin and gives him an old one of his—which is why Coyote has rough, grizzled fur.
>
> Impressed by the badger's ability to dig quickly out of a den, Hopi and other Pueblo Indians sometimes placed a severed paw near a woman in labor to expedite delivery. A Navajo story honors Badger for tunneling the hole that allowed people to climb into the upper world.

These formidable excavators can vanish from sight after only three minutes of digging. They dig new dens with several openings almost daily except when rearing young or during winter snoozing. This skill enables them to dig down into the burrows of prairie dogs, gophers, ground squirrels, mice, and moles. Badgers in Utah have even been observed plugging up secondary openings before digging into the main entrance of ground squirrel burrows. Opportunistic feeders, they also eat insects and roadkill.

In spite of their irascible reputation, badgers sometimes collaborate with coyotes, who have more acute eyesight and hearing for locating prey. Researcher Steven Minta has observed coyotes waiting at secondary ground squirrel holes while badgers dug out the main entry. By hunting together and covering more escape routes, both badgers and coyotes catch more rodents than they would hunting alone.

After a brief mating season in late summer, badgers go their separate ways. Implantation is delayed so young are not born until late March or April and do not emerge from the den for another six weeks.

Badgers (*Taxidea taxus*) occur throughout the state and prefer open areas. Because they are primarily nocturnal, you are most likely to see them in late afternoon or at dawn. Prairie dog towns are good places to watch. Although badger and prairie dog dens appear somewhat similar, the mound around a prairie dog den is more uniform, whereas the dirt excavated from a badger den is more fanned out and the opening is more elliptical, more "badger shaped."

Where To Go

⅋ Radium State Wildlife Area, near Kremmling.
⅋ Pawnee National Grassland, east of Greeley.
⅋ Piñon Canyon, southwest of La Junta.
⅋ Rocky Mountain Arsenal, near Denver. At this superfund site where aldrin, dieldrin, war gases, and other poisonous substances were once produced, scientists study badgers for dieldrin accumulations in their fat—clues to the health of the ecosystem.

VANISHING AMPHIBIANS

Twenty years ago we were charmed but not surprised to find boreal toads hopping placidly about above timber line. Amphibians were a common component of almost all ecosystems—creatures that had thrived since the age of dinosaurs. But now they are vanishing worldwide, and no one knows why.

Biologists are studying Colorado's boreal toads (formerly called western toads) hoping to find some answers. The immediate cause of some deaths is a bacterium or fungus complex called "red leg." In the past, toads and bacteria existed together with no problem. Then something went wrong. "It seems that the toads' immune system now allows a normally occurring bacteria to cause disease," says John Goettl, the Colorado Division of Wildlife's Boreal Toad Recovery Team Coordinator.

Glacial Relics

North Park in Jackson County is home to several "glacial relics," species such as wood frogs and capshell snails that have survived virtually unchanged since the Pleistocene.

Researchers from Oregon State University recently discovered that ultraviolet-B radiation kills long-toed salamander embryos and suspect that UV-B is a factor in the worldwide amphibian decline.

Goettl and his team are investigating several environmental culprits including ozone depletion with the resultant increase in ultraviolet radiation as well as heavy metal pollution,

The lumpy boreal toad. Note the diagnostic light stripe on its back. (Photo by Glenn Cushman.)

acid rain, destruction of wetlands, habitat fragmentation, and pesticides. Meanwhile they are raising and studying boreal toads and releasing some into the wild. About eight hundred were released in 1995 in Rocky Mountain National Park.

Although boreal toads are on Colorado's endangered species list, they still can be found occasionally in wetlands above 8,500 feet. You can recognize them by a light stripe on their back, running from snout to groin. Usually less than 3.5 inches long, they are gray with dark spots on their chest. Like most toads, their skin is warty. During the breeding season between mid-May and July, the males sometimes chirp softly to attract a mate. If you find these rare toads, notify John Goettl, DOW, 317 W. Prospect St., Fort Collins, CO 80526.

Other amphibians are also declining statewide. "Everything is affected but chorus frogs and bullfrogs," says Goettl. However, it's still possible to see and hear amorous amphibians in Colorado, especially on a June morning when many species are in full voice.

Striped chorus frogs, sometimes called "bubble-gum frogs" because of their inflatable throat patches, begin calling in March and continue sporadically into August. These 1-inch-long inhabitants of wet meadows and ponds range from the plains to the mountains. You're much more likely to hear than to see them as they tend to become silent just when you're in viewing range. If you sit quietly for several minutes, they may resume chorusing. Sometimes they even respond to a tape of frog calls. These meistersingers are advertising their location, hoping to attract a mate.

Bullfrogs are common in wetlands on the plains. Their low, distinctive "b-rumm" resonates in prairie marshes throughout the summer, with calling activity peaking in June or July. According to Geoffrey Hammerson in *Amphibians and Reptiles in Colorado,* they will eat "any animal that can be captured and swallowed, including each other."

Northern leopard frogs, which inhabit marshes and ponds from the plains to the high mountains, call only in early spring but can be seen throughout the summer.

BOREAL TOAD

Hammerson describes their song as "a prolonged snore lasting 2–3 seconds followed by 2–3 series of stuttering croaks each lasting no more than a second."

Wood frogs occur as far north as the Arctic Circle and reach the southwestern extension of their range in Colorado. Although listed as threatened in Colorado, they may be more stable than we think, since they tend to disappear in one pond only to reappear in another.

They breed from mid-May to early June and remain active until September, thriving in north central Colorado between 8,000 and 10,000 feet.

Plains spadefoot toads vocalize throughout the summer and can be heard up to .5 miles away. The "spades" are hard protuberances on the hind feet used for digging burrows. The unusual thing about these toads is that they can lose almost 50 percent of their body water and survive. During the day you can sometimes find them resting under rocks or logs.

Woodhouse's toads frequent the plains and foothills and are often seen in urban areas. They are able to pump up their body by gulping in air—a ploy to prevent them from becoming dinner. Both Woodhouse's and spadefoot toads breed on nights following warm rains.

FIREFLIES

It's a little-known paradox that fireflies—beetles associated with hot, moist lowlands—do occur in the dry, high state of Colorado. But if, on a late June or early July evening you venture out into muggy wetlands at lower elevations, sacrificing a little blood to mosquitoes, you may be rewarded by fireflies twinkling like stars in the air and in the grass.

The larvae, which gladden gardeners by feeding on snails and slugs, glow gently but do not flash like the adults. In *Bagging Big Bugs,* Whitney Cranshaw and Boris Kondratieff say nonluminescent, day-flying adults predominate in the Rocky Mountain region but that luminescent species are expanding their ranges because of irrigation and expanding gallery forests along rivers and streams. When Marc Epstein studied Colorado fireflies in 1978, he found two genera present: *Photuris* and *Photinus.*

Each species of lampyrid beetle has its own unique light signal, which varies in color and timing and is used to find a mate. The family name, Lampyridae, is from the Greek word for *bright.* Males fly several feet off the ground flashing a greenish yellow light at regular intervals, while the females perch on grass, flashing a response with different timing. They continue blinking until they find each other and mate. The warmer the evening, the more rapid the signaling. It's possible to induce flashing in at least one species, *Photinus pyralis,* by blinking a flashlight two seconds after the male has flashed. One entomologist found that a different species of firefly could also mimic *Photinus*—in order to procure dinner.

Firefly light (composed of the substances luciferin, luciferase, and adenosine triphosphate) intrigues scientists because the bioluminescence is produced without significant heat. The glimmer also inspires song writers and storytellers. According to American folklore, the presence of "lightning bugs" foretells good luck or indicates, perhaps, that a visitor will arrive or a marriage take place. The sixteenth-century British scientist Thomas Mouffet was less romantic. He wrote that fireflies "... being drank in wine make the use of lust not only irksome but loathsome ..." (quoted in Evans, *Life on a Little-Known Planet*).

In the Philippines they say fireflies received lanterns as a reward for finding jewels lost by the insect king. Another Philippine story says that fireflies carry fire so mosquitoes can't bite. And don't we wish that were true!

Where To Go

Look in low-lying wetlands and irrigation ditches, mostly in the eastern part of the state.

🦆 Valley View Hot Springs at the north end of San Luis Valley, a small resort without signs or glitz, has the largest known population of fireflies in the state.

🦆 Comanche National Grassland, Picture Canyon, south of Springfield.

🦆 Bonny State Recreation Area north of Burlington, south shore of reservoir.

🦆 Roxborough State Park, near Denver.

🦆 Sawhill and Walden Ponds, in Boulder.

JUNE EVENTS

MAMMALS

❀ Black bears mate in June or July, but implantation is delayed until November.

❀ Little brown bats, weighing 1.5 to 2 grams (about the weight of six aspirin tablets!), are born in late June or early July; big brown bats in late June.

❀ Marmots are usually born in June and appear above ground in July.

❀ Elk, pronghorn, and mule deer young are born.

❀ Bighorn lambing peaks early in June.

BIRDS

❀ White pelicans arrive and begin nesting.

❀ Burrowing owlets appear above ground.

❀ Golden eaglets leave nest.

❀ Common nighthawks perform aerial courtship displays, "booming" as air passes through the wings on their descent.

❀ Dippers nest behind waterfalls, cavity-nesters in aspen groves, and ptarmigan and American pipits on the tundra.

OTHER CRITTERS

❀ Fireflies glimmer in low-elevation wetlands.

❀ Many frog and toad species mate.

PLANTS

❀ Showy milkweeds flower at lower elevations.

❀ Forget-me-nots, moss campion, rockjasmine, and other alpine flowers begin to bloom.

❀ The first blue columbines appear.

❀ Early cherries ripen, and roses bloom in urban gardens.

SPECIAL EVENTS

❀ Waterfalls flow at peak owing to spring runoff.

IN THE SKY

❀ "Rose Moon" (Pawnee).

❀ Summer Solstice, around June 20, is the longest day of the year. In Latin, *solstice* means "the sun stands still."

❀ The appearance of "Scorpius" in the southern sky marks the beginning of summer. Look for the scorpion just above the southern horizon after 9:00 P.M. MDT. The prominent star Antares, a red giant with a diameter of 504 million miles, was known in mythology as "the rival of Mars."

June

Bighorn sheep pose atop Specimen Mountain in Rocky Mountain National Park.

7

July

Ajaja, it is pleasant,

    it is pleasant at last

    the great world

    when it is summer at last.

          —ESKIMO

JULY IS AS vivid as butterflies nectaring from freshly unfurled flowers, as vibrant as grasshoppers grating out a gavotte on their legs. It's as busy as pikas harvesting hay, as pipits feeding their young, as hummingbirds zooming after rivals, as bats flittering through the twilight. It's a month when summer seems telescoped into a frenzy of activity. On the tundra alpine flowers bloom, are pollinated, and set seeds within a few short weeks. In stands of Gambel oak, hairstreak butterflies mate, lay eggs for next year's generation, then die, all in a few days.

But it's also a month for leisure. Mountain goat kids kick up their heels in uncoordinated capers while their mothers lie in the sun. Marmot babies tussle with each other while we human interlopers watch in delight. In July, the world is, indeed, a pleasant place.

	Grand Junction (4,824 ft.)	Steamboat Springs (6,760 ft.)	Alamosa (7,536 ft.)	Berthoud Pass (11,310 ft.)	Denver (5,282 ft.)	Lamar (3,620 ft.)
Ave. high (°F)	94	82	82	62	88	94
Ave. low (°F)	64	42	48	39	59	64
Max. high (°F)	105	97	95	76	104	111
Min. low (°F)	44	25	33	26	43	43
Ave. prec. (in.)	0.65	1.53	1.19	2.45	1.91	2.24
Max. prec. (in.)	1.92	3.57	3.50	5.98	6.41	5.85
Ave. snow (in.)	0.0	0.0	0.0	0.0	0.0	0.0
Max. snow (in.)	0.0	0.0	0.0	0.0	0.0	0.0

During this month of gradually lengthening nights, lowland temperatures can exceed 110°F. The state record high of 114° occurred in Las Animas in 1933 and in Sedgwick in 1954. Strong thunderstorms continue to form over the mountains. On July 31, 1976, a nearly stationary storm dumped an estimated 12 inches of rain in the Estes Park region. Waters in the Big Thompson River Canyon rose more than 10 feet in minutes, killing 139 people. On July 28, 1997, a stalled thunderstorm inundated parts of Fort Collins with up to 13 inches of rain. A mobile home park was swept away and five people were killed in the ensuing flood.

In the high country, mid-summer snowstorms are always possible. Six inches of snow blanketed Mt. Evans on July 4, 1995. The July average high temperature on Pikes Peak summit is 48°F, and the highest temperature ever recorded there is 64°F.

See "Colorado Climate Summary" (p. 1) for information on averages, extremes, and sources.

july ecosystem

The Tundra, Land of Lilliput

In this high, lonely land where no trees grow, diminutive flowers defy the elements to form improbable gardens from late June through August. Parnassian and Melissa blue butterflies probe the flowers for nectar. Marmots, pikas, and chipmunks sun on the rocks and harvest the grasses, flowers, and seeds. Sometimes a vole or shrew scurries beside a riffle. Mountain goats and bighorn sheep graze on the rich vegetation.

In Colorado, tree line usually occurs at about 11,500 feet, though the level where trees stop growing varies depending on local conditions. Tree line signals the passage from a temperate to an Arctic climate, in which winter air temperature rarely rises above freezing and blizzards may occur any time of year. In Rocky Mountain National Park, researchers study tree line as a barometer for long-term climate change. Global warming should cause tree line to creep higher as patchy forests at the edge fill in.

At this elevation, wind and driving snow prune the last outposts of evergreens into bonsailike hedges called krummholz (a German word meaning "crooked wood"). The krummholz seems to migrate, as the leeward side creeps forward while the windward side dies—a vegetative growth method called layering. These tough trees provide shelter for more tender plants, such as Jacob's-ladder, and for nesting white-crowned sparrows and an occasional Wilson's warbler.

Above the krummholz, willow shrubs form low mounds where white-tailed ptarmigan feast on protein-rich willow buds and on the explosion of insects that flourish during the brief but intense alpine summer. Ptarmigan often nest on the ground in the lee of these willows.

American pipits also nest on the ground with only a bit of projecting turf or a small plant for protection. They often burst from the nest just where you're about to tread. Listen for their joyous songs and piercing alarm calls as they spiral skyward.

Tundra plants have evolved unusual stratagems to cope with their harsh environment. By growing low to the ground, they conserve moisture, escape the shearing effect of the wind,

Global Warming

During the hottest days of summer, people sometimes wonder whether our climate is changing. The variability of Colorado's weather (a midsummer cold front can drop the temperature 30 degrees in minutes) obscures gradual, long-term changes in the earth's climate. For example, while global temperatures rose (steadily) during the early 1990s, some Front Range cities experienced several consecutive years of below-average mean daily temperatures.

Scientists at the University of East Anglia in Norwich, England, and the National Climate Data Center in Asheville, North Carolina, used data collected from land stations, ships, and buoys to plot global average surface temperatures from 1850 to 1997. They concluded that 1997 was the warmest year and 1995 the second warmest. The mean global surface temperature climbed about $0.4°F$ per decade from 1975–1998. In December 1995, the Intergovernmental Panel on Climate Change (IPCC) projected an additional $4°F$ global warming by the year 2100. This increase would cause sufficient melting of the polar ice caps to inundate many of our coastal cities. The IPCC report concluded that pollutants, especially warmth-inducing greenhouse gases such as carbon dioxide, Freon, and methane, have contributed to the recent global warming.

Source: Science News, January 13, 1996, 149:23; Science, January 16, 1998, 279:315.

Old-man-of-the-mountain in its tundra habitat. (Photo by Glenn Cushman.)

and spend less energy producing unnecessary mass. They also benefit from a snow blanket during much of the year. Snowlover (*Chionophilia jamesii*), which is endemic to the southern Rocky Mountains, grows *only* where there is winter snow cover.

Moss campion (*Silene acaulis*) and many other tundra plants have deep tap roots that hold the plant in place, store nutrients, and extend down to water. The fuzzy hairs on some plants protect them from dehydration and burning and, at the same time, hold in the heat like a greenhouse. Other plants, such as stonecrop (*Sedum lanceolatum*), produce fleshy, succulent leaves to retain moisture. It's no surprise that alpine plants are perennials. They save time and energy by not starting from scratch each summer. Also, if they fail to reproduce one summer, there's always another chance. Many of them cope with the short growing season by utilizing runners, rhizomes, or other methods of vegetative reproduction rather than seeding. The only annual in the Rocky Mountain alpine region is the minuscule *Koenigia*, a member of the buckwheat family that grows in running water. Look for its red leaves, which are more conspicuous than its .06-inch white flower.

Cushion plants dominate the sections of the alpine region known as fellfields (*fell* is Norse and Gaelic for "rock"). In fellfields, frost has broken rocks into gravel, which is then colonized by plants. Many visitors marvel at "moss" dotting this gritty, exposed ground. However, the plants are true flowering plants with all the normal parts reduced to elfin size.

Mat plants, such as sandwort (*Arenaria obtusiloba*), are similar to cushion plants but are looser and larger and can take root wherever their spreading branches touch ground. Still other plants, such as big-rooted spring beauties (*Claytonia megarhiza*), form rosettes, permitting maximum exposure to light and minimum exposure to the elements. These flowers are aptly named; only 2 to 3 inches across at the top, their roots go down 10 to 15 feet.

If not disturbed, many of these plants live for centuries. Some tundra lichens are used for dating purposes because of their slow growth and great age. Map lichen (*Rhizocarpon geographicum*) grows only .375 inches in diameter during its first thousand years.

Tundra plants evolved to withstand a severe climate. However, they can be killed by repeated trampling or by mountain bicyclists wearing grooves in the vegetation. Motorized vehicles wreak even greater havoc. Horseback routes used since the late 1600s in Rocky Mountain National Park are still visible and will take many more generations to regenerate.

Where To Go

❧ Rocky Mountain National Park, Trail Ridge Road.

❧ Any of the high mountain passes such as Rollins Pass, Loveland Pass, Cottonwood Pass, Hagerman Pass, Cumberland Pass, or Boreas Pass.

❧ Any of the 14,000-foot peaks such as Mount Evans near Denver or Pikes Peak near Colorado Springs.

THE MOST ANCIENT LIVING THING?

It's not easy to designate the oldest living thing. But if you discount clones, such as creosote bushes and aspen, on the basis that the original individual dies even though genetically identical offspring continue to spread from the initial shoot, then bristlecone pines wear the crown.

When the pyramids were built, some bristlecones that still produce viable seeds were, themselves, seedlings. They thrive best under adverse conditions and attain the greatest age just below timber line, where scouring winds contort them into

Contorted bristlecone pines at Windy Gap, near Hoosier Pass in central Colorado. (Photo by Glenn Cushman.)

grotesquely beautiful shapes, reminiscent of a Walt Disney tree with gnarled trunk, grasping arms, and gargoyle face.

The oldest bristlecones (*Pinus longaeva*) grow on Wheeler Peak in Nevada and the White Mountains of California. "Methuselah," the current patriarch, is more than 4,600 years old. Rocky Mountain bristlecones (*P. aristata*) are closely related but are younger, usually less than 1,600 years old. However, a 2,435-year-old specimen was discovered in 1992 in South Park, near Fairplay. The tree, believed to be the oldest in Colorado, is 30 feet tall, 4 feet in diameter, and grows at an elevation of about 11,000 feet.

At high elevations, bristlecones grow slowly, adding less than an inch to their girth each century. Slow, but sturdy and stalwart. The wood is very dense and resinous, making it resistant to disease and decay. At lower elevations, the trees grow more quickly but die sooner.

Because of their longevity, bristlecones provide a calendar for prehistoric times. Scientists count the growth rings in a core sample and compare the pattern with wood from prehistoric dwellings to establish accurate dates. The pattern also reveals information on the climate of past ages, as narrow rings indicate drought and wide rings indicate wet years.

Bristlecones are easily recognized by the flecks of white resin that dust the branches like dandruff. The distinctive scales on the cone are each tipped with a bristle, hence the name. Another name for the tree is "foxtail," because the inch-long needles, which may live as long as thirty-eight years, are densely arranged in bunches of five at the end of the branch, giving it the look of a fox's tail. Limber pines resemble bristlecones and often grow in association with them. However, limber pines lack the resin flecks and the bristle-tipped cones.

Where To Go

❀ Kenosha Pass, Mt. Sherman, and other areas in the vicinity of South Park.
❀ Windy Ridge Bristlecone Pine Scenic Area, west of Alma.
❀ Independence Pass, west of Twin Lakes.
❀ Mt. Goliath Natural Area on Mt. Evans.

COLUMBINES

On April 4, 1899, the blue columbine (*Aquilegia coerulea*) was designated Colorado's state flower. Twelve years later Arthur J. Fynn composed Colorado's state song, "Where the Columbines Grow," praising the brilliant blue and white flower but forgetting to mention the name of the state! Although he later added a verse lauding Colorado as "the columbine state," the song continued to be controversial but is now largely forgotten.

It's not the petals of the blue columbine that are blue, but the five long, pointed sepals that vary from a deep, purplish blue to white. The five creamy white petals enclose a mass of yellow stamens and extend between the sepals, forming slender spurs behind the flower. Occasionally, both sepals and petals are blue, and sometimes spurless forms occur.

Other Colorado species include dwarf columbine (*A. saximontana*), yellow columbine (*A. micrantha*), and red columbine (*A. elegantula*). These members of the Hellebore family hybridize readily.

The word *Aquilegia* combines the Latin words for *water* and *collect* and refers to the nectar at the base of the spur. This nectar attracts bees and hummingbirds as pollinators. In 1994 botanist Verne Grant reported that seven columbine species had "abandoned" bees for hummingbirds, evolving over the millennia to attract birds more than bees.

Can columbines also attract humans? In *Uses of Plants*, Melvin Gilmore writes that Omaha and Ponca Indians, especially bachelors, made a perfume by chewing the seeds and anointing their clothes with the paste. Pawnee Indians used columbines as both love charm and perfume. After rubbing pulverized seeds into his palm, a man would shake hands with a desired sweetheart, winning her favor. The Pawnee also made an infusion from the seeds to cure fever and headache. Other American Indians made a tea from the roots for diarrhea, coughs, and stomachache and made a paste from the roots to rub on aching joints.

In 1597 British herbalist John Gerard wrote that the seed "beaten to pouder, and given in wine" facilitated labor and was reputed to be good for "stopping of the liver." However, he concluded that this plant was grown chiefly for "the beautie and variable colours of the floures."

Where To Go

Blue or Colorado columbines grow throughout the state from the foothills to the tundra in open forests, aspen groves, and meadows and on talus slopes, reaching their blooming peak in July. The site that inspired Fynn to write our state song was Schinzel Flats near the present-day infamous Summitville Mine.

PAINTBRUSHES

A legend from the Great Plains tells the story of a young man who had a dream vision that he would paint the sunset. After years of frustration, he asked the Great Spirit for help and was given brushes dripping with glowing colors. He captured the brilliance of the last rays of the sun and threw away the brushes. Wherever they landed, they took root and grew into plants flaunting all the colors of the sunset.

From the plains to the tundra various species of paintbrush range from creamy white to yellow to scarlet, with all shades of pink and magenta in between. The inconspicuous greenish-yellow flowers are enclosed and almost hidden in showy bracts, flaming with color. Because these species hybridize readily, you sometimes find both magenta and white on the same plant. Look at the bracts through a hand lens and you will see tiny silver hairs that glisten like diamonds.

As befits such a magic flower, there is an element of the unusual about paint-brushes. Forty-eight of the two hundred species in the genus have evolved to attract hummingbirds in preference to other pollinators, according to botanist Verne Grant. They are also partially parasitic. The roots branch into small rootlets that attach to

MIDSUMMER WILDFLOWER SAMPLER

COMMON NAME	SCIENTIFIC NAME	FAMILY	HABITAT
Western Valleys (4,500–7,500 feet)			
FLEABANE DAISY	*Erigeron* spp.	Sunflower	Throughout
BLANKET-FLOWER	*Gaillardia aristata*	Sunflower	Sagebrush and mountain meadows
SUNFLOWER	*Helianthus nuttallii*	Sunflower	Wet ditches
COMMON SUNFLOWER	*H. annuus*	Sunflower	Roadsides
GOLDEN ASTER	*Heterotheca villosa*	Sunflower	Throughout
SENECIO	*Senecio* spp.	Sunflower	Throughout
GOLDENROD	*Solidago* spp.	Sunflower	Throughout
HORSE MINT	*Monarda fistulosa*	Mint	Streamsides and meadows
Mountain Forests and Meadows (7,500–11,000 feet)			
HEART-LEAVED ARNICA	*Arnica cordifolia*	Sunflower	Moist thickets and woods
BLANKET-FLOWER	*Gaillardia aristata*	Sunflower	Meadows and clearings
GREEN GENTIAN	*Frasera speciosa*	Gentian	Meadows
MONKSHOOD	*Aconitum columbianum*	Hellebore	Moist meadows and forest clearings
COLORADO COLUMBINE	*Aquilegia coerulea*	Hellebore	Aspen groves and forest clearings
FIREWEED	*Chamerion danielsii*	Evening-primrose	Disturbed areas
PARRY PRIMROSE	*Primula parryi*	Primrose	Waterfalls and streams
ELEPHANT HEADS	*Pedicularis groenlandica*	Figwort	Wet meadows and bogs
LOW PENSTEMON	*Penstemon virens*	Figwort	Rocky, gravelly soils
Tundra (above 11,000 feet)			
OLD-MAN-OF-THE-MOUNTAIN	*Rydbergia grandiflora*	Sunflower	Meadows and rocky slopes
CHIMING BELLS	*Mertensia* spp.	Borage	Streamsides and moist meadows
ROSE CROWN	*Clementsia rhodantha*	Stonecrop	Streams and bogs
KING'S CROWN	*Rhodiola integrifolia*	Stonecrop	Moist meadows
DWARF CLOVER	*Trifolium nanum*	Pea	Meadows and rocky slopes
DWARF COLUMBINE	*Aquilegia saximontana*	Hellebore	Cliffs and rocky slopes
ALP LILY	*Lloydia serotina*	Lily	Rock crevices and meadows
ALPINE AVENS	*Acomastylis rossii*	Rose	Hillsides
SNOWBALL SAXIFRAGE	*Micranthes rhomboidea*	Saxifrage	Meadows and rocky slopes
Eastern Foothills and Plains (3,600–7,500 feet)			
CHICORY[a]	*Cichorium intybus*	Sunflower	Roadsides
COMMON SUNFLOWER	*Helianthus annuus*	Sunflower	Roadsides and hillsides
PRAIRIE SUNFLOWER	*Helianthus petiolaris*	Sunflower	Roadsides and hillsides
GOLDEN ASTER	*Heterotheca* spp.	Sunflower	Dry hillsides and fields
PRAIRIE CONEFLOWER	*Ratibida columnifera*	Sunflower	Mesas and hillsides
ROCKY MOUNTAIN BEEPLANT	*Cleome serrulata*	Caper	Sandy soil in disturbed areas
BUSH MORNING GLORY	*Ipomoea leptophylla*	Morning glory	Disturbed soil
COPPER MALLOW	*Sphaeralcea coccinea*	Mallow	Roadsides and dry fields
BLUE VERVAIN	*Verbena hastata*	Vervain	Ditches, marshes, and streambanks

[a]Introduced species.

July

the roots of host plants, robbing them of nourishment. Sagebrush is one of their favorite hosts.

Some American Indians made a decoction from the roots to use as a blood purifier and as a remedy for venereal disease. New Mexico naturalists Bill Dunmire and Gail Tierney have researched plant use by Pueblo Indians and say paintbrushes were most often mixed with other plants to make a red dye for painting deerskins. This dye was also mixed with minerals to make a black paint. The Tewa sometimes ate the blossoms and bathed in a paintbrush solution to cure aches engendered from long outdoor ceremonies.

The term *Castilleja* (the genus name for paintbrush) comes from the name of an eighteenth century Spanish botanist; the plant is in the Scrophulariaceae, or Figwort, family. All *Castilleja* species are native to the Americas, with twenty-four occurring in the Rocky Mountains. Biologist Url Lanham says that Colorado is one of the world's centers of diversity for paintbrushes. A scarlet, narrow-leafed paintbrush, *C. linariaefolia,* is the state flower of Wyoming.

Different species bloom at different elevations from May through August in Colorado. Our favorite is the rosy paintbrush, *C. rhexifolia,* that dominates wet subalpine basins. See the next section, "Subalpine Wildflowers," for a few places where paintbrushes flourish.

SUBALPINE WILDFLOWERS

From July to mid-August, miles and miles of flowers billow in high country breezes. To lose yourself in this expanse of bloom is to feel drugged with happiness. These gardens of delight flourish in wet basins near timber line and are threaded with silvery rivulets and tiny cascades. Look for the flowers mentioned in the table "Midsummer Wildflower Sampler" (p. 141) plus many more and revel in the diversity.

Where To Go

❧ The Flattops, especially Crane Park, northwest of Dotsero.

❧ Red Mountain Pass above Ouray.

❧ Chicago Basin in the Weminuche Wilderness, north of Durango, and other high basins in the San Juan Mountains.

❧ The Rio Grande Valley west of Creede.

❧ Any of the meadows above Crested Butte.

❧ Shrine Pass, just off the summit of Vail Pass.
❧ The meadows below Arapaho Pass in the Indian Peaks Wilderness.
❧ Rocky Mountain National Park.

POLLINATION: YOUR GARDEN OR MINE?

Try this experiment. Sit beside a showy wildflower and count the seconds before a fly, beetle, bee, moth, butterfly, or hummingbird lands on it. The frequency of these visits says a lot about the interdependence of wildflowers and pollinators. Now observe which pollinators visit which flowers. You'll see bumblebees pushing their round heads into the narrow throats of penstemons, flies and beetles clamoring around on the open corollas of roses and buttercups, and hummingbirds hovering over almost anything red.

In *Principles of Pollination Ecology,* K. Faegri and L. van der Pijl describe six basic flower types, each of which has evolved to attract a different group of pollinators (see table, p. 144). Dish or "soup bowl" flowers, such as roses, poppies, and buttercups, attract a host of "unspecialized" insects, including flies, beetles, and wasps. These insects crawl around haphazardly on the flowers, rubbing against the stamens (pollen-bearing parts) and stigmas (pollen-receiving parts).

Gullet flowers, such as penstemons, snapdragons, and monkeyflowers, carry their sexual organs on the upper side and have landing sites on the lower lip. Bees and other insects perch on these landing areas, push their heads into the corolla, and receive pollen on their backs.

Tube flowers look like gullet flowers but have no landing platforms. Their nectar lies at the base of a long tube or spur. Hovering moths or hummingbirds insert their long proboscises or beaks into the tube to lap up the nectar, shaking loose golden grains of pollen in the process. Tube flowers include columbines and bush morning glories.

Evening-primroses, abundant throughout Colorado, have exceedingly long throated corollas whose nectar is accessible only to hummingbirds and long-tongued, night-flying moths. On warm July evenings, it's fun to sit beside an evening-primrose and wait for a sphinx or hawk moth to arrive. The flowers open up just before sunset, and the moths whir in an hour or two later. Watching these delicate, velvety-winged moths quietly "tending" their evening-primrose gardens has even helped us to see beauty in the much reviled tomato hornworm, which, as it turns out, is a larval form of the five-spotted hawk moth.

Flowers also use scent and color to attract pollinators. Some flowers smell like carrion. Beetles and flies, which zoom in hoping to deposit their eggs, leave with a

FLOWER TYPES AND THEIR POLLINATORS

FLOWER TYPE	COLORADO EXAMPLES	TYPICAL POLLINATORS
DISH OR BOWL	Wild rose, prickly poppy, marsh marigold	Flies, beetles, wasps
BELL OR FUNNEL	Common harebell, blue gentian	Bees
BRUSH	Willows	Bees, butterflies, birds
FLAG	Golden smoke	Bees
GULLET	Penstemons, monkey flowers	Bees, hummingbirds
TUBE	Evening-primroses, columbines	Moths, hummingbirds

Sources: K. Faegri and L. van der Pijl, *Principles of Pollination Ecology;* Doris Stone, *The Lives of Plants.*

load of pollen on their legs or backs. Sweet-smelling flowers entice bees, humming-birds, and other nectar-gathering animals, including many tropical dwelling bats.

Bees can discern blue, yellow, and ultraviolet, but not red. For this reason most red flowers in temperate North America are hummingbird pollinated. Many bee-pollinated flowers have "honey guides," spots of ultraviolet on the lower lip that lead bees to the nectar source. These spots are conspicuous on foxglove (*Digitalis purpurea*) but invisible to our eyes on buttercups and black-eyed Susans (*Rudbeckia hirta*).

ECHOES IN THE SUMMER NIGHT

If we could hear the high-frequency echolocating sounds made by most bats, we might go deaf, or crazy. In some species the volume of these vocalizations, made while the bats flit through the darkness with their mouths agape, rivals that of a smoke alarm or jackhammer. The high volume is necessary because only a minute amount of sound, perhaps one one-thousandth of the original vocalization, reflects back to the animals' oversized ears.

TOWNSEND'S BIG-EARED BAT

Some bats do echolocate at frequencies that are barely audible to humans, and all Colorado bats make clicking and chattering noises that we can hear. Bats use these low-frequency calls to communicate with other bats. They use echolocation to navigate through their environment, to maneuver in the roost, and to locate prey. Echolocating bats emit up to two hundred pulses per second. Their large ears amplify the reflected sound. Their sophisticated brains analyze the echo in a microsecond, determining the size, shape, direction, speed of movement, and texture of the target object.

Bats harvest insects with amazing efficiency. Little brown bats, which inhabit coniferous forests throughout the state, catch and eat up to six hundred mosquitoes in an hour. Mammalogists estimated that a colony of 20 million Brazilian free-tailed bats in Bracken Cave, Texas, consumed up to a quarter of a million pounds of insects per night (Armstrong et al., *Bats of Colorado*). Ironically, one of the greatest threats to North American bat populations is the overuse of pesticides. Vandalism of roosts, disturbance of cave habitats, and closing off abandoned mines also threaten bat populations. Of forty-four bat species in the United States, six are endangered, and eighteen others are listed as "species of special concern."

Bat Houses, Counts, and Conservation

The Colorado summer bat trend survey, initiated in 1991 and modeled after a similar survey in Pennsylvania, takes place the last week of June and the first week of July. Participants sit by a body of water on two successive evenings and count "bat passes" —the number of times individual bats descend from the sky to drink. Scientists use information from the survey to chart bat population trends and locate areas with high bat concentrations. Novices are welcome. For information, call or write the Colorado Bat Society, 1085 14th St., Suite 1337, Boulder, CO 80302.

You can also help conserve bat populations by reporting roosts to the Division of Wildlife. Many species roost in abandoned mines. The Division conserves these sites by placing a steel latticework, easily avoided by the bats, over the entrances. You can also erect a bat box in your yard. Most wild bird centers carry bat boxes, and you can order a book on how to construct them from Bat Conservation International, P.O. Box 162603, Austin, TX 78715.

During summer, females of most species gather in maternity colonies where they care for their young. Most Colorado species mate in autumn, and females store the sperm until they emerge from hibernation in spring. They then ovulate one egg, fertilize it, and give birth fifty to sixty days later. Red bats, which roost singly in trees, may produce up to four young.

In other, colonial roosting species, nursing mothers may take their offspring with them on nocturnal hunting forays, but as the young grow larger, they must be left behind in the maternity colony. Since some colonies contain several hundred

BAT FACTS

❦ One-fourth of all mammalian species are bats.

❦ Of the 900 bat species in the world, about 750 feed primarily on insects, 150 primarily on fruit and nectar, and only 3 on blood. None of these "vampire bats" reside in the United States.

❦ Bats may live up to forty years.

❦ Bats can hear sounds up to 200,000 cycles per second (humans can only hear up to 20,000 cycles per second).

❦ The Brazilian free-tailed colony at Carlsbad Caverns National Park has declined in number from 8 to 9 million individuals around the turn of the century to 250,000 to 350,000 individuals today.

❦ No bats are blind.

❦ About .5 percent of bats carry rabies. There have been only sixteen deaths (most *not* from rabies) from bat-borne diseases in the United States and Canada since 1960.

Sources: Mary Taylor Gray, "Bats Are the Good Guys," *Colorado's Wildlife Company* (quarterly published by the DOW), 1996; Armstrong, et al., *Bats of Colorado: Shadows in the Night.*

thousand individuals, locating a single offspring can be a daunting task. However, each youngster produces a high-frequency "isolation" call that identifies it to its mother. Once she gets close, her sense of smell takes over.

After a few weeks of hanging upside down and fattening up on their mother's milk, young bats initiate experimental flights away from the roost. These flights can be awkward and dangerous. Many young die after crash landing. Some, exhausted, settle onto the ground, where they become prey for foxes, coyotes, raccoons, skunks, dogs, and cats. Others abandon flying efforts and walk back to the roost.

Colorado's largest summer bat colony, in an abandoned mine in the San Luis Valley, contains more than a quarter of a million Brazilian free-tailed bats. Wildlife biologist Peggy Svoboda has studied this colony for several years. In *Bats of Colorado,* she describes the spectacle of a giant undulating cloud of bats leaving the mine shaft each evening: "It looks like a river, and it sounds like the wind."

In July look for bats at dusk and dawn around streams, ponds, and lakes. Most bats like to dip down to take a drink before foraging. While foraging they often follow a set route over and over. If insects are swirling around your head, bats may zip by, but the chances of a bat ever colliding with you are slim; anything that can home in on a mosquito in the dark at 30 miles per hour shouldn't have much trouble echolocating and avoiding a species as large as *Homo sapiens.*

In fall most Colorado bats return to their hibernacula in caves or mines. About half of our species migrate south before hibernating. During hibernation, body temperatures of some bats may drop to near freezing, and heartbeats may slow to as few as ten beats per minute.

A WILDFLOWER FEAST TO LAST THE WINTER

As high mountain snowfields melt away in the summer sun, pikas and marmots begin preparing for winter.

Young pikas, fresh out of their mothers' burrows, scramble back and forth across talus slopes trying to establish foraging territories. Once real estate transactions have been more or less sorted out, all members of the pika colony begin the serious business of hay gathering. Each of these hamster-sized lagomorphs (the mammalian order that also includes hares and rabbits) cuts and stores about a cubic yard of plant material each summer and fall. The hay, placed under overhanging rocks, serves as insurance against a late snowmelt in spring and may also help pikas survive the harsh alpine winters. Pikas do not hibernate. Their shrill squeaks under the snow are a special joy of ski touring above timber line.

A pika with a mouthful of vegetation is one of the easiest wild animals to watch or photograph. While dashing back and forth between the tundra and their rocky haunts, these "rock rabbits" often seem oblivious to other stimuli. If you sit quietly on a rock long enough, a pika will inevitably race through your legs or around your foot, its mouth jammed full of grass and wildflowers.

Nevertheless, pikas remain alert to any movement in or around the colony. A loud "eeek" call may signal the approach of a weasel, fox, golden eagle, or prairie falcon. Ecologist Carron Meaney, curator of mammalogy at the Denver Museum of Natural History, once counted two hundred alarm calls given by an adult male as a weasel scurried in and out of the talus. Pikas give a slightly shorter call during territorial disputes. Meaney reports that territorial chasing sometimes leads to battles, "in which two pikas stand up on their hind legs and 'box' at each other."

While pikas dash madly around gathering plant material, marmots lie indolently, on the largest boulders, soaking up the sun. Like many other true hibernators, marmots are imperfect endotherms, whose body temperature fluctuates even during active periods. Morning sunbathing may help them to boost their body temperature before they venture out onto the tundra to forage.

Young yellow-bellied marmots.

During summer these large rodents follow fairly predictable daily routines. They emerge from their burrows around sunrise, and after a period of alert resting or sunbathing, they forage for a few hours. Favorite foods include dandelions, cow parsnips, bluebells, cinquefoils, and a variety of grasses. Around midday they retreat to their burrows or sunbathe on a flat rock near the burrow entrance. By late afternoon they are back out and about, alternating foraging and resting until around sunset.

Unlike pikas, marmots are highly social. A typical colony consists of an older, dominant male, several subdominant females, and young of the year. Marmots that don't belong to a large colony may live singly or in small groups, and some may mate monogamously. Colonial marmots communicate through whistling, screaming, and tooth chattering (to signal aggression). They also scent mark with cheek glands and engage in a variety of social behaviors including play, grooming, sniffing, chasing, and fighting.

Marmots may double their weight in summer as they munch on grasses and wildflowers. The fat they accumulate sees them through six to seven months of hibernation, usually beginning in October. Colorado's yellow-bellied marmots (*Marmota flaviventris*), which are closely related to the eastern marmot or wood-chuck (*M. monax*), are champion hibernators. During their winter torpor, their body temperature falls to around 40°F and their pulse slows to four or five beats per minute.

Though most often seen in the tundra, marmots occur throughout Colorado's mountains and foothills from around 5,000 to 14,000 feet. Pikas occupy a slightly narrower elevation range, from around 8,500 to 14,000 feet.

Mountain goats on Mount Evans.

KINGS OF THE MOUNTAIN

Mid-summer, when access to their craggy homes is relatively easy, is the best time to observe mountain goats. We have lunched in the midst of a herd, so close our telephoto lenses would not focus. Nannies lay nearby watching us with big yellow eyes while newborn kids cavorted toward us for a closer look.

Mingling with mountain goats in such close proximity was unheard of a century ago in Colorado. The goats were considered an exotic when fourteen were introduced into the Collegiate Range in 1948. Introductions continued elsewhere until 1971. By the 1980s, researchers started to worry that these "exotics" might adversely affect the native bighorns (see pp. 239–241, December).

Then in 1993 the Division of Wildlife released the startling news: Mountain goats may be native Coloradans after all. They were described in some early historical accounts, and Teddy Roosevelt was said to have killed one in the state. It is thought they were killed off by miners in the 1880s. However, some zoologists question these accounts and think the goats have been absent from our mountains since the last ice age. Whatever their history, approximately fifteen hundred are now estimated to reign supreme in our high mountains.

Thin, short horns, a white, shaggy coat, and a debonair goatee characterize this goat that is not really a goat. More closely related to European chamois and African antelope, mountain goats are well adapted to their rugged, alpine terrain. A somewhat elastic pad on their hooves gives them good traction on talus and steep slopes. Nevertheless, some goats do fall to their deaths, and entire herds have been killed in avalanches.

The upside to this inhospitable environment is that there are few predators other than an occasional mountain lion, bear, bobcat, or coyote. Even in winter, mountain goats seldom move much below tree line. They breed during the cold months of November and early December, and kids are born in May and June.

When searching for mountain goats, watch for tufts of coarse hair caught on rocks and alpine willows and for the bare patches where they like to wallow and to lick for minerals. Salt-seeking goats dig up the landscape, searching for salt left by the urine of campers to supplement their usual vegetarian menu. They also relish the ground around toilets and have even invaded the outhouses at Summit Lake on Mt. Evans in their quest for salt.

Where To Go

❧ Mt. Evans near Denver.

❧ Grays Peak and Torreys Mountain just east of Eisenhower Tunnel.

❧ Collegiate Mountain Range west of Buena Vista.

❧ Gore Range near Dillon.

❧ San Juan Mountains, especially the Weminuche Wilderness.

COUNTING BUTTERFLIES

Shimmering butterflies can give you an adrenalin rush even more exciting than Fourth of July fireworks. Butterfly Counts, patterned after the Audubon Christmas Bird Counts, are held each year in the weeks just before and after the Fourth to track butterfly populations throughout the United States, Canada, and Mexico.

Sponsored by the North American Butterfly Association and the Xerces Society, the counts monitor changes in butterfly populations from year to year and reveal possible effects of habitat destruction, weather, and pesticide use. Volunteers count all butterflies and caterpillars in a 15-mile-diameter circle, recording numbers of individuals as well as species. A local expert leads each group, but no experience is necessary to participate.

In 1995 over twenty-nine hundred people participated in 296 counts. Eighty-two observers in Colorado counts racked up 106 species and 772 individual butterflies. Colorado netted maximum numbers on 28 species, including new continental highs on Olympia Marble, Bramble Hairstreak, Western Pine Elfin, Green Skipper, Arachne Checkerspot (109 individuals in Gilpin County), and Garita Skipperling (219 individuals in Fort Collins).

The first count was held in 1975, when seventy-six people covered just twenty-eight sites throughout the United States. Two Colorado sites—Gilpin County and High Line Canal—are among only four that have been censused every year since 1975.

To register for a Colorado Count, call the Butterfly Pavilion and Insect Center in Westminster: 303-469-7657.

OUR STATE INSECT: THE COLORADO HAIRSTREAK BUTTERFLY

It took four years of dedicated campaigning, but the schoolchildren of Colorado finally won their battle for a butterfly. On April 17, 1996, Gov. Roy Romer signed a bill declaring the Colorado hairstreak our state insect.

Fourth graders from Wheeling Elementary School in Aurora started to lobby the state legislature in 1992. The children studied the butterfly and reported that it doesn't damage crops; it lives only in Colorado and adjoining states; and it is gorgeous. In addition, they said, the hairstreak wears the politically correct colors of the Broncos and the Rockies. More than a hundred entomologists also voted for the hairstreak, which narrowly defeated the honey-bee, a nonnative that was introduced to America from the Old World around 1638.

Hypaurotis crysalus was first described from specimens collected by J. A. Allen at "Lake Pass, Colorado" in 1871. In *Colorado Butterflies,* F. Martin Brown writes that there's no such place on the map, but "a little detective work" proved that the type location was Palmer Lake in El Paso County.

As the Butterfly Goes ...

Tracking butterfly populations may help track global warming patterns. Camille Parmesan (University of California, Santa Barbara) studied 151 populations of Edith's checkerspot butterfly and found that over the past century these butterflies have been moving north or to higher altitudes. According to an article in the February 1997 issue of National Wildlife, *this orange, yellow, and black spotted butterfly is dying off in Mexico and expanding its range in Canada.*

In Colorado, Edith's checkerspots inhabit the western part of the state and may be found as early as May. Look for them around paintbrushes, one of their host plants, and other members of the figwort family.

COLORADO HAIRSTREAK

About 1.5 inches across, this butterfly makes up for its small size with brilliant colors—deep bluish purple wings with black margins and golden-orange spots and a black eyespot with a red pupil near the tail. The larger female flaunts a wider band extending across the upper edge of the forewings. The bright colors are rarely seen, as these butterflies fly fast and keep their wings closed when at rest, revealing only their camouflaged gray underside. As with other hairstreaks, the hind wings terminate in fancy, hairlike tails, devices that resemble antennae when the wings are closed and may confuse predators into attacking the tail instead of the head.

From egg to adult, the Colorado hairstreak is associated with Gambel oak. Eggs hatch on the bark, caterpillars eat the leaves, and adults take flight in the Gambel oak groves from June to September. They emerge in late June and July at lower elevations and from July to August at higher elevations. Male adults live only about five days; females, nine.

Adults feed only on tree sap, minerals in mud, and—surprisingly—raindrops. They fly while it's raining and suck up the drops to dilute the thick oak sap. They are one of the few butterflies that remain active on cloudy days and even after sunset.

Some caterpillars in the Lycanid family, to which hairstreaks belong, benefit from a symbiotic relationship similar to the bond between ants and aphids. The caterpillars exude a sweet, protein-rich substance called honeydew that the ants lap up. In turn, the ants guard the caterpillars from spiders and parasitic wasps and flies.

Where To Go

Look in stands of Gambel oak in canyons and foothills from 6,500 to 7,500 feet. Hairstreaks are most common in southern Colorado wherever oak occurs. See the distribution maps in the back of Clifford Ferris and F. Martin Brown's *Butterflies of the Rocky Mountain States* for detailed location information.

GRASSHOPPER GIGS, CRICKET CRESCENDOS, CICADA SERENADES

The strident, staccato songs of insects seem to mimic the crackle of grass in a scorched wind. If a hot July day could vocalize, it might sound like grasshoppers.

Heat even accelerates the tempo of some songs. Cricket chirping speeds up when the thermometer rises. Count the number of chirps in fourteen seconds and add forty for a rough estimate of temperature Fahrenheit, although this formula varies greatly with species and individuals.

Long-horned grasshoppers, crickets, and katydids "fiddle" by rubbing a rough "scraper" on the upper surface of one wing against a "file" on the under surface of the other wing. Some fiddlers are "right-handed" with the file on the right wing, and others are "left-handed." Short-horned grasshoppers fiddle using their hind legs as a bow against their folded wings.

Cicadas provide the percussion to the grasshoppers' fiddle. Male cicadas vibrate a membrane called the tymbal (no, that's not a typo for cymbal) that stretches over a pair of sound chambers near their abdomen. Some cicadas also click with their wings. They will continue to "sing" even when being consumed by a bird or while drowning in a pond. About twenty-eight species of cicadas occur in the Rockies. Most of them live as larvae for three to seven years before emerging from the ground. The famous periodical cicadas that emerge in thirteen- or seventeen-year cycles live east of the Mississippi River.

Insects not only provide dinner music for campers, they can also provide dinner. Because grasshoppers and crickets are about 50 percent protein, they were a rich food source for many American Indians. They are still prized food in many countries. Ironically, in the United States, where we shudder at gobbling down grubs, we steam and esteem related arthropods, such as lobsters. Mealworm chocolate chip cookies are quite tasty, and roasted crickets and other bugs taste a bit like stale Fritos but are a lot more nutritious.

JULY EVENTS

MAMMALS

✇ Pikas start making hay piles and continue until snow covers the ground.

✇ Least chipmunks are born by early July and leave the nest about four weeks later.

❋ Mountain lion kittens are born throughout the year, but the birth rate peaks in July.

❋ Bats forage voraciously at sunset to provide for their young.

Birds

❋ American pipit and horned lark young hatch above tree line.

❋ Ptarmigan chicks, under parental supervision, hunt for insects.

❋ Hummingbirds start to return to lower elevations.

❋ Franklin's gulls and shorebirds begin to arrive from the north.

Other Critters

❋ Grasshoppers swarm at low elevations.

❋ Butterfly populations peak in July and August.

Plants

❋ Alpine and subalpine wildflowers carpet the meadows and peaks.

❋ Sunflowers light up the prairie.

❋ Mushroom season begins.

❋ Sweet corn and Colorado peaches hit the fruit stands.

Special Events

❋ Butterfly and Bat Counts are held around July 4.

In the Sky

❋ "Thunder Moon" (Sioux)

❋ Aquarid meteors are visible during the last week in the southeast.

❋ Ursa Major (the Great Bear, or the Big Dipper) is almost straight overhead around 9:00 P.M. The Iroquois, Greeks, and many other peoples referred to this dipper-shaped constellation as The Bear. Some anthropologists have theorized that hunting peoples living in northern Siberia first named the constellation more than 12,000 years ago and carried the name with them as they dispersed across Eurasia and North America. To locate Polaris, the North Star, extend a straight line up from the last two stars of the bowl of the "dipper."

A light dusting of snow is not uncommon in late summer on the high peaks of the Sangre de Cristo Mountains.

8

August

Toward calm and shady places

I am walking

on the earth.

—CHIPPEWA

ON HOT AUGUST walks we seek the shade of cotton-woods in low elevation grasslands where bright asters and sunflowers spill purple and gold across the land. Purple and blue gentians spangle the golden grasses in subalpine meadows. Wildly colored mushrooms spring up through the duff in spruce and aspen forests. The tundra has already shifted into autumn, with the foliage of alpine plants reddening the slopes even as flowers continue to bloom and set seed.

Shorebirds, sensing that the days are dwindling down and the nights are crispening, start to head south. Hummingbirds begin to forsake the mountains for feeders and flowers at lower elevations. Birds are quieter now, but we listen for the soft conversational notes of jays and for the booms of nighthawks, still diving after ubiquitous mosquitoes.

This is a month when seasons collide. It's high summer on the prairie and autumn on the summits. One morning it's just-spring and flowers are budding; that night, frost leaves diamonds on the grass. But by noon, you're back to summer again, looking for shade.

AUGUST WEATHER

	Grand Junction (4,824 ft.)	Steamboat Springs (6,760 ft.)	Alamosa (7,536 ft.)	Berthoud Pass (11,310 ft.)	Denver (5,282 ft.)	Lamar (3,620 ft.)
Ave. high (°F)	91	80	79	60	86	91
Ave. low (°F)	62	40	45	38	57	61
Max. high (°F)	103	98	90	75	101	110
Min. low (°F)	43	22	29	21	41	40
Ave. prec. (in.)	0.81	1.48	1.12	2.63	1.51	1.87
Max. prec. (in.)	3.48	3.38	5.40	6.68	5.85	6.39
Ave. snow (in.)	0.0	0.0	0.0	0.3	0.0	0.0
Max. snow (in.)	0.0	0.0	0.0	3.0	0.0	0.0

Southerly winds aloft bring moisture up the spine of the Rockies from the Gulf of California and the Gulf of Mexico. Persistent thunderstorms drench the San Juan and Elk Mountains in the southwest. Campers beware: Wolf Creek Pass received 10.89 inches of rain in August 1993. It rained on 22 of 31 days.

Violent thunderstorms persist in the east. A flash flood near Pueblo on August 7, 1904, caused a train trestle to collapse, killing eighty-nine passengers. In 1984 a tornado touched down on Longs Peak. At 11,400 feet above sea level, this may have been the highest elevation tornado sighting in U.S. history.

See "Colorado Climate Summary" (p. 1) for information on averages, extremes, and sources.

august ecosystem

Frosted Mountain Grasslands

Autumn creeps down into mountain meadows and grasslands long before the first aspen leaves turn. On late August mornings in North Park, the mountain sage-brush sparkles with frost, migrating shorebirds wade in icy waters of shallow lakes and ponds, and elk descend from the tundra and subalpine forest to feast on grasses and wildflowers. Foraging moose crunch their way through ice-encrusted bogs while beavers, working overtime, ferry aspen and willow saplings to underwater larders.

Colorful gentians begin blooming during this time of shortening days and crisp starry nights. The deep blue, tubular corollas of Rocky Mountain fringed gentians

(*Gentianopsis thermalis*) and blue gentians (*Pneumonanthe affinis*) mirror the color of the late summer sky and contrast with the mauves and russets of the ripening grasses. Wispy seedheads of foxtail barley (*Critesion jubatum*) glow reddish in the morning sun. Golden tufts of Junegrass (*Koeleria macrantha*) shine among fields of mountain muhly (*Muhlenbergia montana*) and Thurber fescue (*Festuca thurberi*). These grasses grow in bunches, rather than forming turf. This adaptation enables their root systems to spread out and make maximum use of the limited moisture available in porous, gravelly soils. They thrive throughout the high mountain valleys where conditions are too dry (less than 20 inches annual precipitation) to support conifers.

As fall approaches, animal activity peaks. Wyoming ground squirrels (also known as "picketpins" and, formerly, as Richardson's ground squirrels) remain outside their burrows for most of the day, munching on grasses, wildflowers, and shrubs. They convert much of this food into fat, necessary to see them through the winter. Fat accumulation apparently triggers hibernation, which may begin long before the first snows sweep across mountain grasslands.

With their upright posture and gregarious nature, these medium-sized ground squirrels resemble prairie dogs. Both white-tailed (in northern Colorado) and Gunnison's (in southern Colorado) prairie dogs also inhabit mountain grasslands and shrublands. These prairie dogs remain active throughout August and early September, and you can often hear their alarm barks as migrating hawks, eagles, and falcons soar by. Rodent colonies also attract a variety of terrestrial predators, including badgers, coyotes, and red foxes. An early morning stake-out of a prairie dog or Wyoming ground squirrel colony offers great wildlife-watching opportunities.

Northern pocket gophers bulldoze their way through the soil, nibbling on wildflowers, wildflower roots, and grasses. In *Rocky Mountain Mammals*, David Armstrong says a single pocket gopher may excavate more than 500 feet of burrows, displacing nearly 3 tons of soil. The gophers use their long, yellowish-orange incisors, which dangle in front of pursed lips, to chip away at rocks and soil. Armstrong says that on favorable sites populations may exceed twenty individuals per acre and that "the soil in such situations may be so completely undermined that it gives way underfoot." Pocket gophers remain active throughout the winter, burrowing in and under the snowpack, subsisting mostly on roots, bulbs, and tubers.

Toward the end of summer, ripening fruits and seeds attract flocks of songbirds, especially sparrows. Some flocks are made up of family groups that have nested in the grasslands, shrublands, and adjacent forests; others are early migrants making their way down from the north. Though drab and difficult to identify, the sparrows are fun to watch as they cling to swaying thistles and flock to seed-bearing shrubs.

Like Darwin's Galapagos finches, these sparrows reveal a lot about specialization and how closely related species have evolved to occupy distinct niches in the natural world. You can see this clearly in the mountain parks where Brewer's and sage sparrows flock to sagebrush shrublands, savannah sparrows frequent wet meadows and irrigated fields, Lincoln's and song sparrows nest and forage in willow thickets, and chipping sparrows flit through the conifers. Noting where each species "belongs" helps a lot with identification.

By mid-September most of the songbirds and shorebirds have headed south or to lower elevations, and many mammals have already begun their winter sleep. Long before autumn invades the lowlands, much of life in the mountain grasslands will have shut down for the winter, as snow swirls over the highest peaks.

Where To Go

🦆 Arapaho National Wildlife Refuge, North Park, near Walden.

🦆 Tarryall Reservoir, Knight-Imler, Tomahawk, and Buffalo Peaks State Wildlife areas, South Park, near Fairplay.

🦆 U.S. Hwy. 285 and side roads, San Luis Valley between Poncha Springs and Villa Grove.

GENTIANS

Even as we glory in their beauty, gentians bring a touch of sadness, as their blooming peak coincides with the waning of summer. Blue bottle gentians (*Pneumonanthe parryi*), creamy Arctic gentians (*Gentianodes algida*), and purple star gentians (*Swertia perennis*) often bloom in mountain meadows into September.

The Gentian family, divided into several different genera, contains hundreds of species worldwide. They usually grow at high elevations, even up to 18,000 feet on Mount Everest. Although we tend to think of gentians as blue, they come in various shades of pink, purple, green, and white. The flowers are radially symmetrical with four or five petals, and the corolla is often funnel shaped. The leaves are usually opposite or whorled.

Most species are perennial; a few are annual; and one, *Frasera speciosa*, is downright bizarre. In both the Eastern Slope and Western Slope versions of *Colorado Flora,* William Weber writes that this plant, also called monument plant or green gentian, can grow for twenty to sixty years before producing a tall stalk with whorls of pale greenish flowers. After flowering, it dies. David Inouye and Orley Taylor, who studied green gentians at four Colorado sites for many years, marked plants with aluminum tags and found the plants generally flowered when the leaves in the basal

MOUNTAIN (OR PARRY) GENTIAN
(PNEUMONANTHE BIGELOVII)

STAR GENTIAN
(SWERTIA PERENNIS)

FRINGED GENTIAN
(GENTIANOPSIS THERMALIS)

ARCTIC GENTIAN
(GENTIANODES ALGIDA)

rosette numbered twenty-five or more. The number of leaves does not exactly correspond to age, as the leaves may not increase for several years and may even regress.

The Roman historian Pliny wrote that gentians were named for King Gentius of Illyria, who made a concoction from the plant's leaves and roots to cure plague. Winnebago and Dakota Indians made a tonic from the roots of some gentians to promote digestion and improve appetite.

Although most gentians grow in high mountain meadows, some species flourish in wetlands on the plains and in the foothills. One unusual species (*Pneumonanthe bigelovii*) resembles the bottle gentian but has more numerous flowers and grows in dry, open forests of the foothills, blooming in September.

Our favorite gentian display is in South Park, just below Kenosha Pass. In mid to late August fringed gentians (*Gentianopsis thermalis*) suddenly appear in the wet fields, their vivid blues contrasting with golden grasses—a last burst of summer in the midst of autumn's encroaching gold.

LATE SUMMER WILDFLOWER SAMPLER

COMMON NAME	SCIENTIFIC NAME	FAMILY	HABITAT
Western Valleys (4,500–7,500 feet)			
ASTER LANCEOLATUS	*Aster lanceolatus*	Sunflower	Wet meadows and ditches
RABBITBRUSH	*Chrysothamnus* spp.	Sunflower	Throughout
GUMWEED	*Grindelia* spp.	Sunflower	Throughout
SNAKEWEED	*Gutierrezia* spp.	Sunflower	Throughout
COMMON SUNFLOWER	*Helianthus annuus*	Sunflower	Roadsides
GOLDENROD	*Solidago* spp.	Sunflower	Throughout
COMMON EVENING-PRIMROSE	*Oenothera elata*	Evening-primrose	Wet meadows and ditches
Mountain Forests and Meadows (7,500–11,500 feet)			
SMOOTH ASTER	*Aster laevis*	Sunflower	Meadows and open woods
SUBALPINE DAISY	*Erigeron peregrinus*	Sunflower	Moist meadows
TANSY ASTER	*Machaeranthera* spp.	Sunflower	Fields and disturbed ground
SMOOTH GOLDENROD	*Solidago missouriensis*	Sunflower	Meadows and forest clearings
BROOK SAXIFRAGE	*Micranthes odontoloma*	Saxifrage	Wet meadows near streams
TWISTED GENTIAN	*Gentianopsis barbellata*	Gentian	Meadows and grassy slopes
FRINGED GENTIAN	*G. thermalis*	Gentian	Meadows and bogs
MOUNTAIN GENTIAN	*Pneumonanthe parrye*	Gentian	Moist meadows and streambanks
Tundra (above 11,500 feet)			
ALPINE HAREBELL	*Campanula uniflora*	Bellflower	Throughout
SIBERIAN GENTIAN	*Chondrophylla prostrata*	Gentian	Meadows
ARCTIC GENTIAN	*Gentianodes algida*	Gentian	Streambanks and wet meadows
FRINGED GENTIAN	*Gentianopsis* spp.	Gentian	Meadows
STAR GENTIAN	*Swertia perennis*	Gentian	Marshes and bogs
GOLDEN SAXIFRAGE	*Hirculus prorepens*	Saxifrage	Bogs
WHIPLASH SAXIFRAGE	*H. platysepalus*	Saxifrage	Rock outcrops
ALPINE SPEEDWELL	*Veronica nutans*	Figwort	Meadows
Eastern Foothills and Plains (3,600–7,500 feet)			
DWARF MILKWEED	*Asclepias pumila*	Milkweed	Grasslands and forest openings
ROUGH WHITE ASTER	*Virgulus falcatus*	Sunflower	Roadsides and fields
GUMWEED	*Grindelia* spp.	Sunflower	Throughout
SNAKEWEED	*Gutierrezia sarothrae*	Sunflower	Dry grasslands
GAYFEATHER	*Liatris punctata*	Sunflower	Grasslands, mostly near foothills
TEN-PETAL BLAZINGSTAR	*Nuttallia decapetala*	Stick-leaf	Sandstone outcrops, foothills
PLAINS EVENINGSTAR	*N. nuda*	Stick-leaf	Sandy soils, plains
COMMON EVENING-PRIMROSE	*Oenothera villosa*	Evening-primrose	Throughout

SUNFLOWERS

The sunflowers we grow in our gardens are direct descendants of the wild sunflowers (*Helianthus* spp.) that thrive in mid- to low-elevation grasslands and forests throughout the state. In fact, it's often difficult to distinguish the natives from the cultivars. Many of the tall sunflowers growing along highways and on other disturbed sites may be hybrids of wild and cultivated plants.

Archaeologists have found evidence that people used sunflowers for food as early as 5800 B.C. Plains Indians ate sunflower seeds raw, roasted, or boiled. They ground the seeds into a flour to make a thin bread or to thicken soup. They also made a drink from sunflower meal and a snack from sunflower dough moistened with bone marrow.

When sunflowers were introduced into Europe during the sixteenth and seventeenth centuries, they caused a sensation. In *The Herbal or General History of Plants*, English herbalist John Gerard wrote that sunflower buds, when boiled and eaten like artichokes, surpassed the artichoke "in procuring bodily lust." The roots of *Helianthus tuberosus,* a sunflower native to the eastern half of North America, became known in Europe as Jerusalem artichokes.

A half dozen species of *Helianthus* grow in Colorado. Blooming peaks in mid to late summer, when swaying blossoms line roadsides in the western valleys, and whole hillsides on the eastern plains turn yellow.

Sunflowers belong to the Asteracea, or Compositae, a plant family that includes more than three hundred Colorado species. Members of this family include asters, daisies, and thistles. They sport showy flower heads that are a composite of many small flowers. These smaller flowers, by themselves, would not easily attract the attention of pollinating insects, but they have evolved to grow in a cluster that resembles a giant, single flower. The flower head of a common sunflower (*H. annuus*) consists of several dozen yellow ray flowers and several hundred purplish disk flowers, each with male and female parts and each producing a separate fruit. Thus, when we eat a sunflower "seed," we actually are eating the entire fruit of an individual flower.

BLAZINGSTARS

On late summer evenings, one of Colorado's gangliest weeds becomes one of the state's loveliest wildflowers. The delicate white, many-petaled blossoms of the plains eveningstar (*Nuttallia nuda*) open a few hours before sunset and close the following morning. This moth-pollinated species blooms in profusion on shale outcrops and in sandhills along Interstate 76, between Brighton and Fort Morgan. Other blazingstars, including several lemon-yellow varieties, bloom on shale outcrops, barren ground, and adobe hills throughout the state.

Most blazingstars (members of the genus *Nuttallia* in the Loaseae, or stick-leaf family) have many-branched stems and hairy foliage that sticks to anything that passes by. Close inspection of the plant hairs reveals that each supports a ring of stiff, downcurved hooks that attach themselves like Velcro to human clothing or

Plains eveningstar.

animal fur. Once embedded in the wool of sheep, the foliage of blazingstars is almost impossible to remove.

Because blazingstars tend to thrive in disturbed soils and overgrazed grasslands, many species may have increased in abundance since European settlement. Considered of little or no economic use today, blazingstars were valued by Plains Indians for their medicinal properties. The Cheyenne used the root of *Nuttallia laevicaulis* as an ingredient in medicines to treat fevers, earaches, rheumatism, and arthritis. The Dakotas extracted a gummy yellow juice from the stems of *Nuttallia nuda* and applied it externally to relieve fevers. The Hopi snacked on a sweet, oily meal made from the ground seeds of *Nuttallia albicaulis*.

MYSTICAL, MAGICAL MUSHROOMS

 There's something mysterious—almost supernatural—about mushrooms. Some of them look like dead men's fingers, brains, phallic symbols, coral, blobs of jelly, or parasols for elves. Many mushrooms produce caps with gills; others have caps with a spongelike or a "toothed" material underneath. Different species fruit at different times of year, but August is when you find the best bonanzas.

Their colors vary from earth tones to red, pink, salmon, orange, yellow, green, violet, white, or black. These strange growths produce no chlorophyll or seeds, and they have no roots. They are even classified into a kingdom all their own: the fungi. The Denver Botanic Gardens has more than seventeen hundred species of Colorado mushrooms in their herbarium, but the curator, mycologist Vera Evenson, says this collection represents less than half the number that could be found in the state.

The mushroom itself is just the fruit of an underground growth called the mycelium. The mycelium spreads underground (or in wood or in a host organism) in an ever-growing network of interconnecting strands, usually white, that draw nourishment from organic matter in the substrate. Species that depend on dead material (saprophytes) are valuable in recycling organic debris. Reproduction takes place through tiny spores that fall to the ground, where, if conditions are suitable, they start a new mycelium that spreads out in filaments from the center. The underground mycelium can live for many centuries, expanding into a weblike growth larger than a blue whale or a giant sequoia. Mushrooms may be the largest life form known, though aspen clones have challenged this claim (see pp. 176–179, September).

Some mushrooms form a symbiotic relationship (called mycorrhiza) with other plants. Boletes, for instance, grow in symbiosis with conifers. The fungus obtains moisture and nutrients from the tree and, in turn, helps the tree absorb nitrogen, phosphorous, and other nutrients.

The taste of succulent wild mushrooms brings gourmands to their knees, scrabbling in the duff for treasure. However, some mushrooms, such as *Amanita verna* (nicknamed the Destroying Angel), are deadly. Anyone harvesting wild mushrooms must be certain of what they pick. The rule is: "Never eat a mushroom unless you know it well enough to call it by its scientific name." Also, be sure it has no look–alike and don't trust old adages such as "poisonous mushrooms tarnish a silver spoon."

There are no shortcuts. Identify the mushroom in a good field guide such as Vera Evenson's excellent *Mushrooms of Colorado and the Southern Rocky Mountains*. Take a spore print. If possible, get a knowledgeable person to confirm its identity. Novices should take a class or join the Colorado Mycological Society (address in Appendix, "Selected Colorado Nature Organizations") and go on forays with experts. A good way to get started in mushroom identification is at the Annual Mushroom Fair, sponsored by the Colorado Mycological Society every August at the Denver Botanic Gardens.

Different species of mushrooms grow in different habitats, ranging from prairie to tundra. Look for *Boletus edulis* (steinpilz) near spruce and fir, *Agaricus campestris* (meadow mushrooms) in meadows, and *Hydnum imbricatum* (scaly urchin) in coniferous forests. Various species of *Calvatia* and *Lycoperdon* (puffballs) grow just about anywhere.

Picking mushrooms, like picking blueberries, is not believed to harm the plant, since the edible part is simply fruit produced by the mycelium. However, avoid disturbing the mycelium, which may lie close to the surface; firm the soil back into the hole; and leave some for wildlife.

To enjoy mushrooms' subtle flavor, simply sauté them in butter. Some people react badly to the most palatable varieties, so follow these steps the first time you sample a new species: Eat only a spoonful or two and wait twenty-four hours before eating more; don't mix with other species; and save some uncooked fresh whole specimens in waxed paper in the refrigerator for twenty-four hours so their identification can be checked if you do become ill. And don't even *think* about eating a mushroom you don't know is safe.

Treated with caution, mushrooms are delicious. However, it's not the feasting but the search and discovery of something strange, beautiful, and slightly mysterious that provides the thrill of mushrooming.

Where To Go

Mushrooms, like love, are where you find them. And that can be most any-where—cemeteries, college campuses, roadsides, streamsides—even the tundra. Each species has its own preferred habitat, so check Evenson's guidebook for suggested elevations and forest types. Here are a few general areas that are especially productive:

❦ San Juan Mountains, especially in vicinity of Telluride, where a mushroom festival is held each August.

❦ Fraser Experimental Forest.

❦ Mt. Zirkel Wilderness.

SUMMER HUMMERS

They've been called "feathered jewels" for their shimmering ruby and emerald colors and "flower kissers" because they sip nectar. We call them red barons (after the German World War I aviator) because they perform aerial acrobatics while engaging in fierce fighting in July and August.

Rufous hummingbirds (reddish with ruby-gold throats) are the most belligerent. They follow a long and complicated migration route, flying north along the Pacific lowlands when spring wildflowers are abundant. After nesting from Oregon to Alaska, they migrate south through Colorado when mountain flowers bloom. They dive mercilessly after other hummers in defense of foraging territories. They even buzz songbirds impertinent enough to sit near "their" feeder and dive-bomb cats snoozing underneath.

Broad-tailed hummingbirds (emerald backs with ruby throats or "gorgets") are Colorado's most common species, usually arriving in late April. Other species include calliope (our tiniest hummer, with purplish-magenta streamers on the throat), magnificent (emerald gorgets, amethyst heads), and black-chinned (black throats bordered with purple). Rare accidentals, such as the blue-throated and Anna's, sometimes occur here. Females are less brilliant and lack the gemlike gorgets. Refraction of light, not pigment, causes the vivid iridescent colors. Watch as a male turns his head and the gorget turns from jewel tints to black.

Hummingbirds, which occur only in the Western Hemisphere, are the only birds in the world able to fly backward and even upside down—a feat once said to be impossible. They beat their wings up to 78 times a second while hovering and up to 200 times a second in courtship dives that may reach 60 miles per hour. In contrast, a vulture flaps its wings about once a second. The sound that gives hummers their name is caused by this rapid wing movement. They also make soft, twittering chirps. However, only males make the insectlike buzz; the shrill trill so familiar to Coloradans belongs only to the male broad-tailed hummer.

A male that climbs out of sight into the sky, then swoops down in a breath-taking dive is either showing off to a prospective mate or warning rivals away from his territory. He seems to be aware of his gorgeous color, orienting the flight so his feathers glitter in the sun. The dives vary in pattern according to species. After a whirlwind courtship, the male leaves the female to rear the young alone. She builds a demitasse-size nest, often disguising it with lichens and lining it with spider webs. The mother faithfully incubates two eggs for up to seventeen days, making frequent forays to feed.

Hummers use needlelike bills to probe into tubular flower corollas or spurs, where they soak up nectar with long spongelike tongues, eating about half their weight in sugar each day. They also consume ants and other small insects. Many species of hummingbird-pollinated flowers, including penstemons, paintbrushes, and columbines, grow in Colorado. In the process of nectaring, the birds pollinate the flowers.

To conserve energy on cold nights, some hummingbirds enter a state of torpor, reducing their metabolic rate to about one-tenth the normal rate. Nevertheless, many freeze during unseasonable blizzards. Rufous hummingbirds usually leave Colorado by late August, but some broad-tails remain until mid-September before flying to Mexico for the winter.

COLORADO HUMMINGBIRDS

SPECIES	COLORADO STATUS	HABITAT
MAGNIFICENT HUMMINGBIRD	Rare summer and early fall migrant; **WS, MT.**	Feeders near ponderosa pine forests and foothills riparian woodlands.
BLACK-CHINNED HUMMINGBIRD	Fairly common summer resident in western valleys and southern foothills; **WS, PL.**	Piñon-juniper woodlands, oak shrublands, and lowland riparian woodlands.
CALLIOPE HUMMINGBIRD	Rare late summer and early fall migrant at low elevations; **WS, MT.**	Mostly seen at feeders or in wildflower meadows.
BROAD-TAILED HUMMINGBIRD	Common summer resident in foothills and mountains; **WS, MT, PL.**	Coniferous forests, riparian woodlands, and shrublands.
RUFOUS HUMMINGBIRD	Common late summer migrant in foothills and lower mountains; **WS, MT, PL.**	Coniferous forests, riparian woodlands, shrublands, and wildflower meadows.

Blue-throated and Anna's hummingbirds have also been seen in Colorado.
MT: Mountains above 7,500 feet; **PL:** Plains and eastern foothills to about 7,500 feet; **WS:** Western Slope valleys and plateaus to about 7,500 feet.

Source: Robert Andrews and Robert Righter, *Colorado Birds.*

Where To Go

Hummingbirds are most numerous in the foothills and mountains but also occur in canyons, grasslands, and urban gardens—anywhere they find their favorite flowers. To attract them to your yard, plant flowers such as nicotiana, petunias, double-bubble mint (*Agastache*), and trumpet vine or put up feeders containing four parts water to one part sugar. Commercial solutions are expensive and no better than homemade. Any solution ferments quickly, so change it every few days and clean the container each time. Using honey, too much sugar, or food coloring may harm the birds. Instead of food coloring, use a feeder tinted red, since they are attracted to that color. Hummers will even dive-bomb a person wearing red. That's why we like to wear red hats in summer.

MIGRATING SHOREBIRDS

On hot midsummer days, the shrill cries of migrating shorebirds bring visions of cool, distant shores and a reminder that the season is gradually turning toward fall.

First arrivals, in early to mid-July, include Baird's and least sandpipers who have nested in northern Canada and northern Alaska, greater and lesser yellowlegs who have come down from the prairies and bogs of northern and central Canada, and long-billed dowitchers fresh from their breeding grounds on the shores of the Arctic Sea. These migrants mix with flocks of Colorado summer resident shorebirds, including killdeers, American avocets, willets, spotted sandpipers, mountain plovers, common snipe, and Wilson's phalaropes. A larger second wave flies in from the north in August. Most of the birds in this second wave are young of the year, who migrate separately from their parents. By mid-September, numbers have

Upland sandpiper chick.

begun to thin out as flocks of most species continue southward toward wintering areas in Central and South America.

Some shorebirds complete migrations of up to 8,000 miles in a single uninterrupted flight, attaining speeds of 60 miles per hour. Most make their way south in a more leisurely manner, stopping for weeks at a time to rest and refuel. "Staging areas," such as Cheyenne Bottoms in Kansas or Gray's Harbor in Washington, attract hundreds of thousands of migrants at a time. For a few weeks each year, almost the entire North American population of western sandpipers gathers on a few square miles of mudflats in Alaska's Copper River Delta. Destruction of staging areas and other wetlands by commercial development, water diversion, and pesticide or sewage infiltration currently poses the greatest threat to North American shorebird populations.

Shorebirds time their seasonal migrations to optimize foraging opportunities. Some follow elliptical migration routes. Golden plovers, who breed in the Arctic, fly south via northeastern Canada and the Atlantic Ocean, arriving in Argentina in early fall. Their return trip takes them northward via Central America, the Gulf of Mexico, and the Mississippi Valley. Occasionally, a few stray into eastern Colorado. Their elliptical migration route covers about 20,000 miles.

Migrants gather around low- to mid-elevation lakes and ponds with exposed mudflats. Numbers vary from year to year, depending on water levels. Choose one lake or pond and visit it several times between early July and late September, noting

WILSON'S PHALAROPE

AMERICAN AVOCET

LONG-BILLED DOWITCHER

BAIRD'S SANDPIPER

changes in species composition. With effort you can see up to two dozen shorebird species in eastern Colorado and about a dozen species in the western and mountain valleys.

Where To Go

You can find shorebirds on almost any shallow body of water below 9,000 feet during August. The following places are particularly popular with birdwatchers:

- Highline Lake State Park, near Grand Junction.
- Fruitgrowers Reservoir, northeast of Delta.
- Monte Vista National Wildlife Refuge, near Alamosa.
- Arapaho National Wildlife Refuge, near Walden.
- Lower Latham Reservoir, near Greeley.
- Barr Lake State Park, northeast of Denver.
- Julesburg Reservoir, west of Julesburg.
- Lake Cheraw, north of La Junta.

COLORADO'S NESTING SHOREBIRDS

SPECIES	HABITAT	ABUNDANCE
PIPING PLOVER	Mudflats and shorelines of reservoirs and lakes; **PL.**	Rare and endangered.
KILLDEER	Shorelines, meadows, bare ground; **WS, MT, PL.**	Common.
MOUNTAIN PLOVER	Shortgrass prairie, often in heavily grazed areas or prairie dog colonies; **PL.**	Locally common but declining nationwide.
BLACK-NECKED STILT	Alkali flats around lakes and ponds; **PL.**	Locally uncommon in Arkansas River Valley.
AMERICAN AVOCET	Shorelines of lakes and marshes; **WS, MT, PL.**	Locally common in east; uncommon to rare elsewhere.
WILLET	Grassy marshes, **MT, PL.**	Fairly common in North Park; rare on northeastern plains.
SPOTTED SANDPIPER	Shorelines of lakes, ponds, and streams; **WS, MT, PL.**	Fairly common in west and mountains; uncommon in east.
UPLAND SANDPIPER	Tallgrass and midgrass prairies; **PL.**	Fairly common in northeast.
LONG-BILLED CURLEW	Shortgrass and midgrass prairies, **PL.**	Fairly common southeast; rare northeast.
COMMON SNIPE	Marshes, wet meadows, and streambanks; **WS, MT, PL.**	Fairly common statewide to 10,500 feet.
WILSON'S PHALAROPE	Grassy areas and marshes near ponds and lakes; **WS, MT, PL.**	Locally uncommon in western valleys, in mountain valleys, and on eastern plains.

Common migrants to look for in spring and late summer: semipalmated plover, greater yellowlegs, lesser yellowlegs, least sandpiper, Baird's sandpiper, long-billed dowitcher.
MT: Mountains above 7,500 feet; **PL:** Plains and eastern foothills to about 7,500 feet; **WS:** Western Slope valleys and plateaus to about 7,500 feet.

BARN OWLS: MASTERS OF THE DARK

The hisses, shrieks, and rattles of nesting barn owls haunt lowland canyons on both sides of the Divide throughout the summer. At night their primary call, an ear-piercing hiss, sounds like a locomotive venting steam. The rattling, produced by a rapid clapping together of beaks, suggests a sorcerer performing incantations in the darkness.

Barn owls can capture their prey, usually mice, voles, or shrews, in total darkness. Enormous ears located on either side of a broad facial disk pick up the minutest sounds. The ears are positioned asymmetrically, an adaptation that may help these owls triangulate on their targets. Studies have shown that barn owl hunting success falls off on rainy nights, possibly because wet vegetation muffles the rustling sounds made by foraging rodents.

Colorado's barn owls may begin laying eggs as early as February and as late as May. The eggs hatch after about 32 days, and the young barn owls leave the nest about 55 days later. Late nesting probably works for barn owls because their target prey produce several litters throughout the summer and reach peak populations in late summer or early fall. In southern parts of their North American range, and possibly in southeastern Colorado, barn owls produce two or more broods, with the last brood leaving the nest as late as November.

Barn owl pairs nest in cliff hollows, tree hollows, burrows in embankments, and ledges in silos, barns, and abandoned buildings. Scattered pairs breed throughout the eastern plains, in the lower Colorado and Gunnison River valleys, and in low elevation mountain valleys. Good places to watch for them include sandstone canyons in the Comanche National Grassland, dry washes on the northeastern plains, and embankments along the Colorado River, near Grand Junction. Look for whitewash (excrement) on cliff or wall faces and listen for the soft hissing of owlets begging for food.

WHINING AND DINING

Only female mosquitoes, who need the protein in blood to develop eggs, whine and bite. They beat their wings up to 600 times per second, producing a high-pitched whine that attracts males. The faster the wing-beat, the higher the pitch. Males respond to a broad range of frequencies, usually between 250 and 500 cycles per second, and have even been attracted to tuning forks. In *Life on a Little-Known Planet,* Howard Evans wrote that there was once talk of trapping mosquitoes by playing recordings of their love songs, but since females are not attracted to sound, the attempt bagged only males.

Mosquitoes belong to the same order as the common housefly: Diptera or two-winged flies. Forty-three species flourish in Colorado (more than two thousand worldwide) wherever there is standing water for the larvae. Since some species go from egg to adult in three to four days, even a mud puddle will do. The eggs of one of our most common mosquitoes, *Aedes vexans,* can survive more than two years after the mud dries. The larvae, or "wrigglers," live just below the water surface, breathing through a snorkellike tube on their tail.

In Colorado, mosquitoes are rampant from late May to the end of August, even when snow is on the ground. Their ubiquitousness is evidenced by place names such as Mosquito Pass, Mosquito Peak, Mosquito Creek, and Mosca Pass. *Mosca* is the Spanish word for "fly," and *mosquito* is "little fly."

The itch of a bite is actually caused by the mosquito's saliva, which contains an enzyme that acts as an anticoagulant, preventing our blood from clotting at the bite site. Some mosquitoes inject an anesthetic so you don't even feel the bite until it's too late. Although mosquitoes spread some diseases, the chief risk in Colorado is from the *Culex tarsalis,* which transmits the encephalitis virus, mainly to horses.

So, if mosquitoes prey on us, what preys on mosquitoes? Damselflies and dragonflies are sometimes called "mosquito hawks" because of their insatiable appetite for the tiny fly. They make a sort of basket with their spine-covered legs to strain the air for prey. *Gambusia,* a small fish that eats mosquito larvae, and plains killifish, a minnow, are also good for mosquito control. Electronic bug "zappers" are not effective, but birds, such as nighthawks, are.

Mike Weissmann, co-founder of the Butterfly Pavilion and Insect Center, defends this universally disliked critter, pointing out that mosquito larvae convert coarse organic matter found in water into nutrients readily absorbed by plants and by predators that feed on mosquitoes. "Adults have scales adorning their wings and legs with beautiful patterns of white, gray, gold, silver, and black. Males have delicate feathery antennae that resemble feather dusters or plumes of goose down. The mosquito challenges us to find beauty and purpose in nature, even when it hurts or annoys us," he says.

Nevertheless, pestered people sometimes ask why an omnipotent deity created mosquitoes. A Tlingit story doesn't answer the why but does spin a yarn on how. Long ago a giant killed people to drink their blood. Then a brave man killed him, cut the body into pieces, burned each piece in the fire, and scattered the ashes in the wind. The ashes turned into a cloud of mosquitoes that have been drinking our blood ever since.

AUGUST EVENTS

MAMMALS

✿ Colorado chipmunks, born late May or June, appear above ground.

✿ Elk and deer begin to scrape velvet from antlers that are now full grown.

BIRDS

✿ Mountain chickadees, pine siskins, and nuthatches begin their vertical migration down from the high country.

✿ Hummingbirds fight fiercely at feeders.

✿ Migrating shorebirds feed at lakes and ponds on the plains.

✿ Common nighthawks congregate and swoop erratically after flying insects.

OTHER CRITTERS

✿ In spite of the nighthawks, mosquitoes still abound and bite.

✿ Male tarantulas migrate in search of mates.

PLANTS AND FUNGI

✿ Mushrooms "mushroom."

✿ Blue chicory blooms on the plains and blue gentians in the tundra.

✿ Blazingstars bloom at night at low to mid elevations.

✿ Tundra foliage takes on autumnal colors.

✿ Wild blueberries, raspberries, wintergreen berries, and chokecherries ripen.

IN THE SKY

✿ "Moon of Black Cherries Ripening" (Cheyenne and Sioux).

✿ The Perseid Meteor Shower, possibly the best of the year, peaks around August 12. If you get away from city lights and look to the north, you may see as many as sixty meteors per hour.

✿ Lammas, the time of hot weather, the beginning of the harvest, and the approximate halfway point between the Summer Solstice and the Autumn Equinox, was traditionally celebrated on August 1.

✿ The loosely organized constellation Sagittarius is visible above the southern horizon just to the left of Scorpius around 9:00 P.M. This group of second- and third-magnitude stars is said to represent an archer aiming his arrow at the scorpion.

September ushers in autumn with aspen gold here in the Crystal River Valley near McClure pass.

9

September

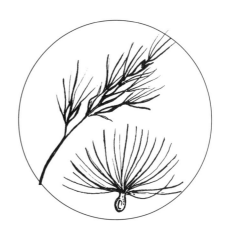

All around the birds in flocks are flying;

Dipping, rising, circling, see them coming.

See, many birds are flocking here,

All about us now together coming.

—PAWNEE

MIGRATION IS IN full swing, and many creatures are on the move. Occasionally a monarch butterfly wafts by on its way to Mexico. Ladybugs come together in bright orange clusters on mountaintops. Bluebirds come together preparing to head south. High overhead sandhill cranes in V-formations utter strange cries.

Knowing it's a silly, anthropomorphic question, we nevertheless wonder: How can they bear to leave when autumn leaves burst into flames of yellow and red? When aspen groves become cathedrals of golden light? When even sumac and poison ivy glow like rubies? This is the month when we cannot get enough of autumn color and agree with poet William Watson, "O be less beautiful or be less brief!"

Red apples and purple grapes hang overhead in orchard and vineyard. Wild currants, plums, and chokecherries ripen, and bears strip the bushes bare. It's a bountiful time of year for food, and all living things are harvesting or fattening up for winter.

Of course, some creatures have other things in mind. The bugling of the elk reminds us that this invigorating season is also a time for starting new life. The elk are now together coming as all around the birds in flocks are flying.

Sep

	Grand Junction (4,824 ft.)	Steamboat Springs (6,760 ft.)	Alamosa (7,536 ft.)	Berthoud Pass (11,310 ft.)	Denver (5,282 ft.)	Lamar (3,620 ft.)
Ave. high (°F)	81	71	73	53	77	82
Ave. low (°F)	53	33	37	31	48	51
Max. high (°F)	100	91	87	73	97	105
Min. low (°F)	28	12	15	4	17	23
Ave. prec. (in.)	0.82	1.64	0.89	2.05	1.24	1.32
Max. prec. (in.)	3.78	8.15	1.94	3.93	4.67	4.42
Ave. snow (in.)	0.1	0.8	0.3	8.7	1.6	0.0
Max. snow (in.)	3.1	19.6	4.2	34.5	21.3	2.0

Some of Colorado's most changeable weather occurs during this month of clear blue skies and cool nights. A storm on September 17, 1971, dumped more than 2 feet of snow on the Front Range foothills. The temperature fell nearly 60 degrees in forty-eight hours. Many Colorado stations have recorded September temperatures in the 100s, including Eads, which reached 107 in 1947.

The first "crest clouds" of the season develop over the Continental Divide as strong westerly winds carry Pacific moisture up the western side of the Rockies and deposit it as snow in the high mountains. These winds often gust to over 100 miles per hour as they rush down the eastern slope of the Rockies.

See "Colorado Climate Summary" (p. 1) for information on averages, extremes, and sources.

september  ecosystem

Aspen in their Glory

American Indians called aspen "the tree that whispers to itself." It's usually called "quaking aspen" or *Populus tremuloides* because the leaves tremble and murmur in the slightest breeze. Early in September an occasional tree turns into a lone golden candle. By the fourth weekend, high country colors reach their peak and brighten mountainsides in warm yellow light. Leaves glitter and glow in luminous tones, sometimes shading into salmon and red. By the end of the month some groves are half bare, and individual leaves—like carefully placed yellow dots—create a living pointillist painting.

Although aspen occasionally reproduce through seeds, their primary method is

FALL COLOR CHANGE

One autumn long ago three hunters and a dog chased a bear who led them faster and faster in all directions. Finally the bear ran high into the sky, where the hunters killed and butchered him on a stack of maple and sumac branches. The leaves, stained by his blood, still turn blood-red every fall, and the Great Bear, followed by three hunters and their dog, can still be seen in the sky at any time of the year. These stars (also called the Big Dipper) can never rest until the hunters and the dog again catch the bear, according to several American Indian legends.

Botanists believe shorter day length, cooler temperatures, drier conditions, bright sunlight, and soil chemistry initiate fall color change. In autumn, a thin-walled layer of cells (the abscission layer) develops at the base of the leaf stem at the point where the leaf will break away from the twig. At the same time, a corky layer develops between the abscission layer and the twig. This layer will prevent an open wound when the leaf falls, and it prevents sugars from moving from the leaf to the trunk. If there is a hard freeze at the wrong time, the process is interrupted, and leaves may hang on until winter winds finally sweep them away. A few trees, such as pin oaks (*Quercus paulustris*), develop no abscission layer and normally hold their leaves well into winter.

Leaves appear green during summer because chlorophyll, the dominant pigment, masks the yellow pigments, carotin and xanthophyll. The green chlorophyll is continually destroyed and replenished during photosynthesis. However, in fall chlorophyll is no longer replenished, and the old chlorophyll bleaches away, revealing the underlying yellow pigments.

Red and purple leaves result when the sugars and starches in the leaves oxidize into chemical substances called anthocyanins. The leaves need sunny days to manufacture sugars but cool nights to form the corky layer that keeps the sugar in the leaf. High acidity in the soil and in the sap contributes to the reddest reds. Alkaline soil and sap produce a bluish red.

to clone by root suckering. They are the most widespread tree species in North America and may also be among the oldest because of this ability to clone. Although the trunk may die, new trees spring from the original root stock. Some cloned clumps are estimated to be ten thousand years old, and some may predate the last ice age. In 1992, botanists reported an aspen clone covering 106 acres in the Wasatch Mountains of Utah and weighing more than 6,000 tons. It consists of some forty-seven thousand connected stems from the root of a single individual.

Viewers are often puzzled to find both yellow and red trees together in the same stand. Although members of a clone share the same genes and bear the same color, they may grow next to trees cloned from a different individual. An entire mountainside of aspen may contain only a few genetic individuals.

The lush understory of an aspen grove includes a wealth of wildflowers in summer. Even in September, black-eyed susans, cinquefoil, asters, fireweed, and harebells still bloom as the foliage of blueberries, wild roses, geraniums, and red-osier dogwood turns red. During a wet year, the floor may be covered with orange, red, and lavender Russula mushrooms—a multicolored mosaic to complement the roof of gold.

Aspen are used by many species, from humans to hummingbirds. Many American Indians made a tonic tea from the bark, which contains substances similar to aspirin, and Paiutes and Shoshones drank aspen bark tea to relieve venereal disease. Aspen groves are home to 55 mammal species and some 135 species of birds. (See p. 122, June, for information on cavity nesters.) In a way, aspen bark acts like a visitor log book, as many creatures, including—unfortunately—humans, record their passing on its surface.

Moose, elk, and deer all seek the shelter of aspen groves and browse on the trees' leaves, bark, twigs, and associated vegetation. The trunks are used by deer and elk to rub velvet from their antlers in early autumn. Black bears devour berries from the bushes that thrive in the understory and scratch the trunks to mark their territory. Look for the scars these animals leave in the soft bark. Aspen also attract porcupines, who may kill a tree by munching off the bark that encircles the trunk.

Beavers can decimate an aspen grove in a season or so, leaving behind stumps chewed into points. In Rocky Mountain National Park, several trails through aspen have been rerouted over the years to avoid areas flooded out by beaver dams. These toothy rodents eat 2 to 4 pounds of aspen twigs and bark each day and can gnaw down a tree 10 inches and more in diameter. They store branches and saplings underwater for winter feasting and use them to build lodges and dams. It takes about twenty aspen per year to support one beaver.

Aspen usually colonize disturbed areas, such as roadsides or sites of forest fires or avalanches. In the absence of fires or other disturbances, conifers eventually replace them in most areas. The complete transition may take a century. Aspen groves occur at altitudes of 7,000 to 10,000 feet, although they are used in landscaping at lower elevations. The most glorious groves occur on the Western Slope.

Where To Go

🐾 Rabbit Ears Pass and other areas near Steamboat Springs.
🐾 Grand Mesa east of Grand Junction.

✽ San Juan Mountains in southwest Colorado.

✽ Cumbres Pass between Antonito, Colorado, and Chama, New Mexico.

✽ Maroon Bells–Snowmass Wilderness and other areas near Aspen.

✽ McClure Pass near Marble.

✽ South Park and Kenosha Pass near Fairplay.

✽ Golden Gate State Park near Denver.

✽ Rocky Mountain National Park.

SETTING SAIL: SEED DISPERSAL

Dandelion and milkweed seeds float down from the heavens like tiny parachutes. Fruits swell and ripen on hawthorns, sumacs, chokecherries, wild plums, and serviceberries. Buffalo burrs cling to our pants, and cheatgrass spears our socks. Plants mature, let go, and cast their fates to the wind, the waters, and the unthinking actions of birds and mammals.

On autumn walks look for the feathery seeds of wind-dispersed plants and note the intricacies of their designs. Fruits of milkweed, fireweed, poplars, and sunflowers all have tiny plumes that carry them off in the gentlest breeze. Plumed fruits of some thistles and sunflowers travel 50 miles or more. Maple, birch, and box elder fruits have papery wings to keep them airborn. These fruits look like miniature helicopter blades spinning through the air.

Orchid seeds don't need parachutes, plumes, or wings. Hardly larger than a grain of dust, they can sail for hundreds of miles on autumn breezes. It's no coincidence that orchids, along with sunflowers, thrive throughout the temperate and tropical zones and are often among the first plants to colonize islands far out at sea. Tumbleweeds, such as knapweed (*Acosta* spp.) and Russian thistle (*Salsola* spp.), use the wind in a different way, allowing it to transport the whole plant until the seeds shake loose.

Open up the dried seed pod of a vetch, milk vetch, or lupine. Seeds of the pea family, including the beans in your cupboard, sport a hard, impervious outer skin and an air space between the skin and embryo. Many are adapted for survival in water and can float great distances. Seeds of some legumes have crossed the oceans and sprouted on continents several thousands of miles away. For Colorado legumes, which do not depend on floatation for dispersal, the impermeability of their seed skins enables the seeds to lie on the ground for years before germinating, a useful trait in an arid and unpredictable climate.

When their seed pods are ripe, legumes forcefully expel their seeds with a small explosion like the popping of a champagne cork. Geraniums, including the ubiquitous filaree (*Erodium cicutarium*) of parking lots, roadsides, and disturbed hillsides, also

Sep

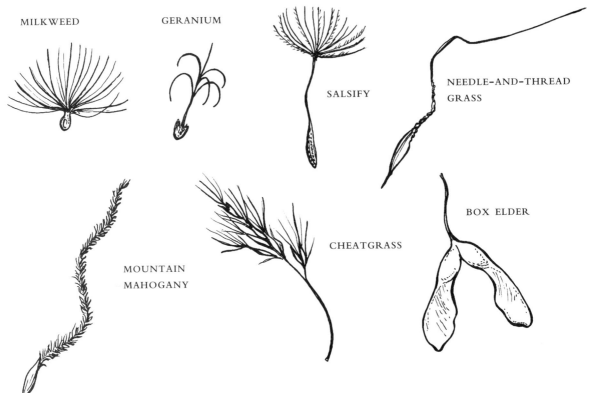

MILKWEED

GERANIUM

SALSIFY

NEEDLE-AND-THREAD
GRASS

MOUNTAIN
MAHOGANY

CHEATGRASS

BOX ELDER

have explosive fruits. Once detached from the host plant, the five-seeded geranium fruits literally plant themselves. Attached to the fruits is a long, pointed remnant of the style, which coils and uncoils with changes in humidity. This springlike object acts like a corkscrew as it pushes up against the grass and wildflower stems, forcing the seeds into the ground. Needle-and-thread-grasses (*Stipa* spp.), known to children as "speargrass," use similar devices, as do mountain mahoganies (*Cercocarpus* spp). The long, delicate attachments give mountain mahoganies their distinctive feathery appearance.

When we go for a walk, we facilitate plant dispersal by getting things stuck on our socks, by eating wild fruits and spitting out the seeds, or by brushing against the ripe seedheads of wildflowers and grasses. Succulent fruits of many plants contain especially hard or poisonous seeds. This adaptation ensures that some seeds will be discarded by birds or mammals or make their way intact through the consumers' digestive systems. A cup of apple seeds can kill a human. Bitter almond seeds contain cyanide, and apricot seeds contain the toxic substance used to manufacture laetrile. Plants with totally edible seeds take advantage of the absentmindedness or profligacy of birds and mammals. Oaks and pines proliferate in part because squirrels and seed-caching birds bury more seeds than they consume.

Many seeds have clinging hooks or spikes that attach readily to animal fur or human clothing. Several species of cheatgrass (*Anisantha* spp.) came to the new world in the socks of immigrants or in the fur of their pets. Arriving by accident on our continent, they found a "cheatgrass heaven" of overgrazed and disturbed grasslands. These and other weeds have taken advantage of our uniquely human ability to create habitat for widely dispersing plants that thrive in arid and semibarren landscapes. We curse these weeds, and try in vain to eradicate them, without giving a lot of thought to how they became established in the first place.

WILD FRUIT HARVEST

During the last days of summer, in the moon of black cherries ripening, Cheyenne women and children would search prairie hillsides and canyons for chokecherries and other ripe fruits. The Cheyenne and other Plains Indians crushed the chokecherries and mixed them with animal fat to create pemmican, a winter staple. They also used chokecherries in a variety of rituals, including celebration of a young woman's first menstruation. The Sun Dance often began on the day of the full moon in the month of ripening chokecherries.

In what is now southwestern Colorado, Ute women gathered serviceberries, which they crushed and molded into round, dry cakes. These cakes were eaten raw or broken up and added to winter soups. The Utes used both serviceberries and chokecherries to make pemmican, and they feasted on fresh serviceberries throughout the late summer and early fall.

> ### On the Pleasures of Eating Rosehips
>
> A traditional Hidatsa story contains a pointed reference to those who would include rosehips in their diet. "We Hidatsa raise corn, beans, sunflower seed, and good squashes to eat. We are not starving, that we must eat roseberries . . . we think they are food for wild men."
>
> Source: *Kelly Kindscher, 1987.* **Edible Wild Plants of the Prairie.**

Although fruit harvesting was usually considered women's work, men often came along to ward off bears and other wild creatures. Wildlife intent on foraging could be oblivious of humans, and accidental encounters commonly occurred. Nineteenth-century European explorers occasionally encountered grizzly bears in plum and chokecherry thickets along prairie rivers.

Today ripening fruits still provide a late summer and early fall feast for Colorado wildlife populations. On a September morning in the Front Range foothills, you can watch bears harvesting chokecherries and raspberries, porcupines munching on red sumac stalks, pine squirrels and Steller's jays chattering and rasping over choice morsels of wild plum. On the Western Slope, extensive serviceberry thickets support the state's highest concentration of foraging black bears. These thickets also entice coyotes, red foxes, porcupines, wild turkeys, and a variety of small mammals.

Unfortunately, there is not enough wild fruit to go around in our overpopulated world. Use moderation in picking wild foods, knowing that many birds and mammals cannot survive without them.

FALL BIRD MIGRATION

For decades ornithologists and naturalists have aimed their telescopes and binoculars at the autumnal full moon to count migrating songbirds. One observer using this method counted more than nine thousand migrants on a single September night.

Night migration helps birds avoid overheating on long flights and renders them relatively invisible to predators. It also enables them to forage during the day, accumulating fat reserves necessary to fuel their journeys. Day migrants include swallows, swifts, and nighthawks, who feed most actively at dusk and dawn; loons and pelicans, who feed underwater; and hawks, eagles, and falcons, who soar on the strong thermal currents produced by solar heating.

Most night migrants probably use the moon and stars to guide them. Ecologist Stephen Emlen observed caged indigo buntings in a planetarium in order to study songbird reliance on stellar cues. Around the time of spring migration, the buntings hopped and fluttered restlessly in the general direction of the North Star. When experimenters rotated the planetarium sky, changing the position of the North Star, the buntings reoriented in that direction. Emlen concluded that young buntings recognize the area of the sky with least stellar rotation (the area around the North Star) and use that part of the night sky as a navigational fix.

Migrating songbirds also home in on magnetic cues (including the earth's magnetic field and ground magnetism), visual landmarks, and smells. Nevertheless, it is mind boggling to contemplate how a pair of Swainson's hawks

A Bird Mystery

Long before the details of migration were known, people speculated on what happened to birds in winter. In 1703 one theory (possibly facetious?) suggested they migrated to the moon. Another theory suggested that small, weak birds rode on the backs of bigger birds. And in the late sixteenth century the preposterous idea was promoted that birds hibernated in mud in lake bottoms or in caves. Preposterous, that is, until December 29, 1946, when an ornithologist found a hibernating poorwill in California. Its body temperature was 40 degrees lower than normal. For the next three years it returned to its hollow rock and remained torpid from late November to late February. Since then, poorwills and some nighthawks have been induced to hibernate in captivity, but hibernation in birds is extremely rare.

wintering in Argentina can return each spring to the same nest tree in eastern Colorado after a northward migration of 6,000 miles. Some trial and error must be involved, and birds must have a remarkable ability to discriminate among geographic features. Birds that have been captured by biologists and released several hundred miles from their nesting sites often fly around randomly until they find a familiar landmark and then take a direct course toward home.

At least half of the birds passing through each fall are young of the year undertaking their first migrations. Since most of these young travel separately from their parents, we know that some of their navigational abilities are innate, rather than learned. However, birds that follow a migration route over several seasons do become more skilled and tend to travel faster than do first-time migrants.

The fall migration comes in waves. Shorebirds begin passing through in July and August, followed by sparrows, warblers, and other songbirds in September and early October, hawks and eagles in late September and October, and ducks and geese from early fall into November. The greatest number of birds often passes through on the heels of Arctic fronts.

Spectacular bird-watching opportunities occur when lingering fronts and low clouds hovering over the mountains and plains "trap" migrants, many of which are warblers. As many as thirty species of warblers have been seen within the state during a single fall migration season. Rare migrants include birds that have been blown far off course by autumn storms. An October storm in 1995 carried an ancient murrelet, a Pacific Ocean seabird, into Louisville. The murrelet was placed on a United Airlines jet and flown to San Diego, where it unfortunately died before being able to continue its southward flight.

Where To Go

Sep

🦆 White River between Meeker and Rangely.

🦆 Gateway Special Recreation Management Area, southwest of Grand Junction.

🦆 Wheat Ridge Greenbelt.

🦆 Valco Ponds, Pueblo.

🦆 Barr Lake State Park, northeast of Denver.

🦆 Crow Valley Campground, Pawnee National Grassland.

🦆 Lake Henry, near Ordway.

See "Vanishing Migrants?" in May (pp. 103–105) and "Greening Woodlands" in April (pp. 68–72) for additional places to go.

THE SOUND OF AUTUMN

The bugling of the elk is the fanfare that heralds autumn. This martial music reaches its peak in late September and early October, though an impetuous elk may sound off as early as August. Sometimes elk bugle during the day, but they are most active at dawn and dusk along forest edges and in adjoining meadows.

Listen for an eerie, high pitched "whinny" ending in a series of snorts. "A-a-a-a-ai-e-eeeeeeeee! e-uh! e-uh! e-uh!" is how Joe Van Wormer transcribes it in *The World of the American Elk*. Because larger bulls have deeper calls, you can guess size and dominance from the pitch. There's nothing like an elk reveille to jolt you out of a down sleeping bag on a frosty September morning!

Cows and young males occasionally bugle, but creating pandemonium is the domain of mature bull elks. These males stand 5 feet high and weigh about 750 pounds. A set of antlers can weigh up to 50 pounds and grow up to half an inch a day. During the rut or mating season, the bulls undergo physiological changes, possibly triggered by decreasing periods of daylight. Their necks and shoulders become swollen, and they vent their lust and stress through bugling and frenzied displays. They attack trees and shrubs. They urinate copiously, drenching themselves and rolling in urine-soaked grass and wallowing in mud. They extend their muzzle upward and draw back their lips to expose their lower incisors. It may look like a smile, but zoologists call it "grimacing."

A bull elk sports a regal set of antlers in Rocky Mountain National Park.

The purpose of all this sound and fury is to collect and keep a harem of five to thirty cows. Posturing or a brief chase usually drives away younger or weaker challengers. But if bluffing fails, combat ensues. Then the two massive males circle, charge, and clash antlers, pushing and shoving until the weaker one gives way. Elk may be injured or killed in these battles. The fourth tine on the antlers is called "the dagger point" because it is so deadly. Van Wormer reports that antlers are occasionally ripped loose along with portions of the skull and that sometimes antlers become so entangled that both elk die.

The victorious harem master mates with all his females, although occasionally an upstart will slip in when His Majesty is busy battling. Naturalist-writer Gary Turbak reports that in New Zealand the roaring of red deer, a close elk relative, causes the cows to enter estrus (the short period when females are receptive) sooner and suggests the same thing may happen with elk bugling. Calves are born late the following May or June.

Between brawling and mating, the dominant male has little time to eat or sleep and may lose up to 100 pounds. When the rut ends in October, he will be a shadow, an echo, of the royal stag that bugled in September.

Elk (*cervus elaphus*) are also called wapiti, a Shawnee word meaning "white rump." They were almost extirpated from Colorado in the early 1900s because of heavy hunting. Fewer than a thousand inhabited the state in 1910. Then 350 were reintroduced to Colorado from Jackson, Wyoming. The current population exceeds 200,000.

Elk feed on shrubs, grasses, and forbs and have actually become a nuisance in such places as Estes Park, where gardeners must erect 8-foot fences around their vegetables. Elk also impair the regeneration of aspen and willow stands by eating the bark, twigs, and seedlings. Gashes and other damage attributed to bears are often the work of elk. In Rocky Mountain National Park, where some groves have disappeared since the 1970s, researchers are simulating elk browsing patterns in fenced areas to determine what effect elk have on the park vegetation.

Where To Go

Elk are widespread from the eastern foothills to the tundra, all the way to the Utah border. In the fall they migrate down to midelevations. Look and listen for them at dusk in mountain meadows, but if the elk become nervous, back away to avoid disturbing them. Especially large herds congregate at:

🐾 Gunnison State Wildlife Area.
🐾 Stonewall Wintering Elk Range, just north of the New Mexico border.
🐾 Mount Zion Wintering Elk Site, north of Leadville.
🐾 Rocky Mountain National Park.

BEAR BINGEING

Bears preparing for hibernation consume about 20,000 calories a day. They spend twenty hours a day gorging on fruits, nuts, grasses, forbs, insects, small mammals, carrion, garbage—just about anything and everything. They're not called "omnivorous" for nothing. They relish something as tiny as a blueberry or a sunflower seed or as large as road-killed elk.

Because of abundant food, Western Slope black bears are among the largest in the West. Females have been weighed at nearly 250 pounds; males, at 350 pounds. However, northern Front Range bears who forage in habitats fragmented by rural subdivisions are undersized, according to a recent study.

This is a dangerous time of year for bears, as they are most likely now to come in contact with humans, their only real enemy. When natural food crops are low, they venture into our yards, raid our trash cans and bird feeders, and even enter our houses in search of food. We can protect both the bears and our property by keeping garbage and other temptations inside.

In August 1995, a bear wandered into a home in Pinewood Springs, and wildlife officials estimated there was one bear for every thirty residents in that area. That same month, a bear was captured on the field of the Grand Junction Airport. In August 1994, a bear was removed from a Denver mall and another bear from a Boulder mall dumpster. And then there was the "Fair Bear," who wandered onto the Renaissance Festival Grounds in Larkspur and was lured to a trap with blueberry pie and doughnuts.

These interactions are more detrimental to bears than to humans, as Colorado has a "Two strikes and you're out" policy. The first time a bear becomes a nuisance, it is trapped, tagged, and relocated. The second time, the bear is killed. A total of 811 bear complaints were received in the state in 1994. By 1995 the number of complaints grew to 1,056, and 101 bears were relocated. Forty-two were killed by the Division of Wildlife.

For more bear stories, see p. 22 (January) and 222–224 (November).

LADYBUGS BY THE MILLIONS

It's mid-September, and you've just attained the summit—only it's been taken over by a million other vigorous mountaineers. The annual assemblages of ladybugs cover mountaintops with what looks like pulsating orange paint. Ladybugs, also called ladybird beetles, perform a reverse vertical migration to high elevations in preparation for winter.

By November many will have crawled under debris or into bark or rock crevices to overwinter in a state of dormancy called diapause. In spring the survivors emerge to mate, fly downslope into the valleys and plains, and lay eggs, which hatch into larvae in about five days. Adult ladybugs can live for about a year.

Both adults and the larvae (usually spotted with blue, black, and orange dots) gorge on aphids and other soft-bodied garden pests and are one of the chief enemies of the notorious Colorado potato beetle. One ladybug can eat up to five thousand aphids in a lifetime. However, when birds or other predators try to turn the tables, a ladybug's blood pressure rises, causing foul-smelling blood to ooze from the leg joints. Ladybugs' bright orange color warns predators they are not a tasty snack.

The number of dots and how they are arranged on the back helps differentiate among the more than two thousand ladybug species known worldwide. More than sixty species occur in Colorado, but entomologist Boris Kondratieff says introduced exotics have reduced the numbers of natives. The seven-spotted ladybird, introduced to control aphids, is now one of our most widespread species. Although ladybugs are beneficial insects, Kondratieff says there is a "bad apple" in the group: the Mexican bean beetle, which eats bean leaves and pods. The adult has eight dark spots in transverse rows on a yellowish back.

No one knows for sure why ladybird beetles assemble on mountain peaks. The easy answer—that they huddle together for warmth—does not seem to be true. Pheromones (distinctive odors) bring members of the same species together and may expedite finding a mate when they emerge from diapause. They often concentrate in areas of higher moisture and on sunlit sites. The same "hilltopping" phenomenon occurs in the Sierra Nevada, the Swiss

Spiderlings Aloft

Young spiders of many species disperse in autumn by means of a strange aerial technique called "ballooning." They climb to the tip of a twig or other high point and spin a single thread that becomes airborne on just a breath of wind. Hanging to the bottom of the long strand of silk, hatchlings may float for hundreds of miles before landing in a new territory. Or, they may snag on an obstacle only a few feet from take-off. In September and October look for their draglines gleaming like gold in the air or caught in fences, grasses, and shrubs.

Sep

Alps, and other parts of the world. Entomologist Edwin Way Teale wrote that one mass in the Sierra Nevada contained about 750 million individuals.

In California, ladybugs are harvested to sell to gardeners. In *Broadsides from the Other Orders,* Sue Hubbell wrote that just two collectors on a one-day "bugging" expedition bagged about 2,325,000 beetles and considered their haul disappointing. Most entomologists say that using collected or mail-order ladybugs for insect control in outdoor gardens is useless because the beetles arrive at the wrong time in their life cycle and simply fly away upon release. Collecting also interferes with natural processes and could have a ripple effect throughout the ecosystem.

Don't Eat Me

For years the similarity between monarchs and viceroys was cited as an example of Batesian mimicry, a protective mechanism named after Henry Bates, the British naturalist who described how edible butterflies escape predation by looking like distasteful species. Scientists thought willow-feeding viceroys had evolved to resemble monarchs, who absorb toxins from milkweeds. However, Lincoln Brower conducted "taste tests" with caged red-winged blackbirds, offering them abdomens, minus telltale wings, of both viceroys and monarchs. The birds tasted and violently rejected both species but consumed other butterfly abdomens. The similarity between the two butterflies thus seems to be an example of Mullerian mimicry (named for German naturalist Fritz Muller) in which unpalatable species flaunt bright colors and mimic one another, thus reinforcing the "don't eat me" lesson.

Where To Go

Almost any summit in the Front Range may harbor ladybug gatherings, but large aggregations have not been reported west of the Continental Divide. If you know of areas outside the Front Range, please contact us, via the publisher. Places where they are frequently spotted include:

- Thorodin Mountain near Golden.
- Green Mountain and Bear Peak near Boulder.
- Mt. Falcon Park near Denver.

MONARCH MIGRATION

The word *ephemeral* could have been coined to describe the life of butterflies. Most live less than two weeks as adults; some only a few days. But the strange life history of the brilliant orange-and-black monarch butterfly contradicts orthodoxy. The first monarchs to emerge in spring lead conventional lives. They mate, lay eggs, and die—all within a period of about two weeks. Three to four generations are born and die throughout the summer.

Then in late summer or early autumn a generation of larger butterflies takes flight. These monarchs are reproductively immature and may live up to ten months. Only these late-hatching monarchs migrate. Most monarchs from the western United States migrate to California, while monarchs from the eastern part of the country head for Mexico. On arrival, the butterflies congregate by the millions in a state of semihibernation.

In spring they start the return journey, though most will die before reaching "home." Along the way, the females lay eggs on their host plant, the milkweed. The caterpillars gorge on the milkweed and undergo metamorphosis. And new generations continue the age-old migration route, mysteriously finding their way home without any discernible guidance.

Monarch butterfly on milkweed.

The reason for this mass migration is unknown but may lie in the insect's evolutionary past. One theory says that the monarchs, which probably originated in South America, followed the milkweed as it spread northward as the glaciers retreated. Natural selection may have favored individuals that returned to warmer climates in winter. The butterflies that cleverly avoided freezing passed on their genes to succeeding generations, also "programmed" for migration.

The largest monarch wintering site is in the Mexican state of Michoacán in fir forests at elevations of 9,000 to 11,000 feet. Unknown to scientists until 1975, this 6,400-square-mile area is now a reserve harboring some 10 to 50 million monarchs per acre. Some migrating monarchs fly as far as 3,100 miles to cluster together in masses so thick they can bend tree branches. In cold weather, the clusters are denser and may help conserve heat and protect the butterflies from wind and rain.

Logging near the Michoacán preserve threatens the protective forest canopy. When the surrounding forests are cut, snow becomes more prevalent in the central area. Lincoln Brower, who studied monarchs for two decades, predicts they could become extinct within twenty years if logging continues at present levels.

Monarch migration in Colorado is only a trickle, not a tidal wave, as the population is small compared to that of many other states, and the migration route is still a mystery. Monarchs from the Western Slope probably head for California, but no one is sure where the eastern slope population goes. In Colorado the generation that migrates usually hatches in September, sometimes as late as October.

Tarantulas

The large, hairy tarantulas that inhabit the southern part of Colorado suffer from an unwarranted bad reputation. This docile spider, called the Texas Brown, rarely bites, and its venom is virtually harmless to humans. A relative of the Texas Brown, the rose-haired tarantula, is petted by hundreds of people each day at the Butterfly Pavilion and Insect Center in Westminster.

Tarantula horror stories may stem from the town of Taranto, Italy. According to folklore, people bitten by a type of wolf spider were driven to dance until they died or recovered. The dance was called the Tarantella. Many of us have been haunted by a version we were forced to hammer out on the piano as children.

Usually tarantulas live in burrows, emerging to hunt small insects. Females can live for 25 to 30 years; males, 10 to 15 years. On August and early September nights in places like Comanche National Grassland, watch for male tarantulas migrating short distances in search of mates.

Researchers from the Butterfly Pavilion have been tagging and releasing local monarchs since 1996 in an effort to find where they go.

The Entomological Society of America is lobbying to have the monarch, the most familiar and loved butterfly in the country, declared our national insect.

Where To Go

Anywhere milkweeds are growing, monarch butterflies may congregate. Although the larvae must feed on milkweed, the adults nectar from many different flowers. See the distribution maps in the back of Clifford Ferris and F. Martin Brown's *Butterflies of the Rocky Mountain States* for detailed location information.

SEPTEMBER EVENTS

MAMMALS

⌘ Mule deer bucks begin to lose velvet from antlers and start playful sparring.

⌘ Elk start to bugle in the high country and continue through October.

⌘ Fox families go their separate ways in September and October.

BIRDS

⌘ Large flocks of songbirds gather together prior to flying south.

⌘ Hummingbirds usually leave by second week.

⌘ Hawk migration peaks by last week.

OTHER CRITTERS

⌘ Ladybugs head for the hills.

🦋 Praying mantises and crickets become more active and conspicuous.

🦋 Young spiders balloon to new territories.

PLANTS

🦋 Aspen color reaches peak, usually by fourth week in the high country.

🦋 Shrubs, leafy plants, and grasses in the foothills start to change color.

🦋 Wild plums, berries, grapes, and "escaped" apples ripen.

IN THE SKY

🦋 "Moon When Deer Paw the Earth" (Ogallala Sioux).

🦋 Harvest Moon, the full moon nearest the Autumnal Equinox, occurs in late September or early October. For several successive days, the moon rises soon after sunset, giving farmers additional light for harvesting crops.

🦋 The Autumnal Equinox, when the sun is directly over the equator, occurs around September 22. Day and night lengths are approximately equal all over the earth.

🦋 Look for Cassiopeia (the Lady in the Chair) in the high northeastern sky around 8 P.M.

Sep

Sandhill cranes cross a gibbous moon during their fall migration.

10

October

Wings of birds invisible
Are now fluttering above you.
You stand with face uplifted
And quietly listen there.

—PIMA

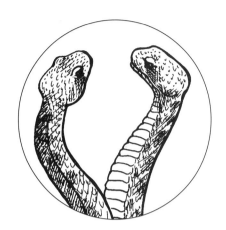

O N FOGGY MORNINGS we stand by a pond and listen for the gabbling of ducks, for the wild cry of Canada geese, and for the swoosh and splash of unseen waterfowl. On other mornings the sky is the bluest of the year, and we look overhead for soaring hawks and for unusual migrants like snow geese or sandhill cranes.

Early in the month colors are still vibrant at lower elevations. Oak woodlands, burnished to rich tints of copper and rust, bring a glow to the hillsides. Along creeks and river bottoms cottonwoods turn to old gold. Later in the month their brown leaves clap in a winter-on-the-way wind. Most flowers are gone, but their seedheads delight us with entrancing shapes and textures. To release a pod of milkweed seeds into the wind is to be a child again.

Now that plants are dying back, the bones and structure of the earth become more prominent. The crisp weather invites us to explore the canyon country for arches, petroglyphs, and dinosaur tracks. Who knows what wonder waits around the next bend or what fossil lies entrapped in the dull matrix of slate?

Oct

In the animal world it's action time for rutting moose. For other creatures, it's time to sleep. Marmots start to hibernate, and rattlesnakes seek dens where they sometimes pile up by the hundreds to quietly snooze away the winter. As the animal and plant world prepares to rest for winter, October is a perfect time to look back on ourselves, tracing prehistoric inhabitants and quietly listening for their ghostly voices.

OCTOBER WEATHER

	Grand Junction (4,824 ft.)	Steamboat Springs (6,760 ft.)	Alamosa (7,536 ft.)	Berthoud Pass (11,310 ft.)	Denver (5,282 ft.)	Lamar (3,620 ft.)
Ave. high (°F)	68	59	63	42	66	72
Ave. low (°F)	42	24	25	21	36	37
Max. high (°F)	88	81	81	63	89	98
Min. low (°F)	16	−4	−10	−5	3	8
Ave. prec. (in.)	0.98	1.87	0.70	2.36	0.98	0.71
Max. prec. (in.)	3.45	4.29	2.37	6.84	4.17	4.44
Ave. snow (in.)	0.5	6.2	3.6	28.0	3.7	0.7
Max. snow (in.)	6.1	24.6	20.3	90.0	31.2	7.8

Low humidities contribute to azure skies and remarkable temperature ranges. Snowstorms often follow on the heels of hot, summerlike days. On October 20, 1995, the weather station at Brown's Park, in northwestern Colorado, recorded a comfortable high of 69°F and a frigid low of 5°F. During that single day, Brown's Park experienced more variation in temperature than San Francisco and many other coastal cities usually experience during an entire year.

Eastern plains residents needed a full complement of summer and winter clothing during October 1993 when Holyoke reported a high of 90°F and a low of 3°F.

See "Colorado Climate Summary" (p. 1) for information on averages, extremes, and sources.

Amidst the Fiery Oaks

Colorado's oak woodlands capture the essence of autumn. Whole hillsides turn fiery orange and red. Drying oak leaves crackle in the wind. Birds and mammals feast on the acorns and on nearby berries and seeds.

The Ute and other mountain Indians depended on oak woodlands for a major portion of their food supply. They ground the acorns into a meal and leached it in water to remove the bitter-tasting tannins. When mixed with cornmeal, acorn meal added protein and flavor to soups, breads, and pancakes. Indians also gathered serviceberries, chokecherries, sumac berries, rosehips, and other wild fruits that grew in profusion.

Eighteenth- and nineteenth-century European explorers had little use for these woodlands. The dense, gnarled vegetation made horseback travel all but impossible. For foot travelers, confrontation with foraging black bears was a gnawing concern. In his 1776 *Journal of Expedition and Discovery,* Father Escalante described "impenetrable" brambles of scrub oak, including "a scruboak thicket so dense that in it four horses vanished from our sight while passing through, so that we had to make a halt in order to look for them."

Modern-day travelers seem equally averse to traversing these colorful but contorted thickets of stunted oaks and prickly shrubs. As a result, oak woodlands are peaceful places to visit and wonderful places to view wildlife. Gambel oak acorns attract rock squirrels, chipmunks, woodrats, desert cottontails, wild turkeys, and scrub jays. Ripe berries entice black bears, coyotes, gray foxes, porcupines, and western spotted skunks, along with noisy flocks of resident and migratory birds. Spotted towhees, dark-eyed juncos, and deer mice shuffle and scurry through the leaf litter.

Desert cottontail populations peak in late summer or early fall. These prolific rabbits can produce offspring at the rate of a litter per month from February through August. Only about 15 percent of the young survive their first winter. The rest succumb to cold, starvation, and predation. Look for cottontail trails crisscrossing the hillsides, small round scat pellets, and small depressions, known as forms, where the cottontails sleep throughout much of the day.

Rock squirrels burrow beneath boulders and shrubs. They feed on acorns, seeds, and other fruits. During autumn, these large ground squirrels are busy fattening up prior to entering a state of torpor or hibernation. Look for them in ravines, quarries, or other areas with exposed rock piles.

Scrub jays squawk and rasp constantly as they squabble over acorns and other choice morsels. These slim-bodied, crestless jays also feed on piñon nuts, wild fruits, eggs, nestling birds, reptiles, and small mammals. Flocks remain on foraging territories

Oct

year-round, defending the acorn crop from other birds. By burying acorns and failing to recover all of them, scrub jays help oak woodlands to spread. These jays also cache piñon nuts and other fruits. They and magpies sometimes perch on the backs of mule deer, hitching a ride while enjoying an easy meal of juicy woodticks.

Oak woodlands occur extensively in western Colorado from about 5,500 to 10,000 feet and sporadically in the foothills of the southern Front Range from about 4,000 to 8,000 feet. Gambel oak is the dominant oak species throughout, although it hybridizes with other oaks in southern Colorado. This scrub oak has leathery, deeply lobed leaves and grows to a height of about 20 feet. It often thrives in areas where fire or other disturbances have killed off conifers, but it may form climax stands at low to mid elevations (usually below 7,000 feet). Biologists estimate that some Gambel oak stands in Utah are more than four thousand years old.

Gamble oaks produce bumper acorn crops every few years. These "mast" years often follow a low production year caused by a late spring freeze.

Where To Go

✿ No Name Canyon, near Glenwood Springs.
✿ Roaring Fork River Valley, Glenwood Springs to Aspen.
✿ Black Canyon of the Gunnison National Monument, near Montrose.
✿ Chimney Rock Archaeological Area, west of Pagosa Springs.
✿ Santa Fe Trail, Air Force Academy, Colorado Springs.
✿ Castlewood Canyon State Park, south of Denver.

FALL WATERFOWL MIGRATION

You can gauge the progression of autumn by observing the size and composition of flocks of migrating waterfowl. First to fly through are the dabblers (surface-feeding ducks)—mallards, northern shovelers, pintails, gadwalls, American wigeons, and green-winged, blue-winged, and cinnamon teal—that have nested in the state or to the north. By late October the blue-winged teal have departed for South America, and populations of other dabblers have begun to thin out. Diving ducks, including common goldeneyes, buffleheads, redheads, lesser scaups, and ring-necked ducks, make their way down to the western valleys and eastern plains from breeding areas in the mountains and far to the north. These species form giant rafts in the middle of our largest lakes and reservoirs until the waters freeze completely over, forcing the ducks to fly farther south.

A few tundra swans, which breed in the Arctic, and trumpeter swans, which breed from Wyoming and northern Nebraska to central Canada, generally pass through in late November or early December. These swans, though locally rare, appear almost annually on large bodies of water on the eastern plains, including Baseline and Valmont Reservoirs, near Boulder; Bonny Reservoir, near Burlington; Chatfield Reservoir, south of Denver; and Pueblo Reservoir.

At Sawhill Ponds Wildlife Refuge, just east of Boulder, you can see a dozen species of migrating ducks and hundreds of Canada geese on a late October morning. These waterfowl attract bald eagles and osprey, who swoop low over the water, prompting an explosion of whirring wings and a frenzy of quacking, whistling, and honking. As the ponds freeze over, red foxes venture out onto the ice to stalk wounded or careless waterfowl.

Because of the constant threat of predation, ducks must remain alert throughout the day. Along with many other kinds of birds, ducks and geese have two sleep patterns: "active-sleep," usually at night, and a type of dozing known as "quiet-sleep." During "quiet-sleep" ducks open their eyes, or peek, at two- to six-second intervals. Males peek more frequently than females, and males in colorful breeding plumage peek more frequently than males sporting the drabber eclipse plumage of summer and early fall.

Persistent quacking and flying in V-formation enable ducks and geese to maintain

Oct

contact with the flock and warn one another of approaching predators. For years scientists believed that V-formation flight enabled waterfowl to conserve energy by "drafting" off one another. However, motion pictures taken of Canada geese revealed that the structure of typical formations is not tight enough to significantly increase flight efficiency. Perhaps V-formation flight serves some other purpose yet to be discovered by scientists.

North American populations of many waterfowl species have declined in recent years. The total estimated breeding duck population in north-central and eastern North America was 37 million in 1996, down from 42 million in 1956, but considerably higher than the low of 25 million in 1962, 1989, and 1990.

Short-term fluctuation in breeding waterfowl populations results largely from weather cycles, which cause ponds to dry up or proliferate. Prairie potholes (shallow, naturally occurring ponds) produce about half of North America's ducks. In North Dakota, more than half of the original 5 million acres of wetlands have been lost, mostly as a result of agriculture.

Some remaining lakes and wetlands become death traps for waterfowl when migrating populations become too concentrated. Each year avian botulism and avian cholera kill thousands of ducks. An avian botulism outbreak in Manitoba's Whitewater Lake in the early 1960s killed fifty thousand waterfowl. Toxic runoff from farms and cities and increasing pressure from urban edge predators, such as crows, red foxes, and domestic dogs, also threaten waterfowl populations.

In parts of Colorado, migrating waterfowl populations have increased as a result of reservoir construction and improved conservation practices. Previously rare species, such as snow geese and wood ducks, have begun to appear regularly at urban ponds and reservoirs, along with hordes of Canada geese. Conversion of reclaimed gravel pits to lakes and ponds has benefited waterfowl along the Front Range urban corridor and in Western Slope valleys. In Boulder County the change in waterfowl populations has been particularly dramatic. On the 1951 Boulder Audubon Christmas Count, observers reported a single waterfowl species, the mallard, whereas observers on the 1993 count reported nineteen species, including snow geese, wood ducks, buffleheads, and hooded mergansers.

Where To Go

❧ Browns Park National Wildlife Refuge, north of Rangely.
❧ Highline State Park, near Grand Junction.
❧ Fruitgrowers Reservoir, Harts Basin, near Delta.

✖ Monte Vista National Wildlife Refuge, near Alamosa.

✖ Pueblo Reservoir.

✖ Big Johnson Reservoir, southeast of Colorado Springs.

✖ Barr Lake State Park, northeast of Denver.

✖ Julesburg Reservoir, west of Julesburg.

✖ John Martin Reservoir, east of La Junta.

For additional places to go, see "Waterfowl Saunas," p. 000 (January).

MOOSE ON THE MAKE

Bull moose bark and moan and occasionally lock horns as they challenge one another for the right to mate with receptive females. These jousts usually involve more pushing than actual combat, but slip-ups can result in serious injury or even death to combatants. As fiercesome as bull moose may appear, it is the cows who usually cause problems for hikers. Cows fiercely protect their young and sometimes charge (and occasionally "tree") curious observers who get too close.

Except for mating and the social interactions between cows and their calves, moose remain solitary throughout the year. Each adult occupies a home range of up to ten square kilometers, usually in areas containing mature coniferous forests, meadows, shrub thickets, and standing water. Home ranges typically shrink in winter, and the animals sometimes "yard up," or aggregate, in riparian thickets where the trampled snow makes travel and foraging easier.

Moose forage in high mountain forests, shrub thickets, meadows, and shallow ponds, munching on grasses, sedges, aquatic plants, wildflowers, willows, and deciduous tree leaves. Weighing up to twelve hundred pounds and consuming as much as fifty pounds of plant material a day, they cut a noticeable swath of broken twigs and trampled vegetation. Adept swimmers, moose can dive up to eighteen feet under water to feed on aquatic plants.

Moose belong to the Cervidae, or deer, family. Their antlers can measure more than four feet from tip to tip. The hairy flap that hangs from a moose's neck is called a "bell" or a "dewlap." Biologists are not sure of its purpose, if any. During cold winters, dewlaps may freeze and fall off.

Although moose occasionally wandered into Colorado from the north, they did not become established within the state until 1978, when the Division of Wildlife introduced two dozen animals into North Park. Since then the Division has used helicopters and trucks to transport moose from North Park to the Creede area in the San Juan Mountains. In addition, animals from the original North Park group have wandered into Middle Park, South Park, and the upper Cache la Poudre drainage. Colorado's moose population currently stands at around 850.

Oct

A recent Division of Wildlife study found that North Park moose spend about two-thirds of their time in montane willow carrs (thickets). These willows provide a year-round food supply as well as shelter from the elements. The Division has erected moose and cattle exclosures along several North Park streams to study the impacts of these herbivores on willow carrs.

Where To Go

🦆 Illinois River Moose Viewing Site, Arapaho National Wildlife Refuge, near Walden.

🦆 Colorado State Forest, near Gould. Moose viewing platform and Moose Visitors Center.

🦆 Silver Thread Scenic Byway (SH 149) between Creede and Lake City.

RATTLESNAKE AGGREGATIONS

The story is told of how a well-known trapper of pioneer days once took refuge from a violent thunderstorm under a shelf of cliff. Rattlesnakes started to go by, first in small groups, and finally in hundreds and thousands, on their way to a den. The ground was alive with them, and he and his horse were cornered until the swarm had passed.
—Lawrence M. Klauber, *Rattlesnakes*

In September and October, western rattlesnakes bask in the sun near the entrances of rodent burrows and small caverns. With the arrival of cold weather, the snakes slither into their dens and enter a state of deep sleep. Late-nineteenth- and early-twentieth-century observers who excavated dens claimed to have found masses of entangled snakes "as large as a watermelon." Herpetologists don't know whether rattlesnakes really entangle themselves in this manner or merely share crowded quarters. They do know that some rattlesnakes travel 10 miles or more from summer foraging areas to hibernacula and that individuals return to the same den site year after year.

Why these cold-blooded reptiles hibernate en masse remains somewhat of a mystery. Winter aggregation may help individuals to conserve moisture and a small amount of heat. It's possible that the practice of aggregation offers no particular

MALE RATTLESNAKES "JOUSTING"

advantages and that rattlesnakes are simply programmed to seek out and return to a limited number of favorable sites (dens with sunny exposures and narrow openings to exclude predators) year after year. Herpetologists have determined that young western rattlesnakes, typically born in late summer or early fall, often follow their mother's scent trail to her hibernaculum.

One of the many myths about rattlesnakes holds that these predators coexist peacefully with other inhabitants of rodent burrows, including prairie dogs and burrowing owls. In truth, rattlesnakes prey on young prairie dogs and young burrowing owls, and these species will abandon their burrows once the snakes take up residence. However, biologists have observed mammals and other animals sharing dens with hibernating rattlesnakes. One observer excavated a den that contained thirteen rattlesnakes, four turtles, two skunks, and a swarm of honey bees.

Another myth states that rattlesnakes become more venomous during late summer and early fall. This assertion has never been verified, but the amount and toxicity of the venom varies among species, subspecies, and individuals within each population. Large snakes tend to carry more venom than small snakes. Of the several thousand rattlesnake bites that occur in the United States each year, fewer than 1 percent are fatal. According to the Colorado Department of Health, four people died of rattlesnake bites in Colorado between 1970 and 1987.

Many bites occur when people inadvertently step on or place their hands next to a basking snake. Most rattlesnakes are shy, retiring creatures who hunt by ambushing rather than stalking their prey. Western rattlesnakes and other pit vipers locate their prey using heat-sensitive pores (known as loreal pits) on the sides of their heads, their eyesight, and their constantly flicking, odor-sensing, tongues. After striking its prey and injecting its venom, the rattlesnake withdraws. Rather than trying to finish the prey off on the spot and risking injury to its eyes or face, the snake waits for the poison to take effect. Usually a mouse or other small rodent wanders off for several yards, well out of range of the snake's thermal sensors or eyesight, before it dies. The rattler uses its chemical senses, sniffing the air and the ground with its tongue to find the dead rodent.

University of Colorado ethologist David Chiszar, who has studied rattlesnake behavior for twenty-five years, says rattlesnake hunting strategy is well suited to life in an exposed environment. "If rattlesnakes are all curled up in a hiding place, a shady spot, they're not burning up energy, they're not fighting thermo-regulatory battles, they're not exposing themselves to hawks. By being in ambush they're not investing calories."

After emerging from their dens in early spring, rattlesnakes disperse to individual foraging territories. Males and females get back together during early summer to mate. Young rattlers, which measure about 6 inches long at birth, become independent of their mothers within a week or so. During the breeding season male rattlesnakes occasionally engage in a "dance." Two males rear up, entangle their necks, and weave from side to side. This ritualized fighting occurs only when a receptive female is nearby. Larger males or males with a prior history of dominance usually prevail and win the right to mate with the female.

Of the nineteen North American rattlesnake species, two, the Western rattlesnake (*Crotalus viridis*) and the massassauga (*Sistrurus catenatus*), occur in Colorado. Western rattlesnakes, which occur at low to mid elevations throughout Colorado, concentrate in areas of sparse human population, such as the Comanche National Grassland, in southeastern Colorado, and the Piceance Basin, in northwestern Colorado. Massassaugas inhabit a small area in southeastern Colorado around Lamar and Kit Carson. This massassauga population is isolated from the rest of the North American population, which inhabits parts of New Mexico, Texas, Oklahoma, Kansas, and the upper Midwest. On summer evenings, look for massassaugas basking on dirt roads north of the Arkansas River.

COLORADO ARCHITECTURE

A deep secret of Colorado is that you don't have to go to Utah for natural arches, windows, and weirdly eroded canyons. October's crisp weather is the perfect time to search for these geological wonders that usually occur in some of the hotter parts of the state.

Arches and windows are most common in sandstone fins (vertical slabs of rock), though one of the largest arches in Colorado (the Del Norte Arch or La Ventana) is in a volcanic dike. Arches are formed when the weaker parts of a rock mass disintegrate. Water, not wind, is the chief architect. Water percolates through porous rock, dissolving the calcium carbonate that cements the sand grains together, and forms fissures. Freezing and thawing enlarge the cracks. Eventually the pull of gravity causes small chunks to fall from the center, creating small holes and windows that continue to erode until they expand into arches. Appropriately, many arches occur in the Jurassic Entrada (meaning entryway) sandstone formation.

Only stone openings at least 3 feet wide that allow light to pass through are

Oct

Arches in Rattlesnake Gulch in western Colorado, near Grand Junction. (Photo by Glenn Cushman.)

considered true arches. If the span was carved by running water, it's called a natural bridge.

Because arches are often tucked away in relatively inaccessible places, many of them have not yet been discovered and many discoveries have not been recorded. Searching for these pieces of air surrounded by stone is a favorite pastime for some canyon connoisseurs. In Arches National Park, just a few miles across the Utah border from Grand Junction, only 83 were listed in 1947. In 1989, park officials announced the discovery of the 1,000th arch. Now more than 1,700 arches are officially listed for this 73,234-acre jumble of sandstone. The lure of the unknown arch still exists.

Where To Go

⚑ Rattlesnake Canyon, near Grand Junction, contains the largest assemblage of windows and arches in the United States, outside of Utah.

⚑ South Shale Ridge, near DeBeque.

⚑ Natural Arch, near Del Norte.

⚑ Comanche National Grassland, especially Holt Canyon, southeast of La Junta.

ROCK ART GALLERIES

A bison seems poised to amble from the surface of an orange cliff in Dinosaur National Monument. Antlered animals, human figures, and abstract designs cover many panels at Mesa Verde National Park. And a graceful, long-necked horse in Picture Canyon sets our imaginations spinning back to a time when bands of American Indians hunted and farmed in these canyons. Their hand prints on canyon walls reach out to us from centuries past.

The artisans who created these petroglyphs usually chose sandstone formations that weather into smooth, vertical walls. At the base of these walls they often cut their glyphs into the dark mineral wash called "desert varnish," revealing the color of the underlying stone through the etching. For pictographs or paintings (more vulnerable to the elements), they chose sheltered spots such as alcoves, caves, and overhangs.

Petroglyphs were usually incised or pecked out by gouging the stone with a harder rock, sometimes using a hammer and chisel technique. Researchers who

The La Garita Volcano

What may have been the largest volcanic eruption in earth's history exploded in southwest Colorado about 28 million years ago, spewing lava and ash over a 10,000-square-mile area. The La Garita eruption was twenty thousand times larger than that of Mount St. Helens in 1980 and may have lasted for several weeks. This cataclysm left a caldera, 45 miles across, that provided a site for younger volcanism and led to formation of about a billion dollars worth of silver ore near Creede, according to Peter Lipman, a geologist who has studied the eruption site for thirty years. Volcanic rocks from these eruptions underlie most of the present-day San Juan Mountains. However, the La Garita caldera is difficult to recognize as the remnant of a volcano because of its vast size, heavy forest cover, and strong erosion by rivers and glacial ice since it formed.

The best viewpoint for the caldera is from just west of Salt House Pass at the north edge of Saguache Park, where the northern quarter of the caldera basin can be seen: It is the vast expanse from the old Salt House cabin toward the La Garita Mountains 12 miles to the southwest. The La Garita Mountains are an updomed part of the caldera floor, and the southern boundary is in the Weminuche Wilderness, 35 to 40 miles to the south. Smaller calderas at Silverton, Creede, and Lake City are easier to discern.

have tried to duplicate this method estimate that 25 to 100 strikes were required to make a 1-inch line. Pictographs were painted with minerals such as hematite, ores, clay, and vegetable dyes with binders made from blood, eggs, plant resins, and other natural substances. Finger painting was one of the earliest techniques. Later, brushes were devised from animal hair, plant fibers, and yucca spines. Numerous other methods were also used, including a type of spray painting in which the artist blew a mouthful of pigment out through a hollow reed.

Interpreting petroglyphs and pictographs puzzles even anthropologists. For instance, do the anthropomorphs (humanlike figures) with elaborate headdresses represent supernatural beings or men in costumes? Is the man aiming a bow at a line of antlered animals an entreaty to the gods for luck in hunting? Or does it mean that a successful hunt actually took place? Or is it just art for art's sake?

Certain representational images recur throughout the Southwest. Animals are a favorite motif and include large and small creatures ranging from bison to bats, horses to humans, cranes to centipedes. The most prolific images show favored game species such as antelope, bighorn sheep, deer, and elk. One of the most endearing and enigmatic characters is the hump-backed flute player popularly known as Kokopelli.

Although no one but the original artist will ever know what the glyph really meant, it's possible to draw some inferences. Because of the frequency of supernatural-looking figures and ceremonial apparel, many of the sites were probably religious and used for such purposes as sympathetic or protective magic. Most anthropologists think the craftsmen were probably adult males, possibly shamans or medicine men, because most of the actions portrayed were male activities.

Dating rock art is difficult and usually depends on

Oct

radiocarbon dating of something associated with the rock, such as charcoal from an ancient pit, or on estimating the growth of lichens or the minerals in the desert varnish. In her book *Indian Rock Art of the Southwest,* Polly Schaafsma says that the oldest drawings in the Southwest can be safely documented at more than two thousand years of age. The art continued into historic times, as is evidenced by horses, introduced by the Spanish explorers, and men in top hats.

Rock art has withstood many centuries of weathering, rock slides, and other natural calamities, but it may not be able to survive the modern world. Proliferating power plants that generate air pollution and acid rain accelerate deterioration. Development and dams destroy, bury, and drown many sites. Artifact hunters and vandals scrawl their own names across antiquities and use the drawings for target practice. Even those of us who stand in awe before these pictures can unintentionally harm them by touching them (oil in our fingers is the culprit) or by making rubbings or by outlining them in charcoal.

Where To Go

Whenever you're hiking in canyon country, investigate likely looking spots. You just might find yourself face to face with Kokopelli.

- Dinosaur National Monument.
- Cañon Pintado near Rangely.
- Colorado National Monument west of Grand Junction.
- Dolores River Canyon near Cortez.
- Hovenweep National Monument.
- Mesa Verde National Park.
- Comanche National Grassland (especially Picture Canyon and Picketwire Canyon) southeast of La Junta.

TRACKING DINOSAURS

Dinosaurs may not have been the slow-moving, slow-witted brutes most of us have envisioned from childhood, and the evolutionary line that produced them may not have ended at the close of the Cretaceous Period. Many paleontologists, led by Colorado dinosaurologist and iconoclast Robert Bakker, believe some dinosaurs were agile, warm-blooded creatures and that birds may be their direct descendants. Duckbilled dinosaurs may even have made music through resonating chambers in their heads, and many dinosaur tracks resemble bird tracks.

October is a good time to combine canyoneer-ing, rock art viewing, and dinosaur tracking, as pet-roglyphs and dinosaur tracks are frequently found in desert or semidesert canyons.

Picketwire Canyon in Comanche National Grassland, for instance, contains the longest set of dinosaur tracks in the world, as well as petroglyphs. The tracks are part of a so-called Dinosaur Freeway where dinosaurs walked along the shoreline of an interior seaway extending 30,000 square miles along the Front Range and into Oklahoma. According to Colorado paleontologist Martin Lockley, this migra-tion route contains billions of tracks, suggesting that dinosaurs traveled in herds. Early morning and late afternoon are the best times to look for tracks, because the lower angle of the sun creates shadows.

Colorado has been a hotbed of dinosaur research since 1877 when Arthur Lakes, a minister and schoolteacher in Golden, discovered a quarry of bones, including the first Stegosaurus, at Dinosaur Ridge, near Morrison. In 1909 Earl Douglass uncovered the largest concentration of Jurassic Period dinosaurs ever found at what is now Dinosaur National Monument. Eventually 350 tons of bones were shipped to museums worldwide from this site.

Colorado has even designated the Stegosaurus as the state fossil. Thornton school children backed this 30-foot-long, plant-eating dinosaur, but legislators balked (per-haps they had one of their own members in mind for the honor). The designation became official by executive edict signed by Gov. Richard Lamm in 1982.

Every year new specimens are discovered throughout the state. In 1994 a dinosaur nest with intact eggs was uncovered in the Garden Park Fossil Area near Canon City. In 1993 a Denverite dug up a Triceratops bone while putting in a retaining wall, and a dinosaur rib turned up right behind home plate at Coors Field in Denver. In 1992 a man walking his dog through a new housing development in Jefferson County found one of the rarest dinosaur bones ever located in the state—the shin bone of a *Tyrannosaurus rex*.

During their heyday, dinosaurs spread over the entire earth, including what is now Antarctica, and were the dominant life form for some 130 million years. Will *homo sapiens* endure for even a fortieth of that span? Regarding dinosaurs—and humans—there are more questions than answers.

Other Fossils

Marine fossils, including giant ammonites, nautiloids, clams, and gas-tropods, are embedded in the Pierre Shale at the Kremmling Cretaceous Ammonite Site, which was designated a Research Natural Area in 1983. Leaf and some insect fossils are found in lay-ers of shale on Douglas Pass, north of Grand Junction. Many fossil insects, leaves, and seeds as well as petrified sequoia tree stumps abound along nature trails at Florissant Fossil Beds National Monument west of Colorado Springs. Collecting is not allowed at the Kremm-ling or the Florissant sites.

Where To Go

🦆 Dinosaur National Monument exhibits bones *in situ* at the quarry and offers many miles of nature trails.

🦆 Rabbit Valley Research Natural Area, west of Grand Junction, contains the Mygatt-Moore Quarry and a 1.5 mile "Trail Through Time."

🦆 Cactus Park, south of Grand Junction, is the site of many recent discoveries.

🦆 Dinosaur Ridge, north of Morrison, contains many footprints and some bones. Take a self-guided tour or arrange a tour through the Morrison Natural History Museum.

🦆 Garden Park Fossil Area, north of Canon City, is where many dinosaurs have been excavated for museums worldwide.

🦆 Picketwire Canyon, in Comanche National Grassland, contains the longest dinosaur trackway in the world, accessible only by reserved four-wheel drive tours or by hiking or mountain biking.

🦆 Museums with excellent dinosaur exhibits include the Museum of Western Colorado, Grand Junction; the Denver Museum of Natural History; and the Henderson Museum at the University of Colorado, Boulder.

OCTOBER EVENTS

MAMMALS

🦆 It's rut season for moose, elk, white-tailed deer, and pronghorns.

🦆 Marmots hibernate, sometimes starting as early as September.

BIRDS

🦆 Unusual migrants, such as sandhill cranes and snow geese, pass through.

🦆 Flicker pecking increases as critters crawl into crevices.

🦆 Hooded mergansers, buffleheads, and common goldeneyes arrive at ponds.

🦆 Juncos and mountain chickadees move to lower elevations.

OTHER CRITTERS

ꕤ Rattlesnakes converge on communal hibernating sites in rocky hillsides and prairie dog towns.

ꕤ Brown trout spawn.

PLANTS

ꕤ Scrub oaks, cottonwoods, maples, various species of ash, and variegated shrubs reach peak color at lower elevations.

ꕤ Pumpkins ripen.

ꕤ Asters, gumweed, rabbitbrush, and some senecios continue to bloom.

SPECIAL EVENTS

ꕤ Big game hunting season is in progress. Check with the Colorado Division of Wildlife for specific dates and wear bright colors if you go where hunters go.

IN THE SKY

ꕤ "Moon of Falling Leaves" (Cheyenne)

ꕤ The Orionid meteor shower appears in the southeast sky around October 19 through 22.

ꕤ Pegasus (the Winged Horse) is high in the southern sky around 9 P.M. This constellation can be located by drawing a line from the North Star (Polaris) through Cassiopeia and extending the line an equal distance. Pegasus is said to look like the head, neck, and forelegs of an upside down horse. The "Great Square," which might be interpreted as the horse's chest, contains three second-magnitude stars.

Mule deer pause in the foothills west of Denver.

11

November

From the flock an eagle now comes flying;

Dipping, rising, circling, comes she hither.

Loud screams the eagle, flying swift.

—PAWNEE

THE ARRIVAL OF bald eagles transmutes November from a somewhat dull, in-between month to a time of excitement. Sensitized by the eagles, we realize this "pewter" month holds many shining moments.

Short-eared owls and rough-legged hawks arrive from the north to feast on voles and other small mammals that remain active throughout the winter. Some birds reveal their presence with raucous calls, and we find ourselves squawking back at intelligent and mischievous ravens and jays. Wild turkeys, so different from their domestic cousins, enchant us with their ventriloquist-like gobblings and iridescent feathers as they skulk through piñon-juniper woodlands.

While black bears enter a state of dormancy, mule and white-tailed deer find November the most exciting month of the year. It's their rutting season. Hearing the clatter of antlers as bucks duel should be electrifying enough to arouse even hibernating bears from their torpor. These battles convince us that the "ember" in November has been fanned to flame.

Nov

	Grand Junction (4,824 ft.)	Steamboat Springs (6,760 ft.)	Alamosa (7,536 ft.)	Berthoud Pass (11,310 ft.)	Denver (5,282 ft.)	Lamar (3,620 ft.)
Ave. high (°F)	51	41	47	30	53	56
Ave. low (°F)	29	14	12	10	25	24
Max. high (°F)	75	69	71	54	79	85
Min. low (°F)	−2	−28	−30	−28	−8	−18
Ave. prec. (in.)	0.71	2.09	0.43	3.36	0.87	0.52
Max. prec. (in.)	2.39	5.59	1.23	7.67	2.97	5.31
Ave. snow (in.)	2.8	21.3	4.5	49.1	8.2	4.3
Max. snow (in.)	23.6	57.0	19.8	91.5	39.1	38.0

November's reputation for grayness comes in part from rains that fall on the Western Slope, snows and howling winds that batter the high country, and "lenticular," or standing wave, clouds that hover over the Front Range, blocking out the sun for hours. Lenticular clouds form when upper-level winds dip and then rise in waves on the lee side of mountain ranges. As the air rushes upward, its moisture cools and condenses, forming a constantly regenerating cloud at the crest of the wave. The edges of these thin ice clouds sometimes shimmer with opalescent color as sunlight is refracted by the ice crystals. On autumn evenings standing wave clouds turn fiery red, creating some of the most spectacular sunsets on earth.

See "Colorado Climate Summary" (p. 1) for information on averages, extremes, and sources.

november ecosystem

Piñon-Juniper Woodlands

Autumn lingers a little longer on the sunwashed mesas and hillsides where piñon pines and junipers grow. Clamorous flocks of pinyon[1] jays and Clark's nut-crackers fly from tree to tree harvesting pine nuts. Mountain chickadees and red-breasted nuthatches flitter down from the high country to feast on insects. Black bears amble through the brushy canyons searching for a last snack of serviceberries, grubs, and carrion.

[1]The spelling of pinyon jay with a "y" follows the American Ornithologists' Union Checklist of North American Birds.

On the rare days when clouds or snow envelops these woodlands, the soft light gives a bluish cast to the scattered trees and accentuates the contours of their textured trunks. The piñon boughs toss lightly in the wind, while mule deer browse on the shrouded hillsides. Wild turkeys, coyotes, and perhaps a mountain lion or two lurk somewhere in the mist.

By November the pungent, turpentine-like aromas of midsummer have dulled to a faint, resinous perfume. These aromas, strongest when the sap flows freely, result from volatization of terpenes in the junipers and ethyl caprylates in the piñon pines. These naturally occurring toxins protect the trees' foliage from browsing mammals and may also limit growth of competing grasses and shrubs. Because piñon pines produce good seed crops only once every three to seven years, pinyon jay flocks may wander over several hundred square miles searching for productive areas. The jays' long pointed beaks allow them to extract the seeds easily from the upright, partially open cones. A pinyon jay can store up to 60 seeds in its esophagus, and a Clark's nutcracker can store up to 120 seeds in a sublingual pouch. Both species cache seeds for the winter by burying them in the ground in one or more locations. A single Clark's nutcracker may cache as many as 30,000 seeds. Some of the seeds remain uneaten and sprout into young pines. Both the birds and the trees benefit; the woodland spreads, while the jays and nutcrackers expand their potential foraging area.

As autumn progresses and seed-gathering activity subsides, the jays and nutcrackers become less conspicuous and less vocal. By late November the monotonous whistles and complex songs of Townsend's solitaires begin to dominate the landscape. Townsend's solitaires sing throughout the winter as they defend foraging territories containing fruit-bearing junipers. A single male solitaire stakes out several acres of prime juniper habitat and fiercely defends the territory from all comers except female solitaires, who roam freely through the woodland. Solitaires digest the nontoxic portions of the juniper berries. They excrete the terpene-bearing resin sacks and the seeds, which can then germinate.

For centuries piñon nuts were a staple food for peoples living in the Great Basin region. Many people still harvest these seeds each fall, and the pungent aroma of burning piñon logs permeates the pueblos and towns of the Rio Grande Valley. The Navajo have used juniper bark for garments, sandals, and blankets; wood for fuel, fence posts, and hogans; twigs for prayersticks and stirrers; seeds for necklaces, anklets, and wristlets; sap for chewing gum; and berries for green dye and medicine. Gin is flavored with juniper berries, and the word comes from the French *genévrier,* for juniper.

Piñon pine–juniper woodlands grow between 5,000 and 9,000 feet throughout much of southern and western Colorado. Utah Juniper (*Sabina osteosperma*) predominates at lower elevations in western Colorado, and Rocky Mountain juniper (*S. scopulorum*) thrives throughout the southeast and at higher elevations in the west. Disjunct stands occur in Owl Canyon, north of Fort Collins, and on Trout Creek Pass, near Buena Vista.

Private landowners and government land managers have destroyed thousands of acres of piñon-juniper in the West through a process known as chaining. Two bulldozers, connected by chains, root up everything in their path. But little grass ever grows on the dry, rocky hillsides favored by piñon pines and junipers, and the economic benefits hardly justify the destruction. Fortunately, this chaining practice has fallen out of favor throughout much of the West as people have grown to appreciate the beauty and value of this long-neglected ecosystem.

Where To Go

⌘ Dinosaur National Monument, north of Rangely.
⌘ Colorado National Monument, near Grand Junction.
⌘ Mesa Verde National Park, near Cortez.
⌘ Black Canyon of the Gunnison National Monument, near Montrose.
⌘ Great Sand Dunes National Monument, near Alamosa.
⌘ State Highway 115, between Colorado Springs and Canon City.
⌘ Owl Canyon, northwest of Fort Collins.

CORVIDS: AGGRESSIVE SUBURBANITES

Because jays, crows, magpies, and other members of the Corvid family are adaptable and omnivorous, they thrive around human settlements, eating our garbage, discarded grains, bird seed, and picnic leavings. During the twentieth century, several species from this avian family have expanded their Colorado ranges: ravens from the northern Rockies into most of the state, scrub jays from western and southern Colorado into the northern Front Range, and blue jays from the Missouri Valley into eastern Colorado.

Like humans, coyotes, cockroaches, and other habitat generalists, corvids respond rapidly to changing environmental conditions, proliferating in numbers and outcompeting other species. Crows living near busy highways in the United States have learned to open walnuts by dropping them on the road and waiting for cars to run over them. Common ravens have learned to throw stones at intruders who get too close to their cliff nests. Crows on the Pacific island of New Caledonia make tools out of sticks and leaves and then use them to extract insects from rotting wood. Gray jays in Rocky Mountain National Park sometimes snatch food from the hands, and even from between the teeth, of unwary picnickers.

Clark's nutcracker, Rocky Mountain National Park.

Corvids prey on eggs and nestlings of other birds. In natural ecosystems they perform the necessary role of weeding out weaker individuals. In disturbed ecosystems, especially around human settlements, corvid predation on songbirds often reaches unnaturally high levels. Corvids have been implicated in the recent decline of North American songbird populations. Along the northern Front Range, ravens have disrupted nesting activities of golden eagles and prairie falcons, while scrub jays, Steller's jays, and blue jays have reduced populations of native songbirds nesting on the urban fringe. As human settlements continue to spread and natural habitats become more fragmented, this problem will get worse. See *Where Have all the Birds Gone?* by John Terborgh for more information about how corvids affect native songbird populations.

JAYS, CROWS, AND MAGPIES

SPECIES	HABITAT	COLORADO STATUS
GRAY JAY	Coniferous forests throughout North America.	Fairly common resident in high mountains.
STELLER'S JAY	Pine-oak woodlands and coniferous forests.	Common year-round resident, mountains and plateaus.
BLUE JAY	Gardens and deciduous woodlands throughout eastern North America.	Fairly common and expanding in eastern Colorado.
SCRUB JAY	Shrublands and gardens, mostly western North America.	Common resident west and south; increasing along northern Front Range.
PINYON JAY	Piñon-juniper woodlands of Great Basin and Rockies; ponderosa pine woodlands of southern California and Oregon.	Common resident of high mountain coniferous forests.
CLARK'S NUTCRACKER	High elevation coniferous forests; western United States.	Common resident of high mountain coniferous forests.
BLACK-BILLED MAGPIE	Woodlands and rangelands, western North America.	Common resident and probably increasing throughout most of state.
AMERICAN CROW	Most ecosystems north of Mexico and south of the Arctic Circle.	Common, especially near eastern farms and towns; expanding in west.
COMMON RAVEN	Mountains, deserts, and coasts; Canada, western United States, and Mexico.	Fairly common resident. Expanding in mountains, west, and southeast.
CHIHUAHUAN RAVEN	Deserts and woodlands; Mexico and south-central United States.	Fairly common and expanding throughout southeastern Colorado.

Sources: Hugh Kingery, ed., *Colorado Breeding Bird Atlas;* Robert Andrews and Robert Righter, *Colorado Birds.*

Nov

Wild turkey.

WILD TURKEYS

During autumn wild turkeys gather into large flocks. By day they scour the forests and woodlands for seeds, wild fruits, and insects. At night they roost in tall trees; Colorado's wild turkeys generally favor ponderosa pines with round or flattened tops.

During the spring mating season, toms gather on strutting grounds where they gobble, fan their feathers, and fight fiercely to win the affections of sometimes admiring, but more often disinterested, hens. After mating, the hens nest on the ground in tall grass or pine needles or at the base of a scrub oak or piñon pine. Since a single hen may raise as many as 14 chicks and hens often travel together with their young, maternal flocks may number more than forty birds.

Overhunting, habitat destruction, and importation of European diseases led to the near extirpation of wild turkeys in North America during the late nineteenth and early twentieth centuries. For several decades scientists tried to augment native turkey populations by breeding turkeys in captivity and releasing them into the wild. These efforts failed because turkeys captured from the wild could not survive in captivity, and crossbreeding of domesticated and wild turkeys produced birds that lacked the hardiness and wariness needed to survive in the wild. During the 1940s and 1950s, biologists began to use only wild birds in restocking programs. North American wild turkey populations increased rapidly and now exceed four million birds.

Wild turkeys occur throughout much of southern and eastern Colorado in ponderosa pine forests, oak woodlands, piñon-juniper woodlands, and plains riparian woodlands. Unlike their domesticated cousins, they are wily and fast moving. Search for them at dawn or dusk, and listen for their gobbling throughout the day and year.

Where To Go

🦃 Mesa Verde National Park, near Cortez.
🦃 Dolores River Canyon, north of Cortez.

✽ Santa Fe Trail, Air Force Academy, north of Colorado Springs.
✽ Tamarack Ranch State Wildlife Area, near Sterling.
✽ Comanche National Grassland—Cottonwood, Carrizo, Sand, and Holt Canyons.
✽ Purgatoire River Canyon, south of La Junta.

WILD TURKEY FACTS

Wing span: Up to 5 feet.
Maximum weight: Males, 18 to 25 pounds; hens, 10 to 18 pounds.
Maximum air speed: 55 miles per hour.
Maximum ground speed: 20 miles per hour.
U.S. population in 1920: 20,000 to 30,000.
Current U.S. population: 4 to 5 million.
Nesting period: May–June.
Gobbling season: All year.

Sources: National Wild Turkey Federation; Hugh Kingery, ed., *Colorado Breeding Bird Atlas.*

WINTERING RAPTOR CONCENTRATIONS

During the colder months, raptor prey becomes less abundant as many small mammals head underground and most songbirds head south. Birds of prey, no longer tied to summer nesting territories, congregate near rivers, wetlands, prairie dog colonies, and other areas that support relatively high numbers of visible prey.

Bald eagles that have nested in Idaho, Montana, British Columbia, and southeast Alaska arrive in Colorado in late October or early November and stay until March. The Colorado Division of Wildlife has counted more than one thousand balds in Colorado during January and February. The eagles hunt and scavenge throughout the day and spend nights in nocturnal roosts, usually located near water. Biologists and naturalists have counted as many as fifty bald eagles at Left Hand Creek, north of Boulder, and along the South Platte River near Weldona.

Bald eagles soar over the eastern foothills and western valleys looking for dead deer and other carrion, they search lakeshores and riverbanks for disabled waterfowl, and they perch on the periphery of prairie dog colonies waiting for ferruginous

Nov

A ferruginous hawk takes wing.

hawks or red-tailed hawks to make a kill. Once a hawk has killed a prairie dog, a dozen or more eagles and hawks may appear out of nowhere to share in the bounty. A study of bald eagle foraging habits in southeast Alaska found that an average prey item changed hands a dozen times before it was totally consumed.

A few hundred ferruginous hawks reside in Colorado year-round, but most of our wintering ferruginous hawks come from Wyoming and other points to the west. These majestic, white-breasted raptors are the largest North American hawk; they can kill and carry away prey as large as prairie dogs and rabbits. Ferruginous hawk concentrations occur around prairie dog colonies throughout eastern Colorado. Wintering populations have declined recently in areas where urbanization and poisoning have eliminated prairie dog colonies.

Rough-legged hawks are somewhat smaller than ferruginous hawks and have much smaller talons, so they prey mostly on meadow voles, deer mice, other small rodents, and insects. Since they nest north of the Arctic Circle, they are among the last wintering raptors to arrive in Colorado. Look for them around wetlands and grasslands throughout the state.

Red-tailed hawks nest, migrate through, and winter in Colorado, so it's hard to distinguish the residents from the transients. Numbers peak during the fall and spring migrations, but several thousand red-tailed hawks remain in the state throughout the winter. Look for them in open country, particularly around prairie dog colonies, wetlands, and farmlands.

Since birds of prey have had much longer to adapt to humans than to automobiles, you can get much closer to them in your car than on foot. For some reason, ferruginous hawks seem particularly unwary. We've driven up to within fifty feet or so of ferruginous hawks perched on fence posts and giddily snapped pictures while the birds stared at us through placid yellow eyes.

Where To Go

⅋ Colorado River between Kremmling and Hot Sulphur Springs. Bald eagles and red-tailed hawks.

⅋ Gunnison River between Gunnison and Blue Mesa Reservoir. Bald eagles and red-tailed hawks.

⅋ Monte Vista and Alamosa National Wildlife Refuges, near Alamosa. Bald eagles, red-tailed hawks, rough-legged hawks, and northern harriers.

⅋ Rocky Mountain Arsenal, near Denver. Bald eagles, ferruginous hawks, rough-legged hawks, red-tailed hawks, northern harriers, and long-eared owls. Tours by appointment.

⅋ Boulder Reservoir and Rabbit Mountain, northern Boulder County. Bald and golden eagles, ferruginous hawks, rough-legged hawks, red-tailed hawks, and northern harriers.

⅋ Platte River north of Platteville. Bald eagles, ferruginous hawks, rough-legged hawks, and red-tailed hawks.

⅋ Jackson Reservoir and Platte River, northwest of Fort Morgan. Bald eagles and red-tailed hawks.

VOLES AND VOLE HUNTERS

Find a wetland. Almost any wetland will do, so long as it contains an expanse of cattails, bulrushes, or sedge-grass meadows. Go there at dusk, sit quietly, and listen. The crunching, nibbling, scurrying, and rustling indicate that members of the genus *Microtus*, commonly known as meadow mice or meadow voles, have begun their evening activities. The vole hunters—northern harriers (marsh hawks), rough-legged hawks, short-eared owls, red foxes, and coyotes—can't be too far away.

Mouselike in size and habits, voles are actually more closely related to muskrats than to deer mice or house mice. Most voles, including the common meadow vole (*Microtus pennsylvanicus*) of Colorado's low- to mid-elevation grasslands and wetlands, have specially adapted teeth that grow constantly to compensate for the wearing away of the upper surfaces by coarse grass fibers.

Meadow voles feed on grass and flower seeds as well as on grass stalks. They scurry beneath the grass canopy through an intricate system of 1-inch-wide runways and underground burrows. They raise their young either above ground or underground in spherical nests constructed from grass clippings. Look for these nests under boards, logs, and along runways.

A SHORT-EARED OWL AND MEADOW VOLE

Meadow voles convert plant material into protein at an astronomical rate. They eat almost their own weight daily. They breed as often as ten times per year, producing litters of up to ten young. During peak population years, meadow voles may number more than two hundred per acre.

This productivity is sufficient to cause any self-respecting hawk, owl, or canid to froth at the mouth. The harriers, in particular, seem almost oblivious to other creatures during times of peak vole activity. Shortly before sunset at Boulder Reservoir, we've watched them cruise back and forth within a few feet of our heads, their owlish faces tilting from side to side as they listened for the characteristic rustling in the sedges and cattails.

The harriers' owlish appearance is created by concave facial disks that funnel sound to their oversized ears. Their long tails and narrow, tapered wings enable them to stop or change direction in an instant, so they can quickly and quietly drop on their prey. Except during spring and fall migration flights, harriers spend their entire lives in the grasslands and marshlands, right in the midst of their primary food supply. They nest on the ground on platforms constructed from grasses, sedges, or cattails. During fall and winter, they roost communally on the ground in groups of five to twenty individuals.

Though harriers may hunt into the night, they are primarily diurnal. While they sleep, another winged predator with similar physical features takes over the vole harvest. Short-eared owls glide low over the marshlands and grassland on long (at least for an owl) tapered wings and use acute hearing to help locate their prey. Like harriers, they nest, and usually roost, on the ground. Heavier bodied than harriers, they spend more time flapping and less time gliding. Tilting their bodies upward and flapping their wings, they sometimes hover in a single spot for fifteen seconds or more. Short-eared owls hunt most actively in late afternoon and early evening, but they often continue well into the night.

Northern harriers nest in small numbers at low- to mid-elevation wetlands and grasslands throughout Colorado, but their numbers peak in late fall and early winter when migrants from the north supplement the state's resident population. Short-eared owls nest in a few scattered locations on the northeastern plains, in the San Luis Valley, and in the southwestern valleys. Their numbers increase irregularly during winter months, depending on vole abundance in Colorado and farther north. Loss of wetlands throughout Colorado appears to have resulted in a general decline in populations of nesting short-eared owls and northern harriers throughout this century.

Where To Go

🦆 Fruitgrowers Reservoir, Harts Basin, near Delta. Northern harrriers.

🦆 Monte Vista National Wildlife Refuge, near Alamosa. Nesting and wintering short-eared owls and northern harriers.

🦆 Chatfield State Park, south of Denver. Nesting and wintering northern harriers. Short-eared owls rare in winter.

🦆 Barr Lake State Park, northeast of Denver. Nesting and wintering northern harriers. Short-eared owls rare to uncommon in winter.

🦆 Boulder Reservoir. Nesting and wintering northern harriers. Short-eared owls rare in winter.

🦆 Nee Noshe and Nee Granda Reservoirs, south of Eads. Nesting and wintering northern harriers. Short-eared owls rare in winter.

H**iBEAR**nation

Since our teddy bear days we've all known that bears hibernate the winter away. But do they? Their body temperature drops only a few degrees below the norm of 100°F. Their metabolic rate drops by about half but remains high enough so they can wake in a few minutes when disturbed. However, for the duration of their long winter nap—three to six months—their breathing slows; their heartbeats drop from forty to about eight beats a minute; and they do not eat, drink, urinate, or defecate. They lose no significant skeletal or muscular strength or calcium and very little protein.

No one understands exactly how this complex process works. Hibernating bears produce energy by burning stored fat, not protein, minimizing the buildup of urea. The small amount of urine that is produced is reabsorbed, and the nitrogen is recycled into new protein.

Because bears do not fit the usual pattern of hibernation in which body temperatures drop to almost freezing, some zoologists describe their winter slumber as "dormancy" or "torpidity" instead of "hibernation." In Colorado animals considered "true hibernators" include yellow-bellied marmots and various species of bats and ground squirrels. In contrast to a bear, a ground squirrel's pulse slows from 350 beats a minute to around 2, and its temperature can drop from 98° to 34°F.

A NAPPING BLACK BEAR

To avoid freezing to death, true hibernators must rouse occasionally, raising their body temperature back to normal. Every time they rouse, they use up energy and fat reserves necessary for survival. Under extremely cold conditions an animal needs to rouse more frequently to warm up, losing additional energy each time. As a result, true hibernation is feasible primarily in midlatitudes, where the duration of extreme cold is shorter.

Scientists believe information from hibernation studies will have applications in treating human ailments, such as kidney failure, bone disease, muscle atrophy, and sleep disorders. Finding the hibernation induction trigger, which appears to be related chemically to morphine, is the goal of several researchers around the country. If the trigger is found, it could be used to preserve organs during transplantation, to slow the human body down during surgery, and to prevent heart fibrillation.

Nov

Grizzlies

Although black bears are our common Colorado bear species, a few grizzlies may still inhabit remote areas in the San Juan mountains. A grizzly sow was killed when she attacked a bow hunter there in 1979. Researchers examined the layers in her teeth, which are used like tree rings to establish age. Close-together rings indicate physiological stress, which occurs when a sow nurses cubs and shortchanges her own nutrition. This sow's teeth showed she had borne cubs; the cubs were never found.

Grizzlies usually hibernate from November to April. But in 1996 researchers in Glacier National Park discovered fresh tracks in January and February near fresh wolf and mountain lion kills. The increased availability of food may be changing grizzly hibernation patterns.

Colorado's eight to twelve thousand black bears usually begin their nap between mid-October and mid-November, though some insomniacs wait until December. Physiological changes within the bear are timed to correspond with shortages of food and seem to be unrelated to variations in climate from year to year. Bear specialist Tom Beck studied black bears in west-central Colorado from 1979 to 1986 and discovered that females enter dens about two weeks earlier than males and leave about two weeks later. He also found that denning bears prefer rock caverns with very small entrances, though they also dig dens under shrubs, often choosing serviceberry bushes. Sometimes they simply go into dormancy on the surface of the ground. The purpose of dens appears to be isolation and defense against predation rather than thermal insulation.

Where To Go

Black bears snooze throughout the state, all the way from the foothills to above tree line, although they seem to prefer higher elevations for their hibernacula. The den may be a cave, a hollow log, a rock crevice, or the hollow under tree roots or in thick brush. However, we don't recommend crawling into a den and arousing the bear, especially with a rectal thermometer in the manner of researcher Tom Beck!

For more bear stories, see pp. 22 (January) and 186 (September).

DUELING DEER

Mule deer bucks begin to shed the soft brown velvet from their antlers in September and often indulge in playful sparring. By November the sparring is no longer playful. With all the style of a Cyrano de Bergerac engaging the enemy, they wield their antlers fiercely in duels for the favors of a doe. Earlier in the year the bucks ignored the females and traveled together—a perfect example of male bonding. But now they travel separately searching for does in estrus. And when two males want the same doe, the battle begins.

Much of the battle is bluff. The stiff-legged combatants shake their heads and lay back their mulelike ears, showing off magnificent antlers and heavy, swollen necks and shoulders. Sometimes they charge. Usually the less dominant buck retreats. If not, the fencing begins, with antler points as sharp as stilettos. It's usually not a duel to the death, though they may wound each other. On rare occasions the antlers interlock, and both warriors die in a grisly embrace.

Unlike elk, deer do not collect harems. Instead, a buck will follow a female in estrus until she is ready to mate (at which point you might say, the buck stops here), and he will fight other interested males. This type of behavior is called "tending."

By late December the rut is over, and the pregnant does, whose fawns will be born in June and early July, separate from the males until another autumn. In February and March the bucks shed their antlers and begin to grow a new set for a new season.

Where To Go

Mule deer can be seen in almost all habitats throughout the state, especially in brushy and riparian areas and along edges between forests and meadows. According to Fitzgerald, Meaney, and Armstrong in *Mammals of Colorado,* the highest densities are in the Piceance Basin in northwestern Colorado, the Gunnison River drainage, and the foothills of the Front Range. However, it would be easier to tell where they are *not* found than to enumerate the areas they inhabit.

In fact, there are more deer now than a century ago. In *Rocky Mountain Mammals,* David Armstrong quotes Merritt Cary, an early biologist, who wrote that a few mule deer had been reported in the Estes Park region in 1895 and none in the foothills of Boulder and Larimer Counties in 1906. Today Colorado has one of the largest mule deer populations of any state. The Division of Wildlife estimates the current population at about 600,000.

YARDING

Deer and elk frequently cope with deep snow by a process called "yarding," in which they gather together, usually in a forest opening, and trample down the snow cover. This strategy gives them more freedom of movement, relieving them from floundering in the drifts. However, food becomes scarce in these areas, and the animals are especially vulnerable if they are spooked or chased away from the firm-floored yard by domestic dogs or other predators. They can't afford to squander energy in winter.

Because of food scarcity, both deer and elk expand their diets in winter to include more woody shrubs. In hard winters they also consume more conifer needles, which contain chemical compounds from which turpentine is derived. In *Winter,* Jim Halfpenny and Roy Ozanne write that some American Indian tribes made a drink from pine needles to induce abortion and that a diet high in needles during fall and early winter may cause spontaneous abortion in deer—a way of limiting population during times of food scarcity.

For more information on deer and elk, see pp. 184–186 (September) and 224–226 (November).

November Events

MAMMALS

- Mule and white-tailed deer spar and mate.
- Most black bears become dormant.
- Some bighorn sheep begin to court and fight.

BIRDS

- Ducks put on their brightest nuptial plumage.
- Bald eagles and rough-legged hawks arrive.
- Tundra swans, various loon species, and snow geese may appear on reservoirs on the eastern plains.

OTHER CRITTERS

- Box elder bugs, spiders, and crickets try to move indoors.

PLANTS

- Some plants, such as asters, rabbitbrush, gumweed, and harebells, may continue to bloom.
- Creeping mahonia, sulphur flower, and prairie grasses retain fall color.
- Seed pods, cattails, and mountain ash berries remain decorative.

IN THE SKY

- "Moon of Storms" (Sioux).
- The Leonid meteor shower (look toward Leo) peaks around the 14th; the Andromedids (look toward Andromeda and Pegasus) between the 17th and 27th; the Orionids (look toward Orion) around the 19th.
- Cygnus (the Swan or Northern Cross) lies just above the western horizon around 10 P.M. This constellation contains Deneb, a first-magnitude star with a luminosity ten thousand times greater than that of our sun.

December snows blanket Boulder Creek.

12

December

In beauty may I walk.

All day long may I walk.

Through the returning seasons may I walk. . . .

In old age wandering on a trail of beauty,

   living again, may I walk.

It is finished in beauty,

It is finished in beauty.

—NAVAJO

THE YEAR FINISHES in the beauty of Douglas-fir trees decked with ice and snow. Their pendant cones attract flocks of crossbills and waxwings more decorative than any Christmas tree ornament. Juncos make vertical migrations down to lower elevations, and birders revel in their favorite holiday outing—tallying birds for the Audubon Christmas Count.

Bighorn sheep show off during this, the peak of their mating season. Each ram tries to appear more magnificent, more macho than the rest. Other animals just try to blend in. As we ski tour through freshly fallen snow, we watch for subtle differences in the white-on-white landscape. That mound of snow may turn into a weasel, a snowshoe hare, or a ptarmigan. Still other creatures are engaged in a long winter nap, and some have become living icicles. Through the season we are constantly amazed at the strange and diverse ways plants and animals cope with winter.

	Grand Junction (4,824 ft.)	Steamboat Springs (6,760 ft.)	Alamosa (7,536 ft.)	Berthoud Pass (11,310 ft.)	Denver (5,282 ft.)	Lamar (3,620 ft.)
Ave. high (°F)	39	29	35	25	45	45
Ave. low (°F)	19	3	−1	3	17	15
Max. high (°F)	66	64	61	47	75	82
Min. low (°F)	−21	−38	−42	−30	−25	−23
Ave. prec. (in.)	0.61	2.57	0.44	3.77	0.64	0.38
Max. prec. (in.)	1.89	7.26	1.52	8.45	2.84	1.75
Ave. snow (in.)	5.3	34.5	7.1	53.0	7.4	4.4
Max. snow (in.)	19.0	92.6	27.7	123.0	30.8	17.4

Bitter cold snaps alternate with periods of remarkably warm weather. In 1983, Denver's temperature remained below zero for nearly five days as Arctic air pushed in from the northeast. Las Animas recorded a December record high temperature of 88°F in 1915.

Nearly 4 feet of snow fell on Denver during a five-day period in early December 1913. This same series of storms dumped 86 inches on Georgetown. A Christmas Eve blizzard that dropped a twenty-four-hour record 23.6 inches of snow on Denver in 1982 contributed to the electoral defeat of Mayor William McNichols after side streets remained unplowed for days. Colorado's record annual snowfall of 837 inches (just under 70 feet) fell at Wolf Creek Pass in the winter of 1978–1979.

See "Colorado Climate Summary" (p. 1) for information on averages, extremes, and sources.

december ecosystem

Christmas Tree Forest

When frosted with snow, Douglas-firs look like perfectly formed Christmas trees neatly arranged on the mountainsides. Douglas-fir forests grow predominantly on shady slopes that retain snow cover throughout much of the winter. These are good places to go tracking or to sit quietly listening for the twitters and squeaks of birds flitting through the forest canopy.

Tracks of chickarees, also called pine squirrels, crisscross the forest floor. These small squirrels scurry from the base of one tree to another, digging up cones they have stored in "middens," great heaps of discarded cone scales. One squirrel can store as many as sixteen thousand cones in a year. The middens provide a cool, moist environment where cones can sit for several years before the chickarees dig them up and harvest their seeds.

Chickarees defend their cone larders ferociously. Anyone sitting within their foraging territory, usually about 1 to 5 acres in extent, is likely to get a severe tongue lashing. On the coldest days, pine squirrels retreat to their nests, conical assemblages of branches and needles placed in the upper third of the forest canopy. In early spring and late summer, they use these nests to raise a litter of two to five young.

Mule deer wander through the Douglas-fir forest to browse on the remaining leaves of small shrubs, such as waxflower and kinnikinick, and to nibble on the green, mosslike lichen, called usnea, that dangles from the bare branches of the Douglas-firs. Usnea, also known as old man's beard, grows in Douglas-fir and Engelmann spruce–subalpine fir forests throughout Colorado. It thrives in dark, moist habitats, often clinging to the north-facing sides of tree trunks and stumps.

Smaller tracks on the forest floor may belong to deer mice, southern red-backed voles, and shrews. Deer mice range from the plains to the alpine tundra, feeding on seeds, flower buds, carrion, bone, insects, and other invertebrates. They stay warm in winter by burrowing under the snowpack, where there is usually plenty to eat, and the temperature rarely falls much below freezing. On the coldest nights they huddle together in aggregate nests or enter a state of short-term torpor in which their heart beats slow and their body temperatures drop. Holes in the snow indicate places where the deer mice have popped up to look around or nibble on a favorite shrub. Southern red-backed voles and montane shrews also forage beneath the snowpack. The voles often hole up in chickaree middens, where they sleep or scavenge conifer seeds.

Burrowing under the snow helps these small mammals escape a variety of predators, including coyotes, foxes, weasels, sharp-shinned hawks, and great horned owls. Coyote tracks in forest clearings often lead to a place where the coyote paused, listened, and then pounced as its prey scurried under the snow. A spot of blood framed by large wing prints tells a different story. Owl supper.

Pseudo Fir

The scientific name for Douglas-fir, **Pseudotsuga menziesii,** *means "false hemlock," but Douglas-fir is neither a hemlock nor a true fir. It belongs to a completely separate North American genus. True firs have upright cones, whereas Douglas-fir cones are pendant. Douglas-firs grow over 300 feet tall in Oregon and Washington and form the old-growth forests that harbor spotted owls and other threatened wildlife. The twigs and the needles of Douglas-firs have been used as a coffee substitute.*

Dec

Douglas-firs produce bountiful cone crops at three- to five-year intervals. High cone and seed production attracts flocks of mountain chickadees, white-breasted and red-breasted nuthatches, pine siskins, and dark-eyed juncos. The chickadees and nuthatches dangle upside down from the fir cones like fluffy Christmas tree ornaments. Mixed flocks often include a hairy woodpecker or two, who peck single-mindedly at the Douglas-fir bark while the smaller songbirds keep a lookout for predators. If you stand under the concealing branches of a tree and whistle in a low monotone, like a northern pygmy-owl, you may soon find yourself mobbed by squadrons of twittering chickadees and nuthatches. The most aggressive birds may perch within a foot or two of your head, chattering shrilly and hopping around frenetically as they try to drive off the oversize "owl."

Douglas-fir forests occur throughout the Colorado mountains from about 5,600 to 9,500 feet. East of the Continental Divide, Douglas-firs often grow in association with ponderosa pines, with the Douglas-firs occupying shadier, moister sites. On the Western Slope, large, relatively uniform Douglas-fir stands occur on mountainsides and in mountain valleys above about 7,000 feet.

Where To Go

🐾 Northstar Nature Preserve, east of Aspen.

🐾 Ouray Amphitheatre Trail.

🐾 Wolf Creek Pass, north of Pagosa Springs.

🐾 Bear Creek Canyon, between Morrison and Kittridge.

🐾 Boulder Mountain Park, including lower Shadow Canyon and upper Bear Canyon.

🐾 Rocky Mountain National Park, especially Beaver Meadows and Horseshoe Park.

WINTER BIRD FLOCKS

Winter birdwatching in Colorado's coniferous forests involves hours of silent searching rewarded by sudden bursts of activity as mixed flocks of woodpeckers, chickadees, nuthatches, juncos, and finches sweep through the trees. These flocks may contain anywhere from a half dozen to several hundred birds.

Biologists do not fully understand why birds group together in winter. Flocks appear to be more adept than individuals at finding areas of seed and insect concentrations, but flocks deplete these food resources much more quickly and must expend precious energy flying from one part of the forest to another. Flocks are better than individuals at detecting predators, but flocks also attract predators. The old adage, "safety in numbers," applies to birds in the center of a flock, but "outlyers" face the constant threat of being eaten.

One theory, first proposed by ecologist W. D. Hamilton in an article entitled "Geometry for the Selfish Herd" (*Journal of Theoretical Biology* 31 [1971]:297–311), suggests that animals may group together for "selfish" reasons rather than to benefit the species as a whole. Hamilton posited that since predators generally attack the nearest prey, an individual always reduces its chances of being eaten by joining together with another of its kind. Once a group of any size has formed, outlying individuals will fly in to selfishly reduce their chances of being eaten. Although birds on the periphery of the flock watch for predators and issue warnings while others forage, all members may jockey constantly for position, seeking out the relatively safe center.

Some of the largest winter flocks consist of irruptive seed and fruit eaters, birds that migrate great distances when food becomes scarce in their usual foraging areas. Red crossbills, white-winged crossbills, red-breasted nuthatches, and pine siskins roam throughout the northern and southern Rockies searching for good cone crops. The crossbills pry open the cones with their uniquely constructed beaks and then extract the seeds with their tongues. Individuals are "right- or left-handed," depending on which way their mandibles cross. They fly swiftly from tree top to tree top, chirping loudly as they hack away at the cones, creating a blizzard of swirling cone scales.

Look for crossbill nests at any time of the year. Crossbills will mate and lay their eggs whenever and wherever conifer seeds abound. In January 1995, Boulder naturalists Mike Figgs and Nancy Lederer found a white-winged crossbill, a Colorado rarity, quietly sitting on her nest in a snowy Engelmann spruce near Brainard Lake, at 10,500 feet.

Bohemian waxwings also travel in enormous flocks. In winter, waxwings feed primarily on fruit and berries. Flocks of several hundred or more will descend on a single juniper tree, chattering shrilly while snatching up the fruits in their conical beaks. They sometimes pass the fruits around in a sort of "berry brigade." Within seconds, they swoop away in a wildly chirping, pulsating mass, leaving the juniper denuded of ripe fruits.

While watching gregarious flocks of crossbills, waxwings, or siskins, we wonder if a mechanistic explanation of bird flocking is really necessary. Just as humans gain comfort by crowding around a blazing fire, birds must experience feelings of security and camaraderie as they flock together during these coldest and darkest months.

Dec

"SNOWBIRDS": SURVIVING THE CHILL

People throughout North America use the term *snowbirds* to describe a variety of species that seem to appear magically with the first snows. Many of these birds are altitudinal migrants that nest in the high country and winter at lower elevations. Others are long-distance migrants from the north who follow the snow line southward during fall and winter.

Dark-eyed juncos travel in flocks, moving slowly southward or to lower elevations as the season progresses. They commonly feed by shuffling backward on the ground, throwing small clouds of dirt and snow out behind them, and then pecking at uncovered seeds and insects. Juncos feed frantically throughout the day, for during the cold nights they may burn as much as 50 percent of their body weight to keep warm.

Horned larks breed both on the tundra and on the plains, so their migration is complicated. Some head south, some remain relatively close to their summer nesting territories on the prairie, and others move down from the high country. In eastern Colorado, flocks of several hundred forage in fallow fields and pastures or perch on dirt roads where both seeds and insects are easy to see.

Snow buntings migrate over great distances, from the arctic tundra to the northern plains. They appear rarely in Colorado, when extreme cold or heavy snows force them farther south than usual. Look for them on the northeastern plains and in the northern mountains.

Black-capped and mountain chickadees seem more affected by food availability than by weather conditions. Some remain in high-elevation spruce-fir and aspen forests throughout the winter, while others flock to bird feeders on the plains and in the western valleys. Their downy white plumage, their gregariousness during the coldest days, and their habit of dangling upside down from snow-encrusted conifer cones make them perfect candidates for our state "snowbird."

All these small songbirds must work hard to make it through the winter. To maintain a body temperature of 108°F, chickadees must consume ten to twenty times as much food in winter as in summer. At night family groups stay warm by roosting in tree cavities or on sheltering conifer boughs. During the coldest nights, the chickadees' metabolisms and heart beats slow, and their body temperatures drop 10 degrees or more to reduce heat loss. Exposed bills are tucked away into fluffed-out feathers. Exposed feet are kept warm by a "countercurrent heat exchange system"; arteries and veins in the birds' feet and legs run close together, allowing the returning venous blood to be warmed by the arterial blood.

To stay warm at night, snow buntings huddle in rock crevices or burrow into the snow. Rosy finches roost communally in small caves or rock outcroppings sheltered from the wind. Goldfinches and tree sparrows huddle at the base of clumps of grass or small shrubs. Despite taking all these precautions, many songbirds shiver continuously to ward off hypothermia during the coldest nights. Because smaller objects lose heat much more quickly than do larger objects (compare the melting time of an ice cube to that of an iceberg), these lightweight songbirds radiate heat about three to four times faster than cottontail rabbits and about ten times faster than humans. Even with several layers of winter clothing, few of us could survive a subzero night in the open, yet these "snowbirds" somehow get along with only a .25-inch layer of soft feathers.

CHRISTMAS BIRD COUNTS

What could be more rewarding than a day in the field learning about nature and helping to conserve bird populations? During the last half of December several hundred Colorado nature lovers brave the elements to carry on a century-old tradition, the Audubon Christmas Bird Counts.

These counts welcome bird-watchers of all abilities and affiliations. Participants go out in groups to search every part of a 15-mile-diameter count circle. Those who cannot go out watch feeders at home. Results, published nationally, are used to track bird populations throughout North America.

Sharp declines in brown pelican and peregrine falcon populations during the 1950s were first reported by the Christmas bird count network. These birds were rescued from extinction when biologists determined that DDT concentrations in their body fat were destroying their ability to lay viable eggs. In Colorado, Christmas counts have documented a disturbing increase in numbers of urban-adapted generalists, including great horned owls, scrub jays, common ravens, and American crows. These species prey on nestlings of other birds and are beginning to reduce populations of some native habitat specialists.

To find out about local counts, call or write the Audubon Society chapter nearest you or the National Audubon Regional Office, 4150 Darley, Boulder CO 80303. Colorado count circles include Aspen, Barr Lake, Boulder, Cortez, Colorado Springs, Douglas County, Denver, Durango, Evergreen, Fort Collins, Grand Junction, Great Sand Dunes National Monument, Gunnison, Holly, Hotchkiss, Lake Isabel, Longmont, Monte Vista National Wildlife Refuge, Nederland, North Park, Nunn, Penrose, Pueblo, Roaring Fork River Valley, Rocky Mountain National Park, Spanish Peaks, Summit County, and Westcliffe.

Dec

ALTITUDINAL MIGRANTS

Almost all birds migrate vertically, which means they move from one elevation to another in response to changes in weather and food availability. This list includes relatively common species that tend to stay within Colorado year-round, summering in the high country and wintering at lower elevations. Many flock to urban bird feeders throughout the winter.

SPECIES	SUMMER HABITAT	WINTER HABITAT
HORNED LARK	Grasslands and tundra.	Western valleys, mountain parks, and eastern plains.
CLARK'S NUTCRACKER	High elevation coniferous forests.	Low- to moderate-elevation coniferous forests and shrublands.
MOUNTAIN CHICKADEE	Deciduous forests and woodlands, 3,600 to 10,000 feet.	Same habitats, but numbers increase at lower elevations.
RED-BREASTED NUTHATCH	Coniferous forests, 5,000 to 11,000 feet.	Same habitats, but numbers increase at lower elevations.
BROWN CREEPER	Coniferous forests, 6,000 to 11,500 feet.	Coniferous and deciduous forests and woodlands, 3,500 to 11,500 feet.
AMERICAN DIPPER	Mountain and foothills streams, 5,600 to 11,500 feet.	Mountain and foothills streams, 5,000 to 10,500 feet.
RUBY-CROWNED KINGLET	Coniferous forests, 7,500 to 11,500 feet.	Piñon-juniper woodlands, riparian woodlands, and urban areas, 3,500 to 6,000 feet.
TOWNSEND'S SOLITAIRE	Coniferous forests, 6,000 to 12,000 feet. Eats mostly insects.	Coniferous forests and riparian woodlands, 5,000 to 9,000 feet. Eats mostly berries.
BROWN-CAPPED ROSY FINCH	Tundra, 11,000 to 13,000 feet.	Coniferous forests and urban woodlands, 6,000 to 11,000 feet.
PINE SISKIN	Coniferous forests, 6,000 to 11,500 feet.	Coniferous forests, shrublands, and urban woodlands, 3,500 to 10,000 feet.

Sources: Hugh Kingery, ed., *Colorado Breeding Bird Atlas;* Robert Andrews and Robert Righter, *Colorado Birds.*

BECOMING INVISIBLE

By late December, weasels, snowshoe hares, and ptarmigan have turned white as winter—a useful camouflage for both predator and prey. Only the black tip of a weasel's tail, the black-tipped ears of a snowshoe hare, or the black beak and eyes of a ptarmigan reveal their presence against the snow.

If the turncoats retain their summer browns and grays too late in the fall or resume them too early in the spring, they will be dangerously conspicuous. Since snow cover is unpredictable, how do they know when to switch? In *Winter,* Jim Halfpenny and Roy Ozanne write, "Changes in photoperiod trigger changes in hormones which are also influenced by cold and snow."

In addition to providing protective coloration, white fur and feathers provide more insulation than dark ones, according to some studies. Whiteness is caused by the absence of the pigment melanin. In *Life in the Cold,* Peter Marchand says that the air spaces that take the place of the pigment granules provide more insulation.

There is more to white coloration in winter, he says, than meets the eye.

Both long-tailed and short-tailed weasels undergo a complete molt, replacing all brown and golden hairs with white ones. When this transformation is complete, weasels are commonly called ermine, though technically only the short-tailed weasel is an ermine. Ermine fur is so highly valued that British royalty use it for coronations. Halfpenny and Ozanne say over fifty thousand pelts were shipped from the United States for King George VI's coronation in 1936. Weasels begin to whiten in October, take about two months to complete the molt, and reverse the process in March.

White-tailed ptarmigan in full winter plumage.

Instead of completely molting, snowshoe hares retain their grayish under-fur, but the tips turn white. Next time you see a snowshoe or "varying" hare, look at the base of the fur, and you'll see that "pure-white" is an illusion. Hares begin their autumnal molt in September and take two to three months to complete it; the prevernal molt (back to summer colors) begins in March or April. A closely related species, the white-tailed jackrabbit, also changes to winter white in the northern part of the state, but in southern Colorado it turns only slightly paler than in summer.

White-tailed ptarmigan start their autumnal molt in mid-September, with white feathers sprouting first on the flanks, then on the neck and back. The area around the eyes is the last to turn. Throughout the winter they remain white except for gray downy feathers next to their bodies. The process reverses starting in late April, with dark feathers appearing around the eyes.

Ptarmigan are feathered even around their eyelids, nostrils, and feet. To stay warm at night, they dive into the soft, insulating snow, where they roost. In spring, females do not begin nesting until completely changed to their summer plumage. The amount of snow cover and light intensity determine the timing of molt and directly affect the start of nesting.

Weasels, hares, and ptarmigan also benefit from cryptic coloration in summer when they are hard to distinguish from rocks and vegetation.

Dec

Where To Go

Ski touring and snowshoeing are the best ways to see these species in their winter coats.

🦡 Short-tailed weasels: coniferous forests, clearings, rock outcrops above 8,000 feet.

🦡 Long-tailed weasels: throughout the state in all habitats if prey species are present.

🦡 Snowshoe hares: coniferous forests from 8,000 to 11,500 feet, especially abundant in willow thickets.

🦡 White-tailed ptarmigan: anywhere above timberline, especially near their preferred food, willow shrubs. Guanella Pass, Mount Evans, Trail Ridge Road, and Independence Pass are easily accessible places to find ptarmigan.

CLASHING BIGHORNS

Snow, sleet, and ice do not dim the amour and ardour of mountain bighorn rams, whose rambunctious duels for females start in November and reach their peak in December. "The usually disorderly and nervous behavior of bighorns gives way to utter chaos," writes mammologist David Armstrong in *Rocky Mountain Mammals*. Bashing, butting, battering, and bluffing each other, the bighorns battle.

In a classic duel, the rams start side by side, facing in opposite directions. Grunting and snorting, they push and kick each other and then pace slowly away. Suddenly they turn and rear up on stiff hind legs. They charge. And their horns clash in a mighty crash that can be heard for up to a mile.

The cartilage at the base of the horns absorbs most of the shock, and after a few dazed moments, the battle starts all over again. Observers have counted up to forty-eight clashes in a single battle, and speed at impact can be over 50 miles per hour. Few bighorns actually die as a result of these fierce fights, though their horns may splinter or break. As in most wildlife battles, the weaker combatant gives way, and the victor, who can weigh up to 350 pounds, mates with the ewe. Sometimes a third ram sneaks in and mates with the ewe while the other two are preoccupied with their quarrel.

How Do You Tell
the Sheep From the Goats?

Female bighorns are sometimes mistaken for mountain goats because of their superficial resemblance in size and shape. However, both male and female mountain goats have whiter coats, more slender spikes, and a spiffy goatee. Although the two species sometimes share the same range, bighorns usually prefer slightly lower elevations.

Some wildlife researchers think reintroduced goats may adversely affect the bighorns. In a five-year study for the Division of Wildlife in the 1980s, Dale Reed found that in one hundred interactions the bighorns were never dominant. Goats forced the bighorns to give up space or food in 30 percent of the cases; 70 percent of the interactions were neutral. See pp. 150–151 for more information on mountain goats.

Desert bighorns also indulge in dramatic duels but may breed as early as July. Desert bighorns, a subspecies of mountain bighorns, are slightly smaller and paler than their cousins, but the main difference between the two is their preferred habitat. Rare in Colorado, desert bighorns are sometimes seen in Colorado National Monument, where they were introduced in 1979, and in the Dolores River Canyon.

The mountain bighorn (*Ovis canadensis*) was designated the official state mammal of Colorado in 1961 and is the logo for the Colorado Division of Wildlife. In the early 1800s there were said to be about 2 million throughout the West; now there are only about 20,000, with 6,000 to 7,000 in Colorado. Many of them formerly migrated to the western edge of the plains for winter. Now that much of their former range has been taken over by humans and livestock and is criss-crossed by roads, they tend to winter at higher elevations; some even stay above timberline throughout the year. Most herds still make short seasonal migrations and prefer rocky slopes above 8,000 feet.

Other than humans, the chief enemy of the bighorns is disease. Lungworm, which often leads to pneumonia, and other parasitic diseases are widespread. Bighorns have no immunity to diseases spread by domestic sheep.

Although both sexes have horns, the ewe's horns are more like small spikes, whereas the ram's spiral horns, weighing up to 35 pounds, grow larger and more curled each year. Like tree rings, the grooves around the horns tell a ram's age. Some American Indian tribes, such as the Havasupai in Arizona, made dippers and ladles from these horns.

In contrast to the massive horns, bighorn hooves are dainty. Like all ungulates, bighorn sheep actually walk on their "toes," two to each foot. The front part is hollow, acting like a suction cup; the sole is rough and springy; and the hard outer shell can cut through mud or snow to gain a purchase on slippery slopes. Dewclaws help protect the foot on stony ground. This foot design enables bighorns to perform with panache as they scramble up sheer cliffs and leap from narrow mountain ledges.

About six months after mating takes place, the young are born, usually on mountain ledges safe from predators. Throughout the summer the sheep stay in bands. However, the older rams remain separate from the ewes and lambs, feeding at higher elevations. They eat chiefly grasses and forbs, and relish salt, often licking the soil to obtain minerals. These ruminants spend much of their time lying down chewing their cud. An idyllic life in June. But who would envy them on a bitter December day?

WHERE TO GO

Horns and Antlers

The words horns and antlers are not synonyms, although both horns and antlers are used for fighting. Horns are permanent, unbranched head gear that continue to grow throughout an animal's life, whereas antlers are usually branched and are shed after the breeding season. Horns adorn mountain goats and bighorn sheep; antlers, deer and elk. The reason you rarely find cast antlers is that rodents nibble them to nubbins for their mineral content.

✗ Cottonwood Canyon in Comanche National Grassland, south of La Junta.

✗ Bighorn Sheep Canyon along the Arkansas River west of Canon City. Five Points Recreation Site provides interpretation and suggests other viewing spots.

✗ Mueller State Park, south of Divide, especially along Four Mile Creek.

✗ Almont Triangle north of Gunnison.

✗ Georgetown. A viewing tower with scope and an interpretive site are south of I-70; about two hundred sheep range north of the highway.

✗ Mt. Evans, south of Idaho Springs.

✗ Poudre River. A viewing station at Big Bend Campground west of Rustic is south of C14; the bighorn sheep are usually north of the road.

The best time for observation is early morning and late afternoon when bighorns are feeding and most active. Scan hillsides with binoculars, looking for their characteristic white rumps. For more information, see *Bighorn Sheep Watching Guide,* available for $3.00 from the Colorado Division of Wildlife.

INSECT ICICLES

Many are cold but few are frozen . . .

Cold-blooded creatures such as insects cannot produce heat internally and must cope with a body temperature that matches their surroundings. To insure that their genes survive, many insects lay eggs and die before the onslaught of winter. In fact, more insects survive the cold in the egg or pupa stage than as larvae or adults.

Dec

A molting grasshopper.

However, some grasshopper nymphs and other arthropods are revved up with "antifreeze" (elevated levels of glycerol) and remain active. Some aquatic insects spend the winter encased in ice—but unfrozen. Mourning cloak and Milbert's tortoiseshell butterflies creep under protective tree bark until spring, and monarch butterflies migrate to Mexico.

Many beetles burrow into holes for the duration of winter. Ants crawl deeper into the ground, sometimes 6 feet under, where they cluster together for warmth. Honeybees cuddle together in a ball in the middle of the hive, constantly shifting position so the bees on the outside move toward the center.

All bumblebees die except for the fertilized queen, who holes up in a hollow log or tree or underground. In spring she chooses a sheltered nest site under boards or grass tufts—even in a mouse nest—and makes a thimble-size wax cup, filling it with honey to feed her newly hatched larvae. These hatchlings, the beginning of a new colony, quickly mature into sterile workers who pamper the queen and care for the succeeding generations that she produces. Fertile queen and male bees are not born until summer's end when the old queen dies and the cycle begins anew. Yellowjacket wasps and hornets have a similar life cycle.

The strangest insect strategies for overwintering are either to supercool or to freeze almost solid—complicated processes described by Peter Marchand in *Life in the Cold*. Some insects can survive having their body fluids fall many degrees below their usual freezing point. Body water remains liquid, and ice does not form. Scientists call this process "supercooling."

Cryobiologist Richard E. Lee writes that ladybugs and springtails can chill to temperatures of 5°F to −31°F without freezing and that some Alaskan species supercool to −76°F. To perform this magic, they undergo physiological and biochemical changes that require several weeks of gradual cold hardening—a process usually induced by shorter periods of daylight and lower temperatures.

Supercooling insects empty their guts to remove impurities that would serve as ice nucleators (particles around which ice crystals grow). They also lose much of the water in their tissues and accumulate certain chemicals, called cryoprotectants, that act like antifreeze in their bodies.

Other insects, such as the goldenrod gall fly and the woolly bear caterpillar, freeze almost solid, with ice forming in the space between cells. These "freeze-tolerant" insects can survive temperatures as low as −94°F. Special proteins act as nuclei around which the ice forms. At the same time these proteins limit dehydration and protect the cells from lethal freezing, which can occur if cells become too dehydrated, if two-thirds of their body water freezes, or if ice crystals puncture cell walls and membranes. Even freeze-tolerant insects will die if the temperature falls below their freezing point—a point that varies among species.

Goldenrod plants harbor insects illustrating both coping strategies: The goldenrod gall fly freezes, whereas the goldenrod gall moth larvae simply supercools.

Some amphibians, such as chorus frogs and wood frogs, and some reptiles, such as garter snakes and painted turtle hatchlings, also freeze and miraculously thaw to life in the sun. However, they seldom survive below −17°F.

Information gained from studying living creatures who turn themselves into icicles may eventually aid in the cryopreservation of human tissue and organs.

WHERE TO GO

To find insects in winter, look under stones and logs, in the crevices of tree bark, and in leaf litter. Examine thistles and look under prickly pear cacti pads for praying mantis egg cases. Check goldenrod and other plants for galls. Check shrubs and trees for chrysalids (hardened butterfly pupae that look like Christmas tree decorations) and cocoons (moth pupae shrouded in silk). Red-osier dogwood, willow, ash, and hackberry are a few favored host species.

To see exotic butterflies flitting through a rain-forest environment, visit the

Butterfly Pavilion and Insect Center, 6252 West 104th Ave., Westminster, CO 80020, phone 303-469-5441. It's a minivacation to the tropics in the midst of winter.

DECEMBER EVENTS

MAMMALS

❦ As mule deer mating ends, the sexes start to move about in separate groups, with the does, fawns, and yearlings staying together and the bucks traveling in bachelor groups.

❦ Bighorn sheep dueling and breeding extends from November to January and peaks in December.

❦ Beavers remain alert in their lodges throughout the winter, eating from the branches they have stored underwater.

❦ Weasels and snowshoe hares turn white.

❦ Even insomniac bears become dormant.

BIRDS

❦ Dippers, chickadees, juncos, and many other birds drop to lower elevations in a vertical migration.

❦ Irruptive seed eaters such as crossbills follow cone crops.

❦ Large flocks of Canada geese congregate around open water as migrants from the north join resident geese.

❦ Northern pygmy owls move to lower elevations and sometimes appear around urban bird feeders.

OTHER CRITTERS

❦ Stone, black, caddis, and crane flies continue their aquatic activities; springtails and snow fleas remain active.

❦ Other insects become dormant, many turning into living icicles.

PLANTS

❦ Easter daisies may begin to bloom on south-facing shales in the Front Range foothills.

❦ Some sages and other mints begin to leaf out.

❦ In urban areas, winter pansies continue to bloom.

SPECIAL EVENTS

✿ The Audubon Christmas Bird Count takes place across the United States, usually the week before Christmas.

IN THE SKY

✿ "Long Night Moon" (Sioux).

✿ Winter Solstice occurs around December 21, and days begin to lengthen. Traditionally, this was a day to celebrate and hope for the sun's "return" from the South.

✿ The Geminid meteor shower, one of the most spectacular of the year, peaks around the 12th.

✿ Look for Sirius, the Dog Star and centerpiece of the constellation Canis Major, low in the southeastern sky around 9 P.M. Sirius is the brightest visible star in the heavens. To locate it, extend a line southeastward from the belt of Orion.

Dec

Earth

always

endures.

—HIDATSA AND MANDAN

Appendixes

1.

WHERE TO GO DIRECTORY

To help locate out-of-the-way places, we recommend the *Colorado Atlas and Gazetteer* by DeLorme Mapping (available at convenience stores and bookstores) and the U.S. Forest Service maps (available at regional Forest Service offices and the Denver Federal Center, 303-202-4700). Region-specific maps with general site locations follow this list (see pp. 258–262). Mileages given in this directory are approximate. Hiking distances are one-way. Phone numbers are included for state parks, national parks, national monuments, and most U.S. Forest Service sites. For information about State Wildlife Areas, call: northeast 970-484-2836, northwest 970-248-7175, southeast 719-473-2945, southwest 970-249-3431.

Note that we have included a few outstanding natural areas in states adjacent to Colorado.

Abbreviations used in this directory are as follows:

BLM—Bureau of Land Management
CDOW—Colorado Division of Wildlife
CG—Campground in vicinity
CR—county road
FR—Forest Service road
I—Interstate highway
NWR—National Wildlife Refuge

SP—State Park
SR—State highway or road
SWA—State Wildlife Area
US—U.S. highway
USFS—U.S. Forest Service
USFW—U.S. Fish and Wildlife Service
$—Entrance fee

Adobe Creek Reservoir SWA, 12 miles north of Las Animas on CR 10. $ CG   CDOW (page 118).

Alamosa NWR, 7 miles east of Alamosa on CR S-116 (2 miles south from US 160). USFW   719-589-4021 (pages 53, 219).

Alberta Falls, .5-mile hike from Glacier Gorge Junction, on Bear Lake Road, in Rocky Mountain National Park. $ CG   970-586-1206 (page 122).

Almont Triangle, 15 miles north of Gunnison on SR 135 and FR 813. USFS   970-641-0471 (page 241).

Animas River, CR 250 north of Durango (page 72).

Antero Reservoir, 15 miles south of Fairplay on US 285.   CG   CDOW 719-836-2361 (page 118).

Arapaho NWR, in North Park 5 miles south of Walden on SR 125. USFW 970-723-8202 (pages 53, 79, 160, 170, 200).

Arapaho Pass, 2.5-mile hike from end of CR 111, 10 miles west of Nederland.   CG (page 142).

🦌 Arkansas River SWA, 6 miles southeast of Holly on CR DD (pages 55, 72).

🦌 Barr Lake State Park, 20 miles northeast of Denver on Piccadilly Road (take Exit 23 east off I-76). $ 303-659-6005 (pages 53, 82, 101, 103, 118, 170, 183, 199, 222).

🦌 Bear Creek Canyon, SR 74 between Morrison and Kittridge (page 232).

🦌 Beecher Island Battle Ground, 19 miles south of Wray on CR LL (3 miles east of US 385) (page 115).

🦌 Big Creek Lakes trail, 30 miles northwest of Walden on FR 600 (go west on CR 6W, 9 miles north of Walden off SR 125). CG USFS 970-723-8204 (page 95).

🦌 Big Johnson Reservoir, 10 miles southeast of Colorado Springs (from US 87 go east on Fontaine Blvd. for 2 miles then north on Goldfield Dr.) (page 199).

🦌 Bighorn Sheep Canyon, Five Points Recreation Site, US 50, 24 miles west of Canon City. CG BLM 719-269-8500 (page 241).

🦌 Billy Creek SWA, 10 miles north of Ridgeway (take CR 2 east off US 550). CDOW (page 105).

🦌 Black Canyon of the Gunnison National Monument, 14 miles northeast of Montrose on SR 347. $ CG 970-641-2337 (pages 196, 214).

🦌 Bonny Reservoir State Recreation Area, 23 miles north of Burlington on US 385. $ CG CDOW 970-354-7306 (pages 37, 53, 55, 72, 103, 105, 115, 118, 120, 129).

🦌 Bosque del Apache NWR, 63 miles south of Albuquerque, New Mexico, along I-25 (page 17).

🦌 Boulder Falls, SR 119, in Boulder Canyon 8 miles west of Boulder. USFS (page 122).

🦌 Boulder Mountain Park, 9th and Baseline, Boulder. 303-441-3408 (pages 22, 35, 59, 94, 99, 105, 188, 232).

🦌 Boulder Reservoir, N. 51st Street, 3 miles north of SR 119, between Boulder and Longmont. 303-441-3468 (pages 219, 222).

🦌 Bowen Gulch trail, 5 miles north of Grand Lake on US 34. CG USFS 970-887-4100 (page 13).

🦌 Bridal Veil Falls, 3-mile hike northwest from Devil's Gulch Rd. in Rocky Mountain National Park. $ 970-586-1206 (page 121).

🦌 Bridal Veil Falls, 3 miles east of Telluride on SR 145 (page 121).

🦌 Bridal Veil Falls and Spouting Rock above Hanging Lake in Glenwood Canyon, I-70, 9 miles east of Glenwood Springs. 1.5 mile hike on steep trail. USFS 970-945-6589 (pages 24, 121).

🦌 Browns Park NWR, 85 miles northwest of Craig on SR 318. CG USFW 970- 365-3613 (pages 53, 198).

✽ Buffalo Peaks and Tomahawk SWA, 16 miles southwest of Fairplay on SR 9. CDOW (page 160).

✽ Butterfly Pavilion and Insect Center. U.S. 36 between Denver and Boulder. Church Ranch Blvd./West 104th Ave. exit. $ 303-469-5441 (pages 152, 243–244).

✽ Buttonrock Reservoir, 9 miles west of Lyons (take US 36 west 4 miles to CR 80 and hike 1.5 miles from end of CR 80, page 22).

✽ Cactus Park, 24 miles south of Grand Junction off SR 141 (turn south on CR KS 20). BLM   970-240-5300 (page 208).

✽ Cameron Pass, 87 miles west of Fort Collins on SR 14. CG (page 81).

✽ Cañon Pintado, along SR 139 south of Rangely. Brochure available from Rangely Chamber of Commerce, 970-675-8469, or from BLM, 970-878-3601 (page 206).

✽ Castle Rock, above the town of Castle Rock (page 35).

✽ Castlewood Canyon SP, 30 miles southeast of Denver on SR 83. $ 303-688-5242 (pages 31, 59, 196).

✽ Cedar Mountain, 7 miles northwest of Craig on CR 7. BLM   970-824-8261 (page 35).

✽ Chatfield SP and Reservoir, 13 miles south of Denver on I-470 or SR 121. $ CG   303-791-7275 (pages 37, 101, 222).

✽ Chicago Basin in the Weminuche Wilderness, 20 miles north of Durango (consult topographic or Forest Service map). Backpacking required (page 142).

✽ Chimney Rock Archaeological Area, 21 miles west of Pagosa Springs (take SR 151 to FR 617). 970-264-2268 (page 196).

✽ Collegiate Mountain Range, west of Buena Vista (several access roads off US 285 between Buena Vista and Salida) (page 151).

✽ Colorado National Monument, 3 miles southwest of Grand Junction off SR 340. $ CG   970-858-3617 (pages 30, 34, 59, 206, 214).

✽ Colorado State Forest, 3 miles east of Gould on SR 14. $ CG.   970-723-8366 (page 200).

✽ Comanche National Grassland, south of La Junta on county roads off SR 109 and US 160. Acquire necessary map at USFS offices in La Junta or Springfield. CG   USFS   719-523-6591 (pages 31, 35, 37, 41, 79, 103, 105, 115, 120, 123–124, 129, 204, 206, 217, 241).

✽ Crescent Lake NWR, 28 miles north of Oshkosh, Nebraska on SR 250. USFW   308-762-4893 (page 79).

✽ Crow Valley Campground, Pawnee National Grassland, 41 miles east of Fort Collins on SR 14. CG   USFS   970-353-5004 (pages 105, 183).

✽ Crystal Mill and Falls, on FR 314 between SR 133 and Marble (page 121).

ᪧ Cumbres Pass, 55 miles west of Antonito on SR 17. CG   USFS (pages 81, 179).

ᪧ Delta Confluence Park, Gunnison River Drive west from Main Street (heron rookery) in town of Delta.   970-874-8616 (page 101).

ᪧ Denver Botanic Gardens, 1005 York St., Denver. $ 303-331-4000.

ᪧ Denver Museum of Natural History, 2001 Colorado Blvd., Denver $ 303-370-6357.

ᪧ Dinosaur National Monument, 18 miles north of Rangely on US 40. $ CG   970-374-3000 (pages 22, 30, 124, 206, 208, 214).

ᪧ Dinosaur Ridge, 3 miles north of Morrison on SR 26 (page 208).

ᪧ Dolores River Canyon, north of Cortez off US 666 between McPhee Reservoir and Gateway.   BLM   970-247-4082 (pages 17, 22, 86, 96, 206, 216).

ᪧ Douglas Pass, 50 miles northwest of Grand Junction on SR 139.   USFS 970-242-8211 (page 59).

ᪧ Empire Reservoir, 30 miles west of Fort Morgan on US 34. $ CDOW (page 101).

ᪧ Escalante SWA, CR G, six miles west of Delta (take 5th Street west off Main Street). CDOW (page 105).

ᪧ Flattops (The), Crane Park. Take CR 17 west off CR 301, 1.5 miles north of Dotsero. USFS   970-328-6388 (page 142).

ᪧ Florissant Fossil Beds National Monument, 17 miles west of Woodland Park off US 24. $ 719-748-3253.

ᪧ Fort Carson, 15 miles south of Colorado Springs on SR 115 (page 124).

ᪧ Fort Collins gravel ponds. From I-25 Exit 265, go west 1.5 miles on CR 38, then north 3 miles on CR 9 to Poudre River Trail (page 86).

ᪧ Fort Collins Greenbelt, on Poudre River between Taft Hill Road and CR 9. 970-482-5821 (pages 37, 72).

ᪧ Fruitgrowers Reservoir Wildlife Viewing Area, Harts Basin north of Delta. From SR 92 take SR 65 north 6 miles to Eckert, turn right on CR N 00 for 2 miles (pages 170, 198, 222).

ᪧ Garden of the Gods, 5 miles northwest of Colorado Springs off US 24. 719-634-6666 (page 31).

ᪧ Garden Park Fossil Area, 5 miles north of Canon City on west side of "Shelf Road" (CR 9). Inquire locally about road conditions (page 208).

ᪧ Gateway Special Recreation Management Area, 55 miles southwest of Grand Junction (take SR 141 to Gateway and turn right on CR 4 40, .5 miles south of town).   BLM   970-244-3000 (page 183).

ᪧ Georgetown bighorn sheep viewing area. Take exit 228 off I-70, 1 mile north of Georgetown. CDOW   303-569-2555 (page 241).

❦ Golden Gate Canyon SP, 25 miles northwest of Golden on SR 46. $ CG 303-582-3707 (pages 22, 179).

❦ Gore Range near Dillon. Take side roads off SR 9, from Dillon to Kremmling (page 151).

❦ Grand Mesa, 42 miles east of Grand Junction on SR 65. CG   USFS 970-874-7691 (pages 81, 179).

❦ Grays Peak and Torreys Peak. Trailhead begins at dead end of FR 248, 7 miles southeast of Georgetown. USFS   303-567-2901 (page 151).

❦ Great Sand Dunes National Monument, 35 miles northeast of Alamosa on SR 150. $ CG   719-378-2312 (pages 22, 59, 214).

❦ Greater prairie chicken leks, on private land north of Wray. Call CDOW (970-484-2836) for access information (page 79).

❦ Guanella Pass, 12 miles south of Georgetown on FR 381. CG (page 238).

❦ Gunnison River along US 50, west and east of Gunnison (pages 86, 219).

❦ Gunnison SWA, 6 miles west of Gunnison. Take US 50 west for 5 miles and turn right on CR 726. CDOW (page 186).

❦ Hamilton Reservoir, 18 miles north of Fort Collins. Take Exit 288 off I-25, go west 2.5 miles, turn right at "Visitors Overlook" sign (page 17).

❦ Henderson Museum, University of Colorado, Boulder campus. 303-492-6892.

❦ Highline State Recreation Area, 20 miles northwest of Grand Junction on SR 139. $ CG   970-858-7208 (pages 170, 198).

❦ Holt Canyon, 30 miles south of Springfield. *See* Comanche National Grassland (page 204).

❦ Horsethief Canyon SWA, Colorado River 5 miles west of Fruita. Take SR 340 south from Fruita for 1 mile, turn right on CR 1.10 and continue on CR 1.30. CDOW   970-248-7175 (pages 17, 37, 72).

❦ Hovenweep National Monument, consists of six ruins in southwest Colorado and southeast Utah accessed by dirt roads that may be impassable in bad weather. Administered by Mesa Verde National Park. CG   970-529-4465 (page 206).

❦ Illinois River Moose Viewing Site. *See* Arapaho NWR (page 200).

❦ Independence Pass, SR 82 between Aspen and Twin Lakes. CG (pages 139, 238).

❦ Jackson Reservoir SP, 15 miles northwest of Fort Morgan on SR 144. $ CG   970-645-2551 (page 219).

❦ John Martin Reservoir SWA, 30 miles east of La Junta on US 50. CG CDOW   719-336-4852 (pages 101, 120, 199).

❦ Julesburg (Jumbo) Reservoir, 22 miles west of Julesburg off US 138. $ CG   CDOW   970-474-2711 (pages 55, 56, 170, 199).

Kenosha Pass, US 285 between Bailey and Fairplay. CG   USFS (pages 139, 179).

Knight-Imler SWA, 12 miles south of Fairplay on US 285. CDOW (page 160).

Kremmling Cretaceous Ammonite Site, 13 miles north of Kremmling via CR 25 and 26. Get map from Kremmling BLM office, 970-724-3437 (page 207).

Kremmling pronghorn viewing site, private land along CR 22, just north of Kremmling. 970-725-3557 (page 124).

La Garita Creek Riparian Demonstration Area, 10 miles northeast of Del Norte on CR 38 (go north on CR 33 off SR 112, 3 miles northeast of town). CG BLM   719-589-4975 (pages 37, 72, 101).

Lake Cheraw, 4 miles north of La Junta on SR 109 (page 170).

Lake Henry SWA, 2 miles northeast of Ordway on CR 20. CDOW (page 183).

Lesser prairie chicken lek, 30 miles southeast of Springfield. *See* Comanche National Grassland (page 79).

Lillian Annette Rowe Audubon Sanctuary, near Kearney, Nebraska. Sandhill crane viewing blinds by reservation. 308-468-5282 (page 57).

Long Lake Nature Trail in Indian Peaks Wilderness, 6 miles west of Ward on CR 102. $ CG.   USFS   303-444-6600 (page 13).

Lower Latham Reservoir, private land 5 miles southeast of Greeley on CR 47 (pages 53, 170).

Manitou Park, 20 miles northwest of Colorado Springs on SR 67. CG USFS   719-636-1602 (pages 94, 99).

Maroon Bells peaks, 9 miles southwest of Aspen on FR 125 (partially closed to private cars in summer). CG   USFS   970-925-3445 (page 179).

Maroon Bells/Snowmass Wilderness, south of Aspen off FR 102 and FR 125. USFS 970-925-3445 (page 179).

McClure Pass, SR 133 between Carbondale and Paonia (page 179).

Mesa Verde National Park, US 160 between Cortez and Durango. $ CG 970-529-4461 or 970-529-4543 (pages 31, 35, 206, 216).

Monte Vista NWR, 15 miles west of Alamosa on SR 15. CG   USFW 719-589-4021 (pages 37, 53, 56, 170, 199, 219, 222).

Morrison Hogback Hawk Watch Site, I-70 and SR 26, 4 miles south of Golden. From parking lot at southeast corner of intersection, take 1-mile trail to top of ridge. 303-697-1893 (page 80).

Morrison Natural History Museum, 501 Highway 8, Morrison. $ 303-697-1873.

✻ Mt. Evans, 28 miles south of Idaho Springs on SR 103 and SR 5. $ USFS 303-567-2901. Road closed in winter (pages 151, 238, 241).

✻ Mt. Falcon Park, 5 miles southwest of Morrison via US 285 and CR 120; the lower portion, from SR 8 (pages 59, 94, 99, 188).

✻ Mt. Goliath Natural Area on Mt. Evans, 19 miles south of Idaho Springs on SR 103 and SR 5. $ USFS 303-567-2901. Road closed in winter (page 139).

✻ Mt. Sherman, 10 miles west of Fairplay on FR 421 (turn west on CR 18 off US 285, 1.5 miles south of town). CG USFS 719-836-2031.

✻ Mt. Zion wintering elk site, 4 miles north of Leadville on SR 91. USFS 719-275-0631 (page 186).

✻ Mueller SP, 4 miles south of Divide (west of Colorado Springs) on SR 67. $ CG 719-687-2366 (page 241).

✻ Museum of Western Colorado History, 4th and Ute Aves., Grand Junction. $ 970-242-0971.

✻ Natural Arch, 10 miles north of Del Norte off FR 659. Get map at USFS office in Del Norte. 719-657-3321 (page 204).

✻ Nee Noshe and Nee Granda Reservoirs, 15 miles north of Lamar on US 287. CDOW 719-473-2945 (pages 53, 55, 222).

✻ No Name Canyon, 2 miles east of Glenwood Springs off I-70 (turn north at Exit 119). USFS 970-945-2521 (page 196).

✻ North Clear Creek Falls, 20 miles west of Creede. Take SR 149 west 17 miles, then turn right on FR 510 for 4 miles to falls. CG USFS 719-658-2556 (page 122).

✻ North, Middle, and South St. Vrain canyons, west of Lyons, US 36 and SR 7. USFS (page 99).

✻ North Platte River near Lewellen, Nebraska. Look for cranes along US 26 between Lewellen and Lake McConaughy (page 57).

✻ Northstar Nature Preserve, 2 miles southeast of Aspen on SR 82. CG (page 232).

✻ Ouray Amphitheatre Trail, Ouray. CG USFS 970-249-3711 (page 232).

✻ Ouray Ice Climbing Park, 1 mile south of town on US 550 (page 24).

✻ Ouzel Falls, 3-mile hike in Rocky Mountain National Park. Wild Basin entrance, SR 7, 15 miles south of Estes Park. $ 970-586-1206 (page 24).

✻ Owl Canyon, 15 miles north of Fort Collins on CR 72 (turn right off US 287) (page 214).

✻ Pawnee Buttes. *See* Pawnee National Grassland (pages 31, 80).

✻ Pawnee National Grassland, northeast of Greeley off SR 14. Acquire necessary map at most USFS offices. CG   USFS   970-353-5004 (pages 31, 41, 80, 103, 105, 115, 120, 124, 126).

        ✗ Picketwire Canyon, 20 miles south of La Junta. *See also* Comanche National Grassland (pages 206, 208, 217).

        ✗ Picketwire Valley, Purgatoire River west of Trinidad along SR 12. CG USFS   719-269-8500 (page 94).

        ✗ Picture Canyon, 35 miles south of Springfield. *See* Comanche National Grassland (page 206).

        ✗ Piedra River, 20 miles west of Pagosa Springs on SR 151. CG   USFS 970-264-2268 (pages 86, 94, 96, 99).

        ✗ Piedra River north of Chimney Rock. Turn north on CR 631, 2 miles west of Pagosa Springs. CG   USFS   970-264-2268.

        ✗ Pikes Peak, west of Colorado Springs on FR 58 (toll road) off US 24. $ 719-684-9383 for road conditions (page 137).

        ✗ Piñon Canyon, 55 miles southwest of La Junta. Acquire $10 pass and map at headquarters, on US 350 near Thatcher, 40 miles southwest of La Junta. U.S. Army 719-579-2752 (pages 124, 126).

        ✗ Platte River, 10 miles north of Platteville on SR 60 and county roads bordering river (page 219).

        ✗ Poncha Hot Springs, on dirt road southeast of Poncha Springs. Inquire locally (page 96).

        ✗ Poncha Pass, 7 miles south of Poncha Springs on US 285 (page 80).

        ✗ Pueblo Greenway and Nature Center, along Arkansas River. Take 11th Street west off SR 45. CG   719-545-9114 (page 105).

        ✗ Pueblo Reservoir, 5 miles west of Pueblo on SR 96. $ CG   719-545-9114 (pages 17, 37, 199).

        ✗ Purgatoire River Canyon. *See* Picketwire Canyon.

        ✗ Rabbit Ears Pass, US 40, 21 miles east of Steamboat Springs.   CG   USFS (page 179).

        ✗ Rabbit Mountain Open Space, 7 miles west of Longmont via SR 66 west, then north on 53rd Street.   303-441-3950 (pages 80, 219).

        ✗ Rabbit Valley Research Natural Area, on I-70 25 miles west of Grand Junction (page 208).

        ✗ Radium SWA, south of Kremmling. Go 2.5 miles on SR 9 to CR 1; then 12 miles southwest (page 126).

        ✗ Rattlesnake Canyon, west of Colorado National Monument near Grand Junction. Requires hiking, either up from Colorado River or down from Black Ridge Road. Acquire map at Grand Junction BLM office.   970-244-3000 (page 204).

❦ Red Lion SWA, South Platte River 33 miles east of Sterling between US 138 and I-76. CDOW (pages 56, 72).

❦ Red Mountain Pass, US 550 south of Ouray. CG   USFS   970-249-3711 (page 142).

❦ Red Rock Lake, 4 miles west of Ward on CR 102. CG $ (summer) USFS   303-444-6600 (page 81).

❦ Rifle Falls SP, 12 miles north of Rifle on SR 325. $ CG.   970-625-1607 (page 23).

❦ Rio Grande Valley, SR 149 west of Creede. CG   USFS (page 142).

❦ Riverside Reservoir, east of Greeley. From US 34, 26 miles east of Greeley, go north 1 mile on CR 87. Park .3 miles before reaching reservoir and walk 1 mile down lane to left. BLM   719-275-0631 (page 118).

❦ Rocky Mountain Arsenal, northeast of Denver. Limited access, phone to arrange tour.   USFS   303-289-8734 (pages 120, 126, 219).

❦ Rocky Mountain National Park, US 34, US 36, and SR 7 from the east; US 40 and US 34 from the west. $ CG   970-586-1206 (pages 59, 86, 94, 96, 137, 142, 179, 186, 232).

❦ Roxborough SP, 22 miles south of Denver on SR 121 to Rampart Road. $ 303-973-3959 (page 129).

❦ Runyon/Fountain Lakes SWA, US 50 and SR 257, Pueblo. CDOW   719-382-5060 (page 55).

❦ Russell Lakes SWA, 10 miles south of Saguache on east side of US 285. CDOW   719-852-4783 (page 118).

❦ Sage grouse leks, north of Craig off SR 13. Map necessary. BLM   970-824-8261 (page 79).

❦ Sand Wash Basin, CR 75 and CR 67 15 miles west of Maybell off SR 318. BLM   970-824-8261 (page 120, 124).

❦ Santa Fe Trail, Air Force Academy, I-25, 5 miles north of Colorado Springs. 719-472-2025 (page 196, 217).

❦ Sawhill and Walden Ponds Wildlife Areas, 5 miles east of Boulder (75th Street between Jay and Valmont roads).   303-441-3408 (Sawhill); 303-441-3950 (Walden) (pages 17, 129).

❦ Schinzel Flats, FR 330, 30 miles southwest of Monte Vista. USFS map helpful. (page 140)

❦ Shadow Mountain Reservoir, US 34 1 mile south of Grand Lake. CG USFS   970-887-4100 (page 82, 86).

❦ Shrine Pass, just off the summit of Vail Pass on I-70 (Exit 190). CG $ USFS 970-925-3445 (page 142).

❦ Snowmass Wilderness. *See* Maroon Bells/Snowmass Wilderness.

❀ South Park, US 285 between Buena Vista and Kenosha Pass (pages 139, 179).

❀ South Platte River at 88th Avenue bridge in Thornton. One mile west of Exit 10, I-76, 9 miles north of Denver (page 17).

❀ South Republican River SWA. *See* Bonny Reservoir.

❀ South San Juan Wilderness Area, many access points from forest roads east and north of Pagosa Springs (USFS map necessary) (page 13).

❀ South Shale Ridge, county roads 10 miles west of DeBeque (BLM map helpful). 970-947-2800 (page 204).

❀ Stonewall wintering elk range, private land along CR 13, south of Stonewall (32 miles west of Trinidad on SR 12). 719-561-4909 (page 186).

❀ Sweitzer Lake SP, 4 miles southeast of Delta off US 50. $ 970-874-4258 (page 17).

❀ Tamarack Ranch SWA, South Platte River 24 miles northeast of Sterling between I-76 and US 138. CDOW (pages 72, 217).

❀ Tarryall Reservoir SWA, CR 77, 15 miles southeast of Jefferson (turn off US 285, 3 miles southwest of Kenosha Pass). CG   CDOW (page 160).

❀ The Flattops. *See* Flattops (The).

❀ Thorodin Mountain, northwest of Golden Gate Canyon State Park, accessible from Gap Road, mostly private land (page 188).

❀ Torreys Peak. *See* Grays Peak and Torreys Peak.

❀ Trail Ridge Road, US 34, Rocky Mountain National Park. $ CG   970-586-1206 (pages 13, 238).

❀ Treasure Falls, US 160, 6 miles southwest of Wolf Creek Pass.   CG   USFS 970-264-2268 (page 122).

❀ Two Buttes Reservoir SWA, 14 miles north of Springfield off US 287/385. CG   CDOW   719-336-4852 (page 115).

❀ Unaweap Seep, on northwest bank of West Creek on SR 141, 10 miles east of Gateway (south of Grand Junction) (page 96).

❀ Valley View Hot Springs, 7 miles east of US 285, on CR GG, 50 miles north of Alamosa. CG $ Private   719-256-4315 (page 129).

❀ Valmont Reservoir, 4 miles east of Boulder on SR 7 (.5 miles west of 75th Street). 303-441-3950 (page 82).

❀ Walden Ponds Wildlife Area. *See* Sawhill and Walden Ponds Wildlife Viewing Areas.

❀ Walker SWA, Colorado River 6 miles west of Grand Junction. Take SR 340 west to CR 20.80. CDOW (pages 17, 37, 72).

❀ Weminuche Wilderness Area, north of Pagosa Springs. Many access points off US 160 (USFS map necessary). 970-264-2268 (pages 13, 151).

❧ Wheat Ridge Greenbelt, Clear Creek between Youngfield Street and Wadsworth Boulevard (off I-70). 303-423-2626 (pages 40, 105, 183).

❧ White River, SR 64 between Meeker and Rangely (page 183).

❧ Windy Ridge Bristlecone Pine Scenic Area, FR 415 west off SR 9, 9 miles north of Fairplay (USFS map helpful). 719-836-2031 (page 139).

❧ Witmore Falls, CR 20, 9 miles west of Lake City on Engineer Pass Road. Also, Treasure Falls on same road 3 miles west of Lake City (page 24).

❧ Wolf Creek Pass, US 160 north of Pagosa Springs (page 232).

❧ Yampa River SWA, US 40 7 miles west of Hayden. CDOW (pages 72, 82, 105).

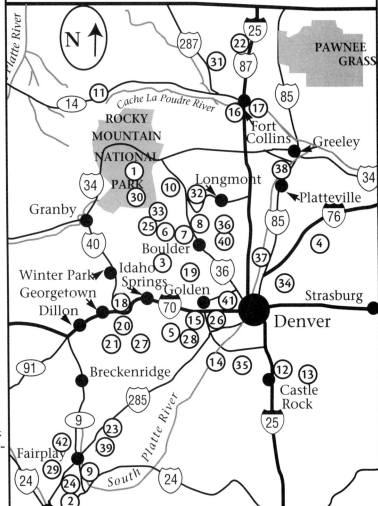

1 Alberta Falls
2 Antero Reservoir
3 Arapaho Pass
4 Barr Lake State Park
5 Bear Creek Canyon
6 Boulder Falls
7 Boulder Mountain Park
8 Boulder Reservoir
9 Buffalo Peaks State Wildlife
   Refuge
10 Buttonrock Reservoir
11 Cameron Pass
12 Castle Rock
13 Castlewood Canyon State Park
14 Chatfield State Park and Reservoir
15 Dinosaur Ridge
16 Fort Collins Greenbelt
17 Fort Collins gravel ponds
18 Georgetown Bighorn Sheep
   Viewing Area
19 Golden Gate Canyon State Park
20 Grays Peak and Torreys Peak
21 Guanella Pass
22 Hamilton Reservoir
23 Kenosha Pass
24 Knight-Imler State Wildlife Area
25 Long Lake Nature Trail
26 Morrison Hogback Hawk Watch Site
27 Mount Evans
28 Mount Falcon Park
29 Mount Sherman
30 Ouzel Falls

31 Owl Canyon
32 Rabbit Mountain Open Space
33 Red Rock Lake
34 Rocky Mountain Arsenal
35 Roxborough State Park
36 Sawhill and Walden Ponds Wildlife Area
37 South Platte River at 88th Ave. bridge
38 South Platte River near Platteville
39 Tarryall Reservoir State Wildlife Area
40 Valmont Reservoir
41 Wheat Ridge Greenbelt
42 Windy Ridge Bristlecone Pine Scenic Area

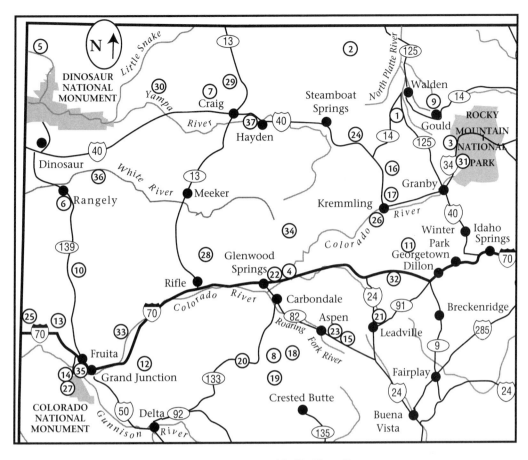

1 Arapahoe National Wildlife Refuge
2 Big Creek Lakes Trail
3 Bowen Gulch Trail
4 Bridal Veil Falls/Hanging Lake
5 Browns Park National Wildlife Refuge
6 Cañon Pintado
7 Cedar Mountain
8 Crystal Mill and Falls
9 Colorado State Forest
10 Douglas Pass
11 Gore Range
12 Grand Mesa
13 Highline State Recreation Area
14 Horsethief Canyon State Wildlife Area
15 Independence Pass
16 Kremmling Cretaceous Ammonite Site
17 Kremmling Pronghorn Viewing Site
18 Maroon Bells Peaks
19 Maroon Bells/Snowmass Wilderness

20 McClure Pass
21 Mount Zion Wintering Elk Site
22 No Name Canyon
23 Northstar Nature Preserve
24 Rabbit Ears Pass
25 Rabbit Valley Research Natural Area
26 Radium State Wildlife Area
27 Rattlesnake Canyon
28 Rifle Falls State Park
29 Sage Grouse Lake
30 Sand Wash Basin
31 Shadow Mountain Reservoir
32 Shrine Pass
33 South Shale Ridge
34 The Flattops, Crane Park
35 Walker State Wildlife Area
36 White River
37 Yampa River State Wildlife Area

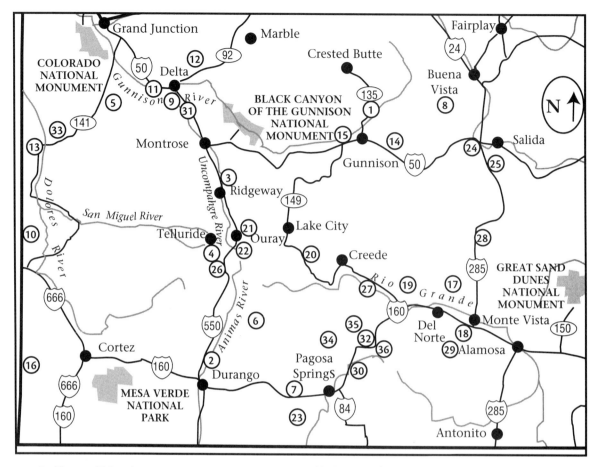

1 Almont Triangle
2 Animas River
3 Billy Creek State Wildlife Area
4 Bridal Veil Falls, Telluride
5 Cactus Park
6 Chicago Basin (Weminuche Wilderness)
7 Chimney Rock Archaeological Area
8 Collegiate Mountain Range
9 Delta Confluence Park
10 Dolores River Canyon
11 Escalante State Wildlife Area
12 Fruitgrowers Reservoir Wildlife Viewing Area
13 Gateway Special Recreation Management
      Area
14 Gunnison River
15 Gunnison State Wildlife Area
16 Hovenweep National Monument
17 La Garita Creek Riparian Demonstration Area

18 Monte Vista National Wildlife Refuge
19 Natural Arch
20 North Clear Creek Falls
21 Ouray Amphitheater Trail
22 Ouray Ice Climbing Park
23 Piedra River
24 Poncha Hot Springs
25 Poncha Pass
26 Red Mountain Pass
27 Rio Grande Valley
28 Russell Lakes State Wildlife Area
29 Schinzel Flats
30 South San Juan Wilderness Area
31 Sweitzer Lake State Park
32 Treasure Falls
33 Unaweap Seep
34 Weminuche Wilderness Area
35 Witmore Falls

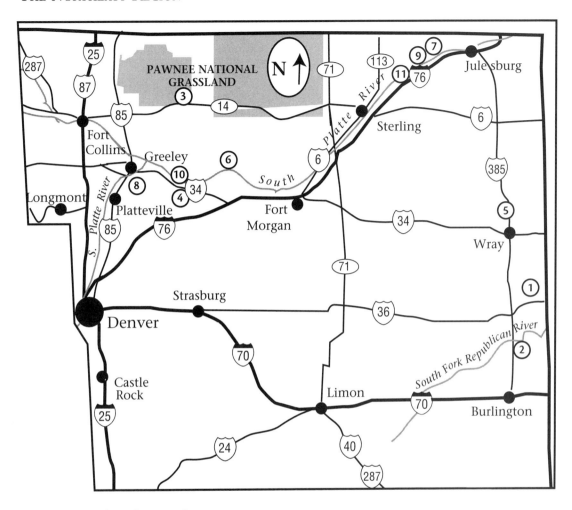

1 Beecher Island Battle Ground
2 Bonny Reservoir State Recreation Area
3 Crow Valley Campground, Pawnee National Grassland
4 Empire Reservoir
5 Greater Prairie Chicken Leks
6 Jackson Reservoir State Park
7 Julesburg (Jumbo) Reservoir
8 Lower Latham Reservoir
9 Red Lion State Wildlife Area
10 Riverside Reservoir
11 Tamarack Ranch State Wildlife Area

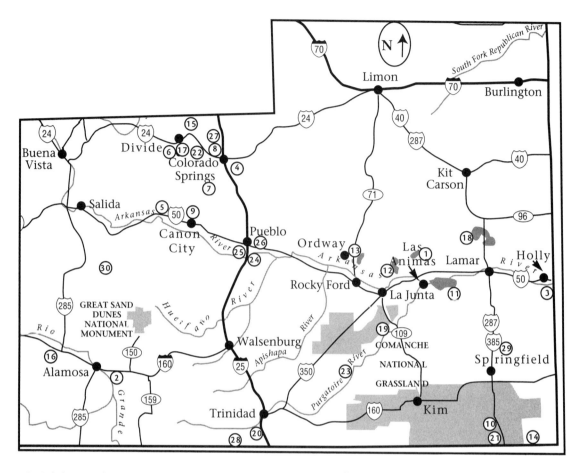

1   Adobe Creek Reservoir
2   Alamosa National Wildlife Refuge
3   Arkansas River State Wildlife Area
4   Big Johnson Reservoir
5   Bighorn Sheep Canyon
6   Florissant Fossil Beds National Monument
7   Fort Carson
8   Garden of the Gods
9   Garden Park Fossil Area
10 Holt Canyon, Comanche National Grassland
11 John Martin Reservoir
12 Lake Cheraw
13 Lake Henry State Wildlife Area
14 Lesser Prairie Chicken Lek
15 Manitou Park
16 Monte Vista National Wildlife Refuge

17 Mueller State Park
18 Nee Noshe and Nee Granda Reservoirs
19 Picketwire Canyon
20 Picketwire Valley
21 Picture Canyon, Comanche National Grass-
    land
22 Pikes Peak
23 Piñon Canyon
24 Pueblo Greenway and Nature Center
25 Pueblo Reservoir
26 Runyon/Fountain Lakes State Wildlife Area
27 Santa Fe Trail at Air Force Academy
28 Stonewall Wintering Elk Range
29 Two Buttes Reservoir
30 Valley View Hot Springs

2.

APPROXIMATE SUNRISE AND SUNSET TIMES, DENVER, COLORADO

Mountain Standard Time

Day	January Rise a.m.	Set p.m.	February Rise a.m.	Set p.m.	March Rise a.m.	Set p.m.	April Rise a.m.	Set p.m.	May Rise a.m.	Set p.m.	June Rise a.m.	Set p.m.
1	7:21	4:46	7:08	5:19	6:34	5:52	5:45	6:24	5:01	6:54	4:34	7:22
2	7:21	4:47	7:07	5:21	6:32	5:53	5:43	6:25	5:00	6:55	4:34	7:22
3	7:21	4:48	7:07	5:22	6:31	5:54	5:42	6:26	4:59	6:56	4:33	7:23
4	7:21	4:49	7:06	5:23	6:29	5:55	5:40	6:27	4:57	6:57	4:33	7:23
5	7:22	4:50	7:05	5:24	6:28	5:56	5:38	6:28	4:56	6:58	4:33	7:24
6	7:21	4:50	7:03	5:25	6:26	5:57	5:37	6:29	4:55	6:59	4:32	7:25
7	7:21	4:51	7:02	5:27	6:25	5:58	5:35	6:30	4:54	7:00	4:32	7:26
8	7:21	4:52	7:01	5:28	6:23	5:59	5:34	6:31	4:53	7:01	4:32	7:26
9	7:21	4:53	7:00	5:29	6:22	6:00	5:32	6:32	4:52	7:02	4:32	7:27
10	7:21	4:54	6:59	5:30	6:20	6:01	5:31	6:33	4:51	7:03	4:32	7:27
11	7:21	4:55	6:58	5:31	6:18	6:02	5:29	6:34	4:50	7:04	4:31	7:28
12	7:21	4:56	6:57	5:32	6:17	6:03	5:28	6:35	4:49	7:05	4:31	7:28
13	7:20	4:57	6:56	5:34	6:15	6:04	5:26	6:36	4:48	7:06	4:31	7:29
14	7:20	4:59	6:54	5:35	6:14	6:06	5:25	6:37	4:47	7:06	4:31	7:29
15	7:20	5:00	6:53	5:36	6:12	6:07	5:23	6:38	4:46	7:07	4:31	7:30
16	7:19	5:01	6:52	5:37	6:11	6:08	5:22	6:39	4:45	7:08	4:31	7:30
17	7:19	5:02	6:50	5:38	6:09	6:09	5:20	6:40	4:44	7:09	4:31	7:30
18	7:18	5:03	6:49	5:39	6:07	6:10	5:19	6:41	4:43	7:10	4:31	7:31
19	7:18	5:04	6:48	5:41	6:06	6:11	5:17	6:42	4:42	7:11	4:32	7:31
20	7:17	5:05	6:47	5:42	6:04	6:12	5:16	6:43	4:41	7:12	4:32	7:31
21	7:17	5:06	6:45	5:43	6:02	6:13	5:14	6:44	4:41	7:13	4:32	7:31
22	7:16	5:08	6:44	5:44	6:01	6:14	5:13	6:45	4:40	7:14	4:32	7:32
23	7:15	5:09	6:42	5:45	5:59	6:15	5:12	6:46	4:39	7:15	4:32	7:32
24	7:15	5:10	6:41	5:46	5:58	6:16	5:10	6:47	4:38	7:15	4:33	7:32
25	7:14	5:11	6:40	5:47	5:56	6:17	5:09	6:48	4:38	7:16	4:33	7:32
26	7:13	5:12	6:38	5:48	5:54	6:18	5:07	6:49	4:37	7:17	4:33	7:32
27	7:13	5:13	6:37	5:50	5:53	6:19	5:06	6:50	4:37	7:18	4:34	7:32
28	7:12	5:15	6:35	5:51	5:51	6:20	5:05	6:51	4:36	7:19	4:34	7:32
29	7:11	5:16	6:35	5:52	5:50	6:21	5:04	6:52	4:35	7:19	4:34	7:32
30	7:10	5:17			5:48	6:22	5:02	6:53	4:35	7:20	4:35	7:32
31	7:09	5:18			5:46	6:23			4:34	7:21		

Official sunrise/sunset is the time when the top of the sun just touches a level horizon. Topography (including mountains) and refraction are not taken into account. Add one hour for Daylight Savings Time.

APPROXIMATE SUNRISE AND SUNSET TIMES, DENVER, COLORADO
Mountain Standard Time

Day	July Rise a.m.	July Set p.m.	August Rise a.m.	August Set p.m.	September Rise a.m.	September Set p.m.	October Rise a.m.	October Set p.m.	November Rise a.m.	November Set p.m.	December Rise a.m.	December Set p.m.
1	4:35	7:32	4:58	7:13	5:28	6:32	5:56	5:43	6:28	4:58	7:02	4:36
2	4:36	7:32	4:59	7:12	5:28	6:30	5:57	5:41	6:29	4:57	7:03	4:36
3	4:36	7:32	5:00	7:11	5:29	6:29	5:58	5:40	6:31	4:56	7:04	4:36
4	4:37	7:31	5:01	7:10	5:30	6:27	5:59	5:38	6:32	4:55	7:05	4:36
5	4:37	7:31	5:02	7:09	5:31	6:25	6:00	5:37	6:33	4:54	7:06	4:35
6	4:38	7:31	5:03	7:08	5:32	6:24	6:01	5:35	6:34	4:53	7:06	4:35
7	4:39	7:31	5:04	7:07	5:33	6:22	6:02	5:33	6:35	4:52	7:07	4:35
8	4:39	7:30	5:05	7:06	5:34	6:21	6:03	5:32	6:36	4:51	7:08	4:35
9	4:40	7:30	5:06	7:04	5:35	6:19	6:04	5:30	6:37	4:50	7:09	4:35
10	4:41	7:30	5:07	7:03	5:36	6:17	6:05	5:29	6:39	4:49	7:10	4:35
11	4:41	7:29	5:08	7:02	5:37	6:16	6:06	5:27	6:40	4.48	7:11	4:36
12	4:42	7:29	5:09	7:01	5:38	6:14	6:07	5:26	6:41	4:47	7:12	4:36
13	4:43	7:28	5:10	6:59	5:39	6:12	6:08	5:24	6:42	4:46	7:12	4:36
14	4:43	7:28	5:11	6:58	5:40	6:11	6:09	5:23	6:43	4:45	7:13	4:36
15	4:44	7:27	5:12	6:57	5:41	6:09	6:10	5:21	6:44	4:45	7:14	4:36
16	4:45	7:27	5:13	6:55	5:42	6:08	6:11	5:20	6:45	4:44	7:14	4:37
17	4:46	7:26	5:13	6:54	5:42	6:06	6:12	5:18	6:47	4:43	7:15	4:37
18	4:46	7:25	5:14	6:53	5:43	6:04	6:13	5:17	6:48	4:42	7:16	4:37
19	4:47	7:25	5:15	6:51	5:44	6:03	6:14	5:15	6:49	4:42	7:16	4:38
20	4:48	7:24	5:16	6:50	5:45	6:01	6:15	5:14	6:50	4:41	7:17	4:38
21	4:49	7:23	5:17	6:48	5:46	5:59	6:15	5:13	6:51	4:40	7:17	4:39
22	4:50	7:23	5:18	6:47	5:47	5:58	6:17	5:11	6:52	4:40	7:18	4:39
23	4:51	7:22	5:19	6:45	5:48	5:56	6:18	5:10	6:53	4:39	7:18	4:40
24	4:51	7:21	5:20	6:44	5:49	5:54	6:19	5:09	6:54	4:39	7:19	4:40
25	4:52	7:20	5:21	6:42	5:50	5:53	6:20	5:07	6:55	4:38	7:19	4:41
26	4:53	7:19	5:22	6:41	5:51	5:51	6:22	5:06	6:56	4:38	7:20	4:41
27	4:54	7:18	5:23	6:39	5:52	5:50	6:23	5:05	6:58	4:37	7:20	4:42
28	4:55	7:17	5:24	6:38	5:53	5:48	6:24	5:03	6:59	4:37	7:20	4:43
29	4:56	7:16	5:25	6:36	5:54	5:46	6:25	5:02	7:00	4:37	7:21	4:44
30	4:57	7:15	5:26	6:35	5:55	5:45	6:26	5:01	7:01	4:36	7:21	4:44
31	4:58	7:14	5:27	6:33			6:27	5:00			7:21	4:45

Adjustments in Minutes for Sunrise/Sunset
in other Colorado Cities

City	December 20	March 20	June 20	September 20
Alamosa	−2/+10	+4/+4	+11/−2	+4/+4
Aspen	+6/+8	+8/+8	+9/+7	+8/+8
Durango	+5/+18	+12/+12	+19/+5	+12/+12
Fort Collins	+5/−1	+2/+2	−1/+5	+2/+2
Grand Junction	+14/+16	+15/+15	+16/+14	+15/+15
Lamar	−13/−5	−9/−9	−4/−13	−9/−9
Pueblo	−4/+4	+0/+0	+4/−4	+0/+0
Steamboat Springs	+10/+5	+8/+8	+5/+11	+8/+8
Sterling	−3/−9	−6/−6	−9/−3	−6/−6

Source: The Nautical Almanac Office of the United States Naval Observatory.

3.

ECLIPSES AND CONJUNCTIONS VISIBLE
FROM COLORADO, *1998-2010*

1998

February 26	Partial solar eclipse.
April 23	Venus and Jupiter only 0.5° apart in east before dawn.

1999

February 23	Venus and Jupiter only 0.3° apart in evening sky.
March 19	Venus, Saturn, and crescent moon cluster in west after sunset.

2000

January 20	Total lunar eclipse, 9:43 P.M. MST.
April 1–10	Jupiter, Saturn, and Mars cluster in low evening sky.

2001

July 17	Venus, Saturn, and crescent moon cluster in east before dawn.
August 6	Venus and Jupiter 1.3° apart in east before dawn.
November 6	Venus and Mercury 0.8° apart in morning twilight.
December 14	Partial solar eclipse.

2002

Apr. 22–May 12	Mercury, Venus, Mars, Saturn, and Jupiter aligned above western horizon at dusk.
May 14	Crescent moon 1° from Venus in low evening sky.
June 3	Venus and Jupiter 2° apart in west after sunset.
June 10	Partial solar eclipse.

2003

May 15	Total lunar eclipse, 9:40 P.M. MDT.
November 8	Total lunar eclipse, 6:19 P.M. MST.

2004

October 27	Total lunar eclipse, 9:04 P.M. MDT.
November 5	Venus and Jupiter only 0.6° apart in east before dawn.
December 7	Crescent moon passes close to Jupiter in east before dawn.

2005

June 25	Venus, Mercury, and Saturn cluster close together in west at dusk.
June 27	Venus just 0.1° from Mercury in west at dusk.

2006

June 17	Saturn only 0.5° from Mars in evening sky.

2007

March 3	Partial lunar eclipse, 4:20 P.M. MST.
May 19	Venus and crescent moon within 1° in west after sunset.
July 1	Venus and Saturn 0.8° apart in west at dusk.
August 28	Total lunar eclipse, 4:47 A.M. MDT.

2008

February 4	Venus, Jupiter, and crescent moon cluster in east before dawn.
February 20	Total lunar eclipse, 8:26 P.M. MST.
December 1	Venus, Jupiter, and crescent moon cluster in west after sunset.

2009

February 27	Venus and crescent moon close together in evening sky.
October 13	Venus 0.5° from Saturn in east before dawn.

2010

December 21	Total lunar eclipse, 1:17 A.M. MST.

Note: The next total solar eclipse visible in our region (total in parts of Wyoming and Nebraska) will occur on August 21, 2017.

Source: Various.

The longest solar eclipse of the century (6 minutes, 25 seconds), as seen in total from the tip of Baja, on July 11, 1991. (Photo by Glenn Cushman.)

4.

FULL MOON DATES, 1998-2010

	1998	1999	2000	2001	2002	2003	2004	2005	2006	2007	2008	2009	2010
JAN	12	1/31	20	9	28	18	7	25	14	3	22	10	29
FEB	11	none	19	7	27	16	6	23	12	1	20	9	28
MAR	12	1/31	19	9	28	18	6	25	14	3	21	10	29
APR	11	30	18	7	26	16	5	24	13	2	20	9	28
MAY	11	29	18	7	26	15	4	23	12	2/31	19	8	27
JUN	9	28	16	5	24	14	2	21	11	30	18	7	26
JUL	9	28	16	5	24	13	2/31	21	10	29	18	7	25
AUG	7	26	14	3	22	11	29	19	9	28	16	5	24
SEP	6	25	13	2	21	10	28	17	7	26	15	4	23
OCT	5	24	13	1/31	21	10	27	17	6	25	14	3	22
NOV	3	23	11	30	19	8	26	15	5	24	12	2	21
DEC	3	22	11	30	19	8	26	15	4	23	12	2	21

Source: Joint Propulsion Lab, Pasadena, California. Ephemeris Generator. JPL On-Line Ephemerides, Horizons.

5.

SELECTED COLORADO NATURE ORGANIZATIONS

Museums are listed in the "Where to Go Directory." Phone numbers are not given here for a few organizations in which there is no permanent phone.

Bureau of Land Management
Colorado State Office
2850 Youngfield St.
Lakewood, CO 80215
303-236-2100

Butterfly Pavilion and Insect Center
6252 West 104th Ave.
Westminster, CO 80020
303-469-5441

Colorado Bat Society
1085 14th St., Suite 1337
Denver, CO 80302

Colorado Division of Parks and Outdoor
   Recreation
1313 Sherman St., Room 618
Denver, CO 80203
303-866-3437

Colorado Division of Wildlife
6060 Broadway
Denver, CO 80216
303-297-1192

Colorado Environmental Coalition
777 Grant, Suite 606
Denver, CO 80203
303-837-8701

Colorado Field Ornithologists
13401 Piccadilly Rd.
Brighton, CO 80601

Colorado Forest Service
Forestry Building
Colorado State University
Fort Collins, CO 80523
970-491-6303

Colorado Mountain Club
710 10th St.
Golden, CO 80402
303-279-5643

Colorado Mycological Society
P.O. Box 9621
Denver, CO 80209
303-320-6569

Colorado Native Plant Society
P.O. Box 200
Fort Collins, CO 80522

Colorado Natural Heritage Program
211 W. Myrtle St.
Fort Collins, CO 80521
970-416-7452

Colorado Wildlife Federation
445 Union Blvd. #302
Lakewood, CO 80228
303-987-0200

Denver Botanic Gardens
1005 York St.
Denver, CO 80206
303-331-4000

National Audubon Society, Rocky Mountain
    Regional Office
4150 Darley Ave., Suite 5
Boulder, CO 80303
303-499-0219

National Park Service, Rocky Mountain
    Region
P.O. Box 25287
Denver Federal Center
Denver, CO 80225
303-969-2000

The Nature Conservancy, Colorado Field
    Office
1244 Pine
Boulder, CO 80302
303-444-2950

Rocky Mountain Bighorn Society
P.O. Box 8320
Denver, CO 80201

Rocky Mountain Nature Association
Rocky Mountain National Park
Estes Park, CO 80517
970-586-1258

Sierra Club, Southwest Office
1240 Pine
Boulder, CO 80303
303-449-5595

Sinapu (wolf reintroduction)
P.O. Box 3243
Boulder, CO 80307
303-447-8655

U.S. Fish and Wildlife Service
P.O. Box 25486
Denver Federal Center
Denver, CO 80225
303-236-7904

U.S. Forest Service
11177 W. Eighth Ave.
Lakewood, CO 80225
303-236-9431

6.

OFFICIAL STATE SYMBOLS

STATE FLOWER: Blue columbine, designated April 4, 1899, after vote by school children. See pp. 139–140 (July).

STATE TREE: Blue spruce, voted on by school children in 1892 but not designated by state legislature until March 7, 1939. This spruce was first described in scientific literature from a specimen found in 1862 by Charles C. Parry on Pikes Peak.

STATE MAMMAL: Bighorn sheep, designated January 1, 1961. See pp. 239–241 (December).

STATE BIRD: Lark bunting, designated April 29, 1931. See pp. 101–103 (May).

STATE INSECT: Hairstreak butterfly, designated April 17, 1996. See pp. 152–153 (July).

STATE FISH: Greenback cutthroat trout, designated March 15, 1994. (From 1954 to 1994 the rainbow trout was considered the state fish but was never officially designated.) See pp. 63–65 (March).

STATE FOSSIL: Stegosaurus, designated April 28, 1982, by Gov. Dick Lamm after schoolchildren had unsuccessfully lobbied legislature three times. The first stegosaurus was described by O. C. Marsh in 1877 from a specimen found near Morrison. See p. 207 (October).

STATE GRASS: Blue grama, designated May 20, 1987. See pp. 112–114 (June).

STATE GEMSTONE: Aquamarine, the blue-green variety of beryl (emerald is the green variety), was designated on April 30, 1971. It is fairly abundant in cavities in pegmatite rocks on Mt. Antero, where it has been found since 1884, and on White Mountain.

SELECTED READINGS

GENERAL

Benedict, Audrey. *The Southern Rockies*. San Francisco: Sierra Club Books, 1991.

Borland, Hal, and Les Line. *Seasons*. Philadelphia: J. B. Lippincott, 1973.

Catlin, George. *Letters and Notes on the North American Indian,* edited and with an introduction by MacDonald Mooney. New York: Clarkson N. Potter, 1975.

Cronyn, George W., ed. *The Path on the Rainbow*. New York: Boni and Liveright, 1918. New edition: Cronyn, George W., ed. *American Indian Poetry*. New York: Fawcett Columbine, 1991.

Cushman, Ruth Carol, and Stephen R. Jones. *The Shortgrass Prairie*. Boulder, CO: Pruett Publishing Co., 1988.

Cushman, Ruth Carol, Stephen R. Jones, and Jim Knopf. *Boulder County Nature Almanac*. Boulder CO: Pruett Publishing Co., 1993.

Leopold, Aldo. *A Sand County Almanac*. New York: Oxford University Press, 1966.

Mutel, Cornelia Fleisher, and John C. Emerick. *From Grassland to Glacier: The Natural History of Colorado*. 2d ed. Boulder, CO: Johnson Books, 1992.

Thompson, Stith. *Motif-Index of Folk-Literature*. 6 vols. Rev. and enl. ed. Bloomington: Indiana University Press, 1989.

Zimmermann, John. *Cheyenne Bottoms: Wetland in Jeopardy*. Lawrence: University Press of Kansas, 1990.

ARCHAEOLOGY AND GEOLOGY

Cassells, E. Steve. *The Archaeology of Colorado*. Boulder, CO: Johnson Books, 1983.

Chronic, Halka. *Roadside Geology of Colorado*. Missoula, MT: Mountain Press, 1986.

Cole, Sally. *Legacy on Stone*. Boulder, CO: Johnson Books, 1990.

Schaafsma, Polly. *Indian Rock Art of the Southwest*. Albuquerque: University of New Mexico Press, 1980.

CLIMATE AND WEATHER

Halfpenny, James C., and Roy Douglas Ozanne. *Winter: An Ecological Handbook*. Boulder, CO: Johnson Books, 1989.

Keen, Richard A. *Skywatch: The Western Weather Guide*. Golden, CO: Fulcrum, 1987.

Marchand, Peter J. *Life in the Cold*. 3d ed. Hanover, NH: University Press of New England, 1996.

FLORA AND FUNGI

Craighead, John J., and Frank C. Craighead. *A Field Guide to Rocky Mountain Wildflowers*. Boston: Houghton Mifflin, 1963.

DeByle, Norbert V., and Robert P. Winokur, eds. *Aspen: Ecology and Management in the Western United States*. Fort Collins, CO: U.S. Department of Agriculture, Forest Service, Rocky Mountain Forest and Range Experiment Station, 1985.

Dunmire, William W., and Gail D. Tierney. *Wild Plants of the Pueblo Province*. Santa Fe: Museum of New Mexico Press, 1995.

Evenson, Vera. *Mushrooms of Colorado and the Southern Rocky Mountains*. Englewood, CO: Westcliffe Publishers, 1997.

Faegri, K., and L. van der Pijl. *Principles of Pollination Ecology*. New York: Pergamon, 1979.

Gerard, John. *The Herbal, or General History of Plants*. 1633 (rev. ed.). Reprint, revised and enlarged by Thomas Johnson, New York: Dover, 1975.

Gilmore, Melvin. *Uses of Plants by the Indians of the Missouri River Region*. Lincoln: University of Nebraska Press, 1977.

Guennel, G. K. *Guide to Colorado Wildflowers*. Englewood, CO: Westcliffe Publishers, 1995.

Kindscher, Kelly. *Edible Wild Plants of the Prairie*. Lawrence: University Press of Kansas, 1987.

———. *Medicinal Wild Plants of the Prairie: An Ethnobotanical Guide*. Lawrence: University Press of Kansas, 1992.

Kirkpatrick, Zoe M. *Wildflowers of the Western Plains*. Austin: University of Texas Press, 1992.

Kricher, John C. *Ecology of Western Forests*. Boston: Houghton Mifflin, 1993.

Lincoff, Gary. *Audubon Society Field Guide to North American Mushrooms*. New York: Knopf, 1981.

Long, John C. *Native Orchids of Colorado*. Denver: Denver Museum of Natural History, 1965.

Martin, Laura C. *Wildflower Folklore*. Charlotte, NC: East Woods Press, 1984.

Moenke, Helen. *Ecology of Colorado Mountains to Arizona Deserts*. Denver: Denver Museum of Natural History, 1971.

Nelson, Ruth Ashton. *Handbook of Rocky Mountain Plants*. 4th rev. ed. by Roger L. Williams. Boulder, CO: Roberts Rinehart Publishers, 1992.

Stone, Doris M. *The Lives of Plants*. New York: Scribner's, 1983.

Weber, William A. *Colorado Flora: Eastern Slope*. Rev. ed. Boulder: University Press of Colorado, 1996.

Weber, William A. *Colorado Flora: Western Slope*. Rev. ed. Boulder: University Press of Colorado, 1996.

Weber, William A., and Ronald C. Wittman. *Catalog of the Colorado Flora: a Biodiversity Baseline*. Niwot: Colorado Associated University Press, 1992.

Willard, Beatrice E., and Michael T. Smithson. *Alpine Wildflowers of Rocky Mountain National Park*. Estes Park, CO: Rocky Mountain Nature Association, 1988.

Young, Robert G., and Joann W. Young. *Colorado West: Land of Geology and Wildflowers*. Grand Junction, CO: Self-published, 1984.

Zwinger, Ann H. *Aspen: Blazon of the High Country*. Salt Lake City: Peregrine Smith Books, 1991.

Zwinger, Ann H., and Beatrice E. Willard. *Land Above the Trees: A Guide to American Alpine Tundra*. New York: Harper & Row, 1972.

FAUNA

Allen, Thomas B. et. al. *Field Guide to the Birds of North America*, 2d ed. Washington, DC: National Geographic Society, 1983.

Andrews, Robert, and Robert Righter. *Colorado Birds*. Denver: Denver Museum of Natural History, 1992.

Armstrong, David M., *Rocky Mountain Mammals*. Boulder: Colorado Associated Press, 1987.

Armstrong, David M., Rick A. Adams, Kirk W. Navo, Jerry Freeman, and Steven J. Bissell. *Bats of Colorado: Shadows in the Night*. Pamphlet. Denver: Colorado Division of Wildlife, n.d.

Armstrong, Edward A. *Folklore of Birds*. Boston: Houghton Mifflin, 1959.

Bailey, Alfred Marshall, and Robert J. Niedrach. *Birds of Colorado*. Denver: Denver Museum of Natural History, 1965.

Barbour, Roger William, and Wayne H. Davis. *Bats of America*. Lexington: University Press of Kentucky, 1969.

Beck, Thomas. *Black Bears of West-Central Colorado*. Technical Publication No. 39. Denver: Colorado Division of Wildlife, 1991.

Bent, Arthur Cleveland. *Life Histories of North American Marsh Birds*. New York: Dover, 1963.

———. *Life Histories of North American Nuthatches, Wrens, Thrashers, and Their Allies*. Gloucester, MA: Peter Smith, 1974.

Colorado Division of Wildlife. *Wildlife in Danger: The Status of Colorado's Threatened or Endangered Fish, Amphibians, Birds, and Mammals*. Denver: Colorado Division of Wildlife, 1996.

Craighead, John Johnson, and Frank C. Craighead, Jr. *Hawks, Owls, and Wildlife*. New York: Dover, 1969.

Cranshaw, Whitney, and Boris Kondratieff. *Bagging Big Bugs: How to Identify, Collect and Display the Largest and Most Colorful Insects of the Rocky Mountain Region*. Golden, CO: Fulcrum, 1995.

Ehrlich, Paul R., David R. Dobkin, and Darryl Wheye. *The Birder's Handbook: A Field Guide to the Natural History of North American Birds*. New York: Simon & Schuster, 1988.

Evans, Howard Ensign. *Life on a Little-Known Planet*. New York: Lyons & Burford, 1993.

Ferris, Clifford D., and F. Martin Brown, eds. *Butterflies of the Rocky Mountain States*. Norman: University of Oklahoma Press, 1981.

Fitzgerald, James, Carron A. Meaney, and David M. Armstrong. *Mammals of Colorado*. Denver: Denver Museum of Natural History; Niwot: University Press of Colorado, 1994.

Furtman, Michael. *On the Wings of a North Wind: the Waterfowl and Wetlands of America's Inland Flyways*. Harrisburg, PA: Stackpole Books, 1991.

Gray, Mary Taylor. *Colorado Wildlife Viewing Guide*. Helena MT: Falcon Press, 1992.

Halfpenny, James A. *A Field Guide to Mammal Tracking in Western North America*. Boulder, CO: Johnson Books, 1986.

Hammerson, Geoffrey A. *Amphibians and Reptiles in Colorado*. Denver: Colorado Division of Wildlife, 1982.

Holt, Harold R. *A Birder's Guide to Colorado*. Denver: American Birding Association, 1997.

Hubbell, Sue. *Broadsides from the Other Orders: A Book of Bugs*. New York: Random House, 1993.

Johnsgard, Paul A. *Hawks, Eagles, & Falcons of North America*. Washington, DC: Smithsonian Press, 1990.

————. *North American Owls.* Washington, DC: Smithsonian Institution Press, 1988.

Kingery, Hugh, ed. *Colorado Breeding Bird Atlas.* Unpublished manuscript, 1998.

Klauber, Laurence M. *Rattlesnakes.* Abridged ed. Berkeley: University of California Press, 1982.

Peterson, Roger Tory. *Field Guide to Western Birds.* 3d ed. Peterson Field Guide No. 2. Boston: Houghton Mifflin, 1990.

Pyle, Robert Michael. *The Audubon Society Field Guide to North American Butterflies.* New York: Knopf, 1981.

————. *The Handbook for Butterfly Watchers.* Boston: Houghton Mifflin, 1992.

Ryden, Hope. *Lily Pond.* New York: W. Morrow, 1989.

Selsam, Millicent. *Where Do They Go? Insects in Winter.* New York: Four Winds Press, 1982.

Sparks, John, and Tony Soper. *Owls: Their Natural and Unnatural History.* New York: Facts on File, 1989.

Teale, Edwin Way. *Grassroot Jungles: A Book of Insects.* New York: Dodd, Mead, 1966.

Terborgh, John. *Where Have All the Birds Gone?* Princeton, NJ: Princeton University Press, 1989.

Turbak, Gary. *Twilight Hunters: Wolves, Coyotes and Foxes.* Flagstaff, AZ: Northland Press, 1987.

Tyrrell, Ester Quesada, and Robert A. Tyrrell. *Hummingbirds: Their Life and Behavior.* New York: Crown, 1985.

Urquhart, Fred A. *The Monarch Butterfly: International Traveler.* Chicago: Nelson Hall, 1987.

Van Wormer, Joe. *The World of the American Elk.* Philadelphia: J. B. Lippincott, 1969.

Walker, Lewis Wayne. *The Book of Owls.* New York: Knopf, 1974.

Whitaker, John O., and Robert Elman, text consultant; visual key by Carol Nehring. *Audubon Field Guide to North American Mammals.* Audubon Society Field Guide Series. New York: Knopf, 1980.

Wolfe, Art, and William Ashworth. *Bears: Their Life and Behavior.* New York: Crown, 1992.

Index